Workbook in Nonlinear Phonology
for Clinical Application

Workbook in Nonlinear Phonology for Clinical Application

Barbara Handford Bernhardt
and
Joseph Paul Stemberger

pro·ed
An International Publisher

8700 Shoal Creek Boulevard
Austin, Texas 78757-6897
800/897-3202   Fax 800/397-7633
Order online at http://www.proedinc.com

© 2000 by PRO-ED, Inc.
8700 Shoal Creek Boulevard
Austin, Texas 78757-6897
800/897-3202   Fax 800/397-7633
Order online at http://www.proedinc.com

Library of Congress Cataloging-in-Publication Data

Bernhardt, Barbara Handford.
    Workbook in nonlinear phonology for clinical application / Barbara
  Handford Bernhardt, Joseph Paul Stemberger.
        p.   cm.
      Includes bibliographical references.
      ISBN 0-89079-810-9 (alk. paper)
      1. Articulation disorders in children.   2. Speech disorders in
  children.   3. Language disorders in children.   4. Grammar,
  Comparative and general—Phonology.   I. Stemberger, Joseph P.
  (Joseph Paul)   II. Title.
RJ496.S7B486   2000
618.92'85—dc21   98-50043
                                                                  CIP

This book is designed in Frutiger and New Century Schoolbook.

Production Director: Alan Grimes
Production Coordinator: Dolly Fisk Jackson
Managing Editor: Chris Olson
Art Director: Thomas Barkley
Designer: Jason Crosier
Print Buyer: Alicia Woods
Preproduction Coordinator: Chris Anne Worsham
Staff Copyeditor: Martin Wilson
Project Editor: Jill Mason
Publishing Assistant: John Means Cooper

Printed in the United States of America

1 2 3 4 5 6 7 8 9 10   03 02 01 00 99

Contents

Preface

This workbook is designed for use by clinicians and students in speech–language pathology who work with children with phonological disorders. Over the past 10 years, we have been developing analysis and intervention procedures in nonlinear phonological frameworks for both clinical and research purposes. It is our view that these procedures elucidate a child's difficulties in phonology more clearly than previous phonological frameworks, thus providing a strong foundation for intervention. In their entirety, these procedures are most useful for children who have moderate to severe phonological disorders; however, sections of the analysis procedures are useful for children with mild disorders. They are at this time being piloted with adult subjects with neurogenic disorders, and it is anticipated that they will also be useful for that population.

The workbook begins with a short tutorial on nonlinear phonology as an introduction to the theories and concepts underlying the analysis procedures; it is not an introduction to phonology in general, for which many other textbooks are available. Nonlinear phonology emphasizes the role of groupings of segments into syllables and feet, as well as the independent nature and timing of different features. Its focus on many lines of elements (one line for each feature, for syllables, for feet, etc.) rather than on one line (of whole segment) earns it the name "nonlinear," or sometimes "multilinear." The bulk of the book is devoted to a step-by-step demonstration of the various nonlinear analysis procedures (with a blank form for future analyses in Appendix D). Suggestions are included for intervention based on nonlinear concepts.

The procedures in this book have been presented for several years in university coursework and in many workshops and projects for clinicians. We gratefully acknowledge the insightful comments of students and clinicians in trying to help us find clinically useful, clear, and comprehensible forms and documentation. Where clarity and utility are yet lacking, we encourage users to come up with their own improvements.

To Eva Major, SLP (C), who created the figures for this book and provided much useful feedback over the years, we give particular thanks.

We also acknowledge the children and their families who have participated in phonological intervention projects in British Columbia over the past 10 years, without whom these ideas could not have been put into practice. In addition, we acknowledge the BC Medical Services Foundation and the BC Health Research Foundation for their grant support for those projects.

Finally, we thank our children, Gwendolyn, Morgan, and Larissa Stemberger and Travis and Carmine Bernhardt, for their inspirational speech development and their amazing forbearance in putting up with extensive home computing.

Introduction

Over the 10 years that we have been working with nonlinear phonological theories to describe developmental and disordered data, we have been frequently asked two things:

1. What do the new theories contribute to our understanding of development and disorders?

2. Are there analysis shortcuts that make clinical application feasible?

In terms of the first question, it is our view that nonlinear phonological theories not only describe phonological patterns more precisely than previous theories, but also *explain* many patterns. For children with moderate to severe phonological disorders, progress can be slow in treatment. The better we can describe the patterns, and the more we understand what they mean, the more likely the interventions will be efficient and successful. Nonlinear phonological analysis in particular pays more attention to syllable, word, and phrase structure than previous analysis methods and thus provides more insight into patterns that affect those larger phonological units. Children with moderate to severe disorders often have particular difficulty with syllable and word structure, and thus, the methodologies are especially useful for them.

The most common current phonological analysis method is phonological process analysis. What this type of analysis does is list the "symptoms" of the disorder: a child shows evidence of "velar fronting," "stridency deletion," or "assimilation." These descriptors (or symptoms) have often proven useful for phonological intervention, not in the least because they have led clinicians to think of general phonological patterns rather than focusing on one *segment* (speech sound) at a time. But a process (although general) is just a solution, or *repair,* that circumvents a set of impossible articulations. If fricatives are impossible, substituting stops for fricatives is one way to solve that problem, just as segment deletion is a solution, just as gliding (e.g., [h] or [j] substitutions) is a solution, etc. The nonlinear analyses we present do not ignore the child's repairs but focus on

- what the child *can* do, and
- what is *missing* from the child's system that needs to be there.

For example, when a child produces [j] for fricatives, what is possible for the child is continuous airflow through the oral cavity; what is impossible is a narrow obstruction that causes turbulence in such airflow. On the other hand, if a child produces stops for fricatives, what is possible for the child is obstruction; what is impossible is continuous airflow (without sonorance). The nonlinear analyses we present throughout this tutorial workbook focus on breaking down the possible and the impossible into discrete components. Each component is viewed as an independent unit that can be manipulated in ways that affect other independent units. In other words, the child's strengths are used to facilitate development of those areas in which the child has needs for development. This is the general benefit of nonlinear phonology in our experience. Individual aspects of the various subtheories have their own relevance for intervention, and these will be elucidated as we progress through the analyses. Chapters 1–3 (Part I) present a tutorial on nonlinear phonological theory, beginning with syllable and word structure in Chapter 1 and proceeding through features and sequences in Chapters 2 and 3, respectively.

The major purpose of this workbook is to demonstrate use of a shortcut nonlinear analysis for phonological intervention. This methodology has been piloted extensively over the last several years with practicing clinicians and with students, and a form was developed for that purpose. (A blank form is included in Appendix D, but readers are encouraged to develop their own versions for daily use.) Data are visually scanned, rather than counted. Major patterns are noted for all aspects of the phonological system. Chapters 4–10 (Part II) lead the reader step by step through the scan analysis procedure. (Chapter 5 includes a complete analysis for one child.) As with any new theory or form, the scan will take a while—a few hours—the first time, but after practice it can be done in 20 to 60 minutes, depending on the length and complexity of the data set.

Throughout the analysis chapters, we include examples of quantitative analysis, should the reader decide that some counting would be informative (or necessary for determination of efficacy).

An introduction to intervention strategies and techniques based on nonlinear phonological theory is given in Chapter 11. In addition, the book contains four appendices: a modified IPA (International Phonetic Alphabet) chart (Appendix A), answers to exercises (Appendix B), extra data sets (Appendix C), and a blank scan form (Appendix D).

What This Book Is *Not:*

• This book is not an in-depth tutorial on nonlinear phonological theory or phonological development. Readers who wish to pursue those topics in depth are referred to Bernhardt and Stemberger (1998).

• It is not an introduction to phonology. Readers without any background will probably find it necessary to first work through an introductory text or workbook (such as Stoel-Gammon & Dunn, 1985, or Lowe, 1996).

• It does not provide a full assessment procedure. Clinicians who have determined that a child has a moderate to severe phonological disorder, based on a screening or articulation/phonology test, can use any word list for elicitation (preferably 75 words minimum) as a basis for the scan analysis presented here.

What This Book Provides:

• a short tutorial on nonlinear phonology

• a nonlinear scan analysis and goal-setting procedure that is useful for people with phonological disorders, particularly those with moderate to severe disorders

• an introduction to phonological intervention techniques based on nonlinear phonology

The scan form in Appendix D provides a map for the rest of the book. Taking a look at it first and keeping it with you throughout is probably a good idea. Readers who are familiar with nonlinear theories may wish to skim the tutorial section in order to see which perspectives are presented here before proceeding to the procedural chapters. Readers with some introductory phonology will need to read the theory chapters before proceeding to the analysis chapters and will probably find after doing some analysis that many of the concepts in the theory chapters become more comprehensible. Workshop participants and students have often commented that this is the case. More suggestions for reading the analysis chapters are included in Chapter 4.

Part I
Tutorial on Nonlinear Phonology

Chapter 1
Syllable and Word Structure: Theory

The segments (speech sounds) of a word do not usually appear in isolation. There is generally more than one segment in a word. Further, segments group together in systematic ways that make up what is called a *prosodic hierarchy*. (See Figure 1.A.) Segments are grouped into syllables. Syllables are grouped into feet. Feet are grouped into prosodic words. We address each unit in turn. We then discuss a less intuitive unit (a timing unit, or mora), and the interaction of such units with syllables and feet.

1.1. Syllables

The smallest grouping of segments is the *syllable*. A syllable consists of one prominent phoneme (the *peak*), which is relatively long and of high amplitude, plus additional less prominent phonemes (generally consonants). Native speakers of a language can generally say how many syllables are in a word and where the boundaries between syllables lie (though native speakers may find some syllabification tasks difficult). The peak of a syllable is generally a vowel, although syllabic consonants (particularly the sonorants /n, m, l, r/) are also possible. In general, given a sequence of vowels and consonants, the syllable structure is predictable: we can identify which vowels will be peaks, which vowels will instead be glides, and which consonants will be syllabic.

Nonsyllabic elements (whether true consonants or glides) can appear either before the peak of the syllable or after it. Consonants that appear before the peak of the syllable make up the *onset;* all languages allow syllables to have onsets, and a few languages require every syllable to have an onset. Consonants that appear after the peak of the syllable make up the *coda;* all languages allow syllables without a coda, and some languages do not allow a syllable to have a coda. A syllable without a coda

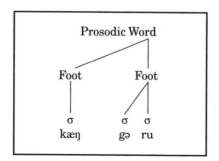

Figure 1.A. Prosodic hierarchy.

is an *open* syllable. A syllable with a coda is a *closed* syllable. Languages prefer open syllables over closed syllables, and open syllables are statistically more frequent than closed syllables.

The peak and the coda are grouped together into a larger unit known as a *rime* (or sometimes "rhyme"). In Figure 1.B, illustrating the word *sit* /sɪt/, note that the Greek letter sigma (σ) is used as shorthand for a syllable. The representation of a monosyllabic word is straightforward. Once we identify the peak, all segments before the peak are in the onset, and all segments after the peak are in the coda.

The order of consonants within an onset or within a coda generally is governed by the *sonority hierarchy,* a scale based on the "sonority" of a segment. Sonority is not well defined, but seems to correspond to how similar a segment is to the most proto-typical segment with high sonority: a vowel. The scale is, roughly (from most sonor-ous to least sonorous):

vowel
glide
liquid
nasal
voiced fricative
voiceless fricative
affricate
voiced stop
voiceless stop

The peak of the syllable is usually the "peak" of sonority, and sonority tends to decrease toward the edges of the syllable. Thus, the first consonant in the onset is low in sonority, the second consonant is higher in sonority than the first, the peak of the syllable is highest, the first consonant in the coda is lower in sonority than the peak of the syllable, and the second consonant in the coda is lower yet. A typical syllable would be *clump* /klʌmp/: stop-liquid-vowel-nasal-stop.

There are exceptions to this generalization. Cross-linguistically, the most com-mon exception involves /s/, which is higher in sonority than a stop but often precedes stops in onsets (in words like *stand* /stænd/) and follows them in codas (in words like *ax* /æks/). We do not know why this is the case, but /s/ creates sequences in onsets and codas with unusual sonority relationships. Some phonologists argue that the /s/ is part of a separate subgrouping outside the syllable: an *appendix.* An appendix may appear only at the edges of words: word-finally in some languages, word-initially in other languages, or at both edges. The appendix allows for one or more additional consonants than would be allowed in the onset or the coda. It has been proposed that

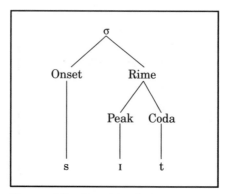

Figure 1.B. Onset and rime.

the /s/ of word-initial /sp, st, sk/ clusters in English is not a part of the onset but is rather an appendix. Although controversial, this proposal would account for the odd sonority of /s/-stop clusters. Furthermore, some children *do* produce elements in word-initial or word-final position (i.e., at word edges) that they do not produce in intervocalic position (longer sequences of consonants, for example).

A further complication concerning intervocalic consonants regards syllabification. All consonants at the beginning of the word before the peak of the first syllable are in the onset of the first syllable. All consonants at the end of the word after the peak of the second syllable are in the coda of the second syllable. But the syllable position of consonants in the middle of the word, between the two peaks, is unclear. In principle, intervocalic consonants could make up either the onset of the second syllable or the coda of the first syllable.

In almost all adult languages, the division of consonants between the two syllables is simple and predictable. If there is only one intervocalic consonant, it makes up the onset of the second syllable, rather than the coda of the first syllable. A word like *bunny* /bʌni/ would be [.bʌ.ni.] (where the periods in the phonetic transcription represent the place where a syllable begins or ends), never *[.bʌn.i.]. This is because onsets are preferred, while codas are avoided to the extent possible. In [.bʌ.ni.], both syllables have an onset, and neither syllable has a coda. In *[.bʌn.i.], the first syllable has a coda, and the second syllable has no onset; neither is optimal. The preference for onsets over codas is reflected in a subtle fashion in the syllabification of an intervocalic consonant as an onset.

In a few languages, the treatment of intervocalic consonants is unclear. In English and other Germanic languages, most native speakers are uncertain about whether [.bʌ.ni.] or *[.bʌn.i.] is correct. As a result, it has been suggested that intervocalic consonants in adult English belong to *both* syllables, making up both the coda of the first syllable and the onset of the second syllable. A consonant that belongs to two syllables in this way is called *ambisyllabic* and is represented as in Figure 1.C.

Not all intervocalic consonants are ambisyllabic. If the second syllable is stressed (as in *balloon*), the intervocalic consonant is strictly a part of the onset of the second syllable. The motivation behind such mushy syllabification may be to increase the size (and hence the prominence; see below) of the stressed syllable. If segments can be ambisyllabic, we can make an interesting prediction that sometimes is true of child phonology: an intervocalic consonant and a word-final consonant are then both in codas, and so both may show patterns that are characteristic of codas rather than onsets.

If there is more than one intervocalic consonant, the syllabification depends on the particular sequence of consonants in the word. As many consonants as possible are placed in the onset of the second syllable, subject to constraints on the sequences of consonants that are allowed within onsets in the language in question. Some languages (and most very young children) allow only a single consonant in an onset. In that case, words like *number* /nʌmbɚ/ and ugly /ʌgli/ would be syllabified as [.nʌm.bɚ] and [.ʌg.li.]. However, the language (or child) may allow two or more consonants within an onset, with the second consonant often restricted to a glide or liquid. For such a language or child, *ugly* would be syllabified as [.ʌ.gli.] (because a

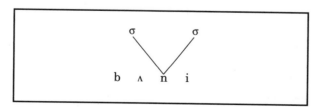

Figure 1.C. Ambisyllabic intervocalic consonants.

syllable is allowed to begin with [gl], such as in *glove* [glʌv]), but *number* would still be [.nʌm.bɚ] (because a syllable cannot begin with *[mb]). Given the sequences of consonants that are allowed in a word-initial onset, and the sequences of consonants that are allowed within a word-final coda, we can accurately divide all sequences of intervocalic consonants into their respective syllables.

If, in a child's phonological system, a word may begin with a consonant (word-initial onset) and end with a consonant (word-final coda), we predict that up to two consonants may appear in a sequence between vowels (with the first in a word-medial coda, and the second in a word-medial onset). This is often the case; the only consonant sequences appear between two vowels. However, some children do not allow any consonant sequences, even between two vowels.

✏️ Exercises (Answers to all exercises are in Appendix B.)

1. Take the following words and syllabify them, identifying onsets, rimes, peaks, and codas:

   snake /sneɪk/   flower /flɑʊɚ/   mistake /mɪsteɪk/
   angry /æŋgri/   whispering /wɪspɚɪŋ/   milky /mɪlki/

2. Rank the following segments from most sonorous to least sonorous:

   m s t u ɑ w v g l n r p θ

3. Identify which segments in the following words might be in appendices:

   smile /smɑɪl/   task /tæsk/   plunk /plʌŋk/
   glance /glæns/   stroll /stroʊl/   sphinx /sfɪŋks/

4. Which consonants are ambisyllabic?

   carry   buckle   coffee   city
   machine   giraffe   believe   support

The syllable structure of a word is entirely predictable from the segments and the timing units (see Section 1.4) that are present. The first step is to identify the syllable peaks, as shown in Figure 1.D for *numbers* and *box*. Onsets are then added to the syllables. As many consonants go in the onset as are allowed in the language, as long as the onsets created are "legal" sequences of consonants, as in Figure 1.E.

In this case, only the /b/ of the intervocalic consonant cluster /mb/ can link to the onset of the second syllable, because English does not allow onsets with the sequence /mb/ (because /m/ is higher in sonority than /b/). The next step is to add consonants to the coda: as many as are allowed in codas in the language (which might be zero if

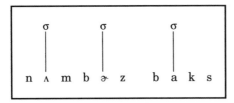

Figure 1.D. Syllable peaks.

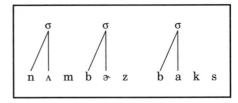

Figure 1.E. Adding onsets.

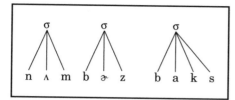

Figure 1.F. Adding codas.

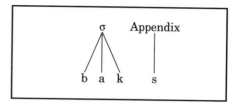

Figure 1.G. Appendix.

the language does not allow codas) as long as the resulting consonant sequences make legal codas in the language. (See Figure 1.F.)

At this point, all the segments in the word *numbers* have been linked to a syllable node. Similarly, we would have *tractors* [.træk.tɚz.]. In contrast, we would expect *ugly* [.ʔʌ.gli], because [gl] (unlike [mb] and [kt]) can begin a syllable in English. For *bunny*, we would have [.bʌ.ni.]. If the intervocalic consonant is ambisyllabic, an additional step at this point makes the [n] a coda as well, so it becomes a part of both syllables.

If the /s/ in *box* is part of the coda, then all consonants have been syllabified at this point. If the /s/ is instead acting as an appendix (because it is higher in sonority than the /k/), then an appendix would be introduced to absorb it, as in Figure 1.G.

At this point in the syllabification process, problems may have arisen, due to the *constraints* (inherent limitations) of the language interacting with the segments in the word. *There are two types of problems: too few consonants and too many consonants.* (See Table 1.1.).

Because constraints limit what can be produced, the pronunciation must be repaired to accommodate those limitations. *Phonological processes* (or *repairs*) are thus observed.

With respect to syllable structure, an extra consonant is needed *for only one reason:* because an onset is required. The high frequency of syllables with onsets in the target language leads to the generalization that an onset *must* be present. This arises in child phonology. Words with no onset in the first syllable (as in *apple* [.a.pu]) or in the second syllable (as in *crayon* [.kweɪ.an]) are altered to give an onset in all syllables. One possible repair is to *insert a consonant* (most often a glottal stop, a glide, or a coronal stop):

Table 1.1. Constraints and Repair Processes in Syllables

Child's Constraint	Target Word Challenge	Resulting Difficulty	Repair
All σs require an onset.	TOO FEW C's	Onsetless σ	• Insert C.
			• (Delete V.)
			• Eliminate σ boundary.
			• Lengthen C.
All C's must be in a syllable.	TOO MANY C's	A C not in a σ	• Delete C.
▬ no coda			• Insert V.
▬ only one C in a coda			• Make C syllabic.
▬ only one C in an onset			• Move C.
▬ impossible sequence of C's			

apple	[.ʔa.pu.] or [.wa.pu.] or [.da.pu.]
crayon	[.kweɪ.ʔan] or [.kweɪ.wan] or [.kweɪ.dan]

Another repair is to delete the syllable without an onset, but this is extremely rare:

apple	[.pu.]
crayon	[.kweɪ.]

Alternatively, a syllable boundary may be eliminated, thus removing the potential locus of an onset.

    drawing   [.drɑ. + .ɪŋ.]   >   [.drɑɪŋ.]

Finally, a consonant or glide elsewhere in the word can be extended in duration to also occupy the onset:

apple	[.pa.pu.]
crayon	[.kweɪ.jan.]

Note that, for [.kweɪ.jan.], the second portion of the glide, when lengthened, is transcribed with the symbol [j]; but the glide [j] and the vowel [i] (or [ɪ]) have exactly the same set of features. Whether the segment is a glide or a vowel is determined by the role it plays in the syllable (see Chapter 2).

If a target word has too many consonants for the child's syllable structure limitations, then one or more consonants will not be syllabified. In order to be pronounced, all segments must be a part of a syllable. There are four possible repairs. Consider words such as *play* and *cat*. First, the unsyllabified consonants can be left unsyllabified, in which case they will not be pronounced. Only [p] of *play* and [k] of *cat* are syllabified, as in Figure 1.H. Second, a vowel may be inserted, thereby creating a syllable to take up the extra consonant ([.pə.leɪ.], [.kæ.tə.], as in Figure 1.I). Third, a consonant may be made syllabic (as in [.pu.eɪ], Figure 1.J); this is likely only with sonorant consonants. Finally, the unsyllabified consonant can be moved to another syllable that has a free syllable position into which the consonant could fit. For example, if an onset is limited to one consonant but codas are allowed, the word *snow* /snoʊ/ could be pronounced [noʊs], as in Figure 1.K.

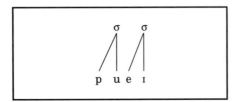

Figure 1.H. Segment deletion.

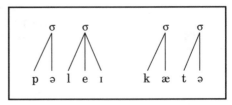

Figure 1.I. Vowel epenthesis.

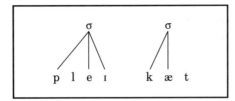

Figure 1.J. Consonant becomes syllabic.

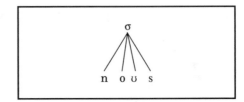

Figure 1.K. Migration of segments.

✏ Exercise

5. Take the following pairs of words and constraints, identify whether there is a problem in each, and if there is, suggest possible repairs:

   a. WORD: *fly* /flɑɪ/   CONSTRAINT: no coda
   b. WORD: *scoot* /skuːt/   CONSTRAINT: no /s/-stop onsets
   c. WORD: *icy* /ɑɪsi/   CONSTRAINT: onset obligatory
   d. WORD: ask /æsk/   CONSTRAINT: no coda
   e. WORD: *swing* /swɪŋ/   CONSTRAINT: no complex onset
   f. WORD: *shower* /ʃɑʊɚ/   CONSTRAINT: onset obligatory

1.2. Feet and Stress Patterns

In English and many other languages, some syllables are more prominent than others, because they are stressed (that is, longer, louder, and of higher pitch), while other syllables are unstressed. Stressed syllables are often called "strong" (S), and unstressed syllables are called "weak" (w). These differences in prominence are represented by grouping syllables into a higher-order unit called a *foot*. There is only one stressed syllable in a foot. We follow the common convention of placing the stressed syllable directly beneath the foot node in nonlinear representations; unstressed syllables are linked up with a slanted line. We illustrate feet with the words *happy* (with stress on the first syllable) and *balloon* (with stress on the second syllable). A foot with stress on the first syllable is *left-prominent* (or *trochaic*): Sw. A foot with stress on the second syllable is *right-prominent* (or *iambic*): wS. (See Figure 1.L.) In English, almost all two-syllable words are left-prominent (with stress on the first syllable), but there are unpredictable exceptions.

The basic foot has at most two syllables. However, feet can have three or more syllables, and when this happens, stress can be on a middle syllable rather than on one of the edge syllables. The English word *banana*, for example, contains a single foot with stress on the middle syllable. Such feet often arise because of constraints on which vowels may be stressed and which may be unstressed.

We can make the following generalization about vowels and stress in (adult) English:

• Schwa (the reduced vowel in narrow transcription) is never stressed.

• The unstressed vowel may not be long or diphthongal, unless it is in an open syllable. Even then, only [iː], [uː], and [oʊ] are possible, as in *happy* [ˈhæpi], *delight* [diˈlɑɪt], *value* [ˈvæljuː], and *yellow* [ˈjɛloʊ]. Further, the word-final unstressed

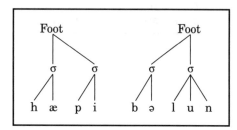

Figure 1.L. Building feet.

tense vowels [i] and [u] are short in many dialects. (Inflectional affixes do not count; in *values* [ˈvæljuːz], the [uː] is in a closed syllable.)

• The only short lax vowel that can be unstressed is the "reduced vowel," which may be [ə], [ɨ], or [ɪ], depending on the dialect or position with respect to the word or particular consonants. The vowels [ɛ], [ʊ], and [ʌ] never occur unstressed.

• The low vowels [æ], [ɑ], and [ɔ] must be stressed. This is true even if they are not as prominent as the vowel in the syllable with primary stress (represented as ˈ) but carry secondary stress (represented as ˌ), as in ˌraˈcoon.

Accounting for the acquisition of English works best if we assume that the child knows where the stressed syllable is in the adult pronunciation and puts unstressed syllables into feet according to general principles.

The child may have constraints that prevent accurate pronunciation of some target words. These constraints may require the addition or deletion of syllables. (See Table 1.2.)

A foot might be *required* to have two syllables: if one syllable is prominent, there might also have to be a nonprominent syllable. Thus, a foot with a single syllable, such as the word *up* /ʌp/, might be augmented with an additional syllable: [ˈʔʌpə]. In contrast, a word with two syllables that ends in the same segment (in this case, /p/) would never be augmented—*ketchup* [ˈkɛtʃəp]—because it already has two syllables.

More commonly, target words have too many syllables for accurate child production, either because there are two unstressed syllables, or because the single unstressed syllable is in the wrong location in the word. In English, the statistically most frequent foot with more than one syllable is Sw. The left-prominent Sw pattern can serve as a powerful constraint, making impossible less frequent alternatives, i.e., the right-prominent wS, center-prominent wSw, and extra-long Sww. There are two types of repairs. Consider the words *balloon* /bəˈluːn/, *banana* /bəˈnænə/, and *rickety* /ˈrɪkəti/. First, the weak syllable can be deleted:

balloon	ˈluːn
banana	ˈnænə
rickety	ˈrɪkə

Second, for target wS feet only, the stress pattern can reverse (stress shift), resulting in a left-prominent Sw:

| balloon | ˈbʌlən |

Table 1.2. Constraints and Repair Processes for Stress Patterns

Child's Constraint	Target Word Challenge	Resulting Difficulty	Repair
Every foot must be Sw.	TOO FEW σs for a foot	A foot with a single σ	Insert V.
Every foot must be Sw. ▬ no Sww feet ▬ no wS feet	TOO MANY σs for a foot	A σ not in a foot	• Delete σ. • Make weak σ strong (Sw, sS, or SS).

Finally, the extra weak syllable can become stressed, so that there are two stressed syllables in the word:

balloon	ˌbʌˈluːn
banana	ˌbʌˈnænə
rickety	ˈrɪkəˌdi

The most frequent repair in child phonology is deletion of the extra syllable(s), but other patterns also occur (see Chapter 6).

Exercises

6. Code the following words in terms of S and w syllables. Identify whether the words are right-prominent, left-prominent, or center-prominent.

oval	machine	tortuous	prominent
department	freckle	purple	today
sanity	novice	phonology	productive

7. Identify the relevant constraints and repairs, if any, for the following:

a. delicious	/dəlɪʃəs/	[lɪʃə]
b. muddy	/mʌdi/	[mʌdi]
c. probably	/prɑbəbli/	[prɑli]

1.3. (Prosodic) Words

Feet are always incorporated into a higher level unit: the *(prosodic) word*. In multi-syllabic words, there may be more than one foot, one of which contains the syllable with the greatest level of stress: the *primary* stress (written as uppercase S). Other feet contain *secondary* stress (written as lowercase s). A word generally constitutes one prosodic word, no matter how long it is, and has only one primary stress. An example of a prosodic word with two feet would be swSw *hibernation* (with the weak foot /haɪbɚ/ followed by the strong foot /neɪʃn̩/). (See Figure 1.M.)

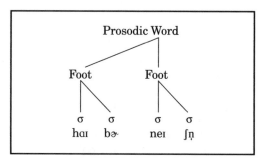

Figure 1.M. Prosodic word with two feet.

Some basic generalizations about English stress patterns for words with two feet are as follows (but note that English has many exceptional words and patterns):

• When the last foot has two syllables (is *binary*), the word is often right-prominent: the last foot has primary stress, and the first foot has secondary stress, e.g., hiberNAtion.

• Similarly, when both feet have only a single syllable (as in sS *raCOON* [ˌræˈkuːn]), primary stress falls on the final foot, with the first having secondary stress. Compound words are exceptions, e.g., *HOTdog*.

• If the first foot has two syllables, but the second foot has only one syllable, the prosodic word is generally left-prominent, as in the Sws *hibernate* [ˈhaɪbɚˌneɪt].

Languages often have a maximal word: an absolute upper bound on the length of a word. If a language has such a fixed length, words tend to be relatively short: either two syllables (limited to a single foot) or four syllables (limited to two feet). Young children often have maximal words, sometimes limited to a single foot. (See Table 1.3.)

A long word may be reduced to a single foot via two repairs. Consider the words *hippopotamus* /ˌhɪpəˈpɑtəməs/, *kangaroo* /ˌkæŋgəˈruː/, and *protein* /ˈproʊˌtiːn/. First, one foot may be deleted entirely—one or more syllables deleted:

hippopotamus	[ˈpɑməs]
kangaroo	[ˈkæŋgə]
protein	[ˈpoʊ]

Second, the foot's syllable(s) might be retained but become unstressed:

kangaroo	[ˈkæŋgəwə]
protein	[ˈpoʊdən]

Deletion of both the foot and its syllables is the more common repair.

 ## Exercise

8. Divide the following words into feet, recoding using S, s, and w:

rhinoceros	driveway	calculator	raspberry
instantaneous	alligator	watermelon	express lane
telephone	transportation	relatively	apple pie

Table 1.3. Constraints and Repairs for Word Length

Child's Constraint	Target Word Challenge	Resulting Difficulty	Repair
Only one foot is allowed.	TOO MANY FEET	Two feet	• Delete one foot. • Make one foot unstressed.

1.4. Timing Units

For various reasons, it is necessary to distinguish between the phonetic content of a segment and an element that simply indicates that a segment is present. We refer to these additional elements as *timing units*. There are competing proposals about the exact details of these timing units and whether all segments have them. In this section, we lay out two proposals.

Timing units commit some amount of real time during speech production to the realization of the segments with which they are associated. They are independent of the segments to which they are attached. This has several consequences:

- There can be more timing units than segments.

- There can be more segments than timing units.

- A segment can be deleted without affecting the associated timing unit, leaving that timing unit free to link to (and thus lengthen) some other segment (compensatory lengthening).

The earliest proposal for timing units assumed that the timing unit encoded not only the presence of a segment but also whether it was syllabic (V) or nonsyllabic (C). The word *sit* is an example of a word with one timing unit for every segment (seen in Figure 1.N). When two timing units are linked to a single segment, that segment takes up two consecutive units of time. As a result, the segment is phonetically long. Long vowels have two syllabic timing units (VV). The word *seat* is an example of a word in which the vowel has two timing units, as in Figure 1.O. The long vowels of "standard" English are [iː] and [uː] and arguably [æː], [ɑː], and [ɔː] (since the low vowels are phonetically the longest vowels of English).

The diphthongs of English (/eɪ/, /oʊ/, /aɪ/, /aʊ/, and /ɔɪ/) also have two timing units; we assume that they are VV. Unlike long vowels, diphthongs contain two segments, each of which is linked to a single timing unit, as in the word *right* (Figure 1.P).

Adult English does not contrast long and short consonants. Young children sometimes produce a single long consonant in place of a consonant cluster: *monkey* /mʌŋki/ [mʌkːi] and *number* /nʌmbɚ/ [nʌmːə]. A long consonant has two timing units (Figure 1.Q). In Section 1.1 above, we noted that consonants can be made syllabic. This is represented by changing the C timing unit into a V timing unit (Figure 1.R). Syllables are built on top of V timing units. This change allows a new syllable to be created.

A more radical view of timing units is expressed in moraic theory (e.g., Hayes, 1989). The timing unit is called a *mora,* represented by the symbol μ. This approach differs from CV theory in that not all segments have moras. Mora theory presupposes the following:

- All vowels have moras.
- Long vowels and diphthongs have two moras.

Figure 1.N. Timing units.

Figure 1.O. Long vowel timing units.

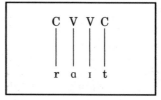

Figure 1.P. Diphthong timing units.

Figure 1.Q. Long consonant timing units.

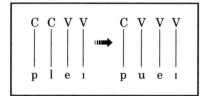

Figure 1.R. Making consonants syllabic.

- A syllable with a coda has an additional mora for the coda in some languages (including adult English after lax vowels, as in words like *bit, bed, foot,* and *duck*).

- Onsets never have moras.

- Most languages do not allow more than two moras in a syllable.

For most purposes, the two views of timing units are equivalent (but see Chapter 11 for intervention techniques).

Stress is often sensitive to the number of moras in a syllable. A *light* syllable has only one mora: it ends in a short vowel with no coda. A *heavy* syllable has two moras: it has a long vowel, a diphthong, or a short vowel with a coda. Stress is a measure of prominence, and heavy syllables are already more prominent than light syllables, because they are longer. In many languages, all heavy syllables must be stressed; adult English has a strong tendency in that direction.

The most optimal stressed syllables are heavy. In an English word such as *bunny* [.ˈbʌ.ni.], the stressed syllable is light. One way to make the stressed syllable heavy would be to shift the intervocalic consonant into the coda of the first syllable: [.bʌn.i.]. It is possible that intervocalic consonants in English are ambisyllabic *because* this increases the heaviness of the stressed syllable.

In most languages, a foot must have at least two moras. Those moras can be either in two syllables or in a single heavy syllable. Adult English is such a language: no word can be made up of a single open syllable with a short vowel (*/bɛ/, */sɪ/, */gʊ/, */mʌ/). The few exceptions involve function words that are unstressed (e.g., *the* /ðə/) and thus are part of some larger foot. However, as long as the foot has two moras, it does not matter whether it is made up of a single syllable that has a long vowel (as in *see*) or a coda (as in *sit*) or of two short open syllables (as in *city*).

Table 1.4 lists constraints and repairs for timing units (which affect *word shape* in terms of CV's—see Chapter 6). A number of constraints on timing units can lead to repairs, as the table shows.

First, if a child's minimal word or foot must have two moras, or a stressed syllable must have two moras, a given target word may have too few timing units. This can be resolved through the insertion of a timing unit. Because a timing unit must be associated with a segment in order to be pronounced, a segment must be supplied. An existing segment can be linked to the inserted timing unit, thereby becoming long:

ticket   /.ˈtɪ.kət./   [.ˈtiː.kət.] or [.ˈtɪkːət]   (vowel or consonant lengthening)

balloon   /.bə.ˈluːn/   [.ˌbʌː.ˈluːn]   (vowel lengthening)

Alternatively, a particular *default* segment (see Chapter 2) can be inserted to supply the new timing unit with a segment:

ticket   [.ˈtɪʔ.kət.] or [.ˈtɪŋ.kət.]   (default segment insertion)

Table 1.4. Constraints and Repairs for Timing Units

Child's Constraint	Target Word Challenge	Resulting Difficulty	Repair
Maximal foot has two μs.	TOO FEW MORAS	Foot with one μ	Insert timing unit.
Stressed σ should be heavy.		Light stressed σ	1. Lengthen V or C. 2. Insert default segment.
Maximal σ has two moras.	TOO MANY MORAS	σ with three μs	Delete timing unit. 1. Delete segment. 2. Shorten long V.
Timing units are not deleted but must have a segment.	STRANDED MORAS	Timing unit but no segment	• Insert segment. • Lengthen segment.

Second, a given target word may have too many timing units, because the child has a constraint limiting a syllable to two moras. A problem will arise if the peak has two moras (a long vowel or a diphthong) and the syllable has a coda (which adds a third mora to the syllable). The extra mora (either in the vowel or in the coda) can be deleted, along with any segment that is left without a timing unit:

write	/raɪt/	[wat] or [waɪ]	(mora and segment deletion)

Finally, if the system does not allow deletion of timing units, a timing unit may be left behind when the segment with which it is associated is deleted for some reason. The presence of a timing unit can lead to lengthening of a nearby segment or to insertion of a particular segment (a *compensatory repair*):

bill	/bɪl/	[bɪʔ]	(default segment insertion)
stinky	/stɪŋki/	[dɪk:i] or [di:ki] or [dɪʔki]	(lengthening or glottal stop insertion)

 ## Exercises

9. Recode the following words as a sequence of C and V timing units, marking syllable boundaries:

cabbage	wander	crane	delightful	boundaries
suffer	mutual	selfish	judge	see

10. Explain the following pronunciations in terms of constraints, using timing units:

fin	/fɪn/	[.fiː.]
feet	/fiːt/	[.fɪt.]
ketchup	/kɛtʃəp/	[.teɪ.təp.]

1.5. Summary: Units of Word and Syllable Structure

• (Prosodic) words are made up of groupings of more prominent and less prominent feet. In English, words of two feet or more are usually right-prominent (i.e., have greater or primary stress at the end of the word).

• Feet are made up of groupings of strong (prominent) syllables and (optionally) weak syllables. Sw feet are common in English.

• Strong syllables are stressed (with primary stress in strong feet and secondary stress in weak feet).

• Syllables contain rimes and usually onsets, also.

• Rimes are made up of peaks and codas. Codas are not preferred.

• Another way to describe word structure is in terms of its timing units. Rimes may be limited to two timing units (or moras).

Chapter 2
Phonological Features and Feature Geometry

Basic to the discussion of this chapter is the notion that *features,* not segments, are the primary phonological elements. Features combine and recombine to form larger units called segments, just as syllables combine to form feet, feet to form words, and words to form phrases. Most of this chapter therefore concerns features, beginning with their definitions, then describing their organization within segments and with respect to each other, and finally, outlining briefly the types of constraints and repair processes that affect them.

2.1. Phonological Features

All speech sounds are composed of smaller units called *features* that encode the phonetic information of the segment. There is currently some disagreement over the optimal set of features for human languages, but the set that we make use of is fairly standard (see Bernhardt & Stemberger, 1998, for discussion). Traditional phonetic labels (such as "fricative" and "glide") are not sufficient for capturing all the important similarities between different speech sounds (such as the continuous oral airflow that occurs in both fricatives and glides). This is a serious matter, because the similarities lead different classes of sounds to take part in similar patterns. We identify a set of features that are, essentially, instructions to the motor component about how to articulate a particular phone. Features are categorical distinctions that are superimposed on continuous phonetic dimensions. Most features are *binary;* that is, there are two possible values for those features: having the characteristic (+), and lacking the characteristic (−). When a feature is used as a feature, it is enclosed in square brackets, and a one-value feature is capitalized, e.g., [+nasal], [Labial]. However, when the same word is used as a noun or adjective, no brackets or capitalization is used, e.g., *a nasal, a labial, nasal stops, labial fricatives.* (Features that have only one value have been identified with [✓], since when they are present, they are automatically positive-valued.) The features that we use are defined here, and Tables 2.1 and 2.2 give the values for all the phones of English. In the following sections, 2.1.1 to 2.1.3, we define first manner features, then laryngeal features, then place features, following the order of analysis suggested in Chapter 7 for features (and also the hierarchical representation of features, presented later in the chapter). In each section the segments that contain the particular features are listed.

2.1.1. Manner Features

1. [+sonorant]: A sound in which the pressure above the larynx allows the vocal cords to vibrate continuously, without any rise in pressure above the larynx.

Table 2.1. All Consonant Features for Adult English

	p	t	tʃ	k	b	d	dʒ	g	f	θ	s	ʃ	v	ð	z	ʒ	m	n	ŋ	l	r	w	j	h	ʔ
sonorant	−	−	−	−	−	−	−	−	−	−	−	−	−	−	−	−	+	+	+	+	+	+	+	+	+
consonantal	+	+	+	+	+	+	+	+	+	+	+	+	+	+	+	+	+	+	+	+	−	−	−	−	−
continuant	−	−	−	−	−	−	−	−	+	+	+	+	+	+	+	+	−	−	−	+	+	+	+	+	−
nasal	−	−	−	−	−	−	−	−	−	−	−	−	−	−	−	−	+	+	+	−	−	−	−	−	−
lateral																				+					
Laryngeal	✓	✓	✓	✓	✓	✓	✓	✓	✓	✓	✓	✓	✓	✓	✓	✓	✓	✓	✓	✓	✓	✓	✓	✓	✓
voiced	−	−	−	−	+	+	+	+	−	−	−	−	+	+	+	+	+	+	+	+	+	+	+	−	−
spread glottis	+/−	+/−	+/−	+/−					+	+	+	+												+	
constricted glottis	+/−	+/−	+/−	+/−																					+
Place	✓	✓	✓	✓	✓	✓	✓	✓	✓	✓	✓	✓	✓	✓	✓	✓	✓	✓	✓	✓	✓	✓	✓	✓	✓
Labial	✓				✓				✓				✓				✓				✓	✓			
round																					+	+			
labiodental									+				+												
Coronal		✓	✓			✓	✓			✓	✓	✓		✓	✓	✓		✓		✓	✓		✓		
anterior		+	−			+	−			+	+	−		+	+	−		+		+	−		−		
distributed		−	+			−	+			+	−	+		+	−	+		−		−	+		+		
grooved		−	+			−	+			−	+	+		−	+	+									
Dorsal				✓				✓													✓	✓	✓		
back				+				+													+	+	−		
high				+				+													+	+	+		
low				−				−													−	−	−		

Note. Cells that are blank indicate that the given feature is irrelevant for that particular segment. The one-valued features have a checkmark, rather than [+] or [−] binary values. [Laryngeal] and [Place] are organizing nodes in the feature geometry. See Figure 2.2.

+ All regularly voiced vowels, glides, liquids (*r*'s and *l*'s), and nasals ([m], [n], [ɲ], [ŋ]) are [+sonorant], because the air that passes through the larynx is quickly vented out through the oral or nasal cavities, and pressure never rises. Voiceless sonorants ([h, ʔ, m̥, n̥]) are [+sonorant], even though they are not voiced, because the supraglottal pressure is low.

− Obstruents (stops, fricatives, and affricates) are [−sonorant], because the constrictions inhibit airflow; supraglottal pressure rises enough during these segments to prohibit voicing unless special measures are taken to keep voicing going.

2. [+consonantal]: A sound with a narrow constriction in the oral and/or pharyngeal cavities that significantly impedes the flow of air by stopping it, redirecting it, or creating turbulence.

Table 2.2. All Vowel Features for Adult English

	i	ɪ	e	ɛ	æ	u	ʊ	o	ɔ	ɨ	ə	ʌ	ɑ/a
sonorant	+	+	+	+	+	+	+	+	+	+	+	+	+
consonantal	−	−	−	−	−	−	−	−	−	−	−	−	−
continuant	+	+	+	+	+	+	+	+	+	+	+	+	+
tense	+	−	+	−	?	+	−	+	?	−	−	−	?
voiced	+	+	+	+	+	+	+	+	+	+	+	+	+
Labial						✓	✓	✓	✓				
round						+	+	+	+				
Coronal	✓	✓	✓	✓	✓								
anterior	−	−	−	−	−								
Dorsal	✓	✓	✓	✓	✓	✓	✓	✓	✓	✓	✓	✓	✓
back	−	−	−	−	−	+	+	+	+	+	+	+	+
high	+	+	−	−	−	+	+	−	−	+	−	−	−
low	−	−	−	−	+	−	−	−	+/−	−	−	−	+

Note. Cells that are blank indicate that the given feature is irrelevant for that particular segment. The one-valued features have a checkmark, rather than [+] or [−] binary values.

+ All "true" consonants are [+consonantal], because they stop the flow of air out of the vocal tract (oral stops and affricates), redirect air out the nasal cavity (nasal stops), narrow the constriction enough to create turbulence (fricatives and affricates), redirect the air around the sides of the tongue (laterals), or briefly block the flow of air (taps and trills). (Occasionally, glides in onsets behave as if they are [+consonantal], but it rarely matters.)

− Only vowels and glides have sufficiently wide constrictions that airflow is unimpeded, and these are [−consonantal]. Note that the (North American) English *r* ([ɹ]) is a glide (see Appendix A), and thus [−consonantal]. The glottal phones [h] and [ʔ] have constrictions only at the larynx, and by definition lack constrictions in the oral or pharyngeal cavities; they are thus [−consonantal] and for this reason have sometimes been called glides.

3. [+continuant]: A sound in which air continues to move through *the oral cavity*.

− Oral stops and affricates, nasal stops, and glottal stops entirely block airflow through the oral cavity and are [−continuant]. *Note that nasals are [−continuant] even though air continues to be vented through the nasal cavity;* nasals pattern with oral stops in adult languages and in language acquisition, not with fricatives.

+ All other segments are [+continuant]: vowels, glides, liquids, and fricatives. (Note that no *single* feature defines fricatives. They are

19

defined via the *feature combination* [−sonorant,+continuant]. However, for purposes of simplicity in the scan analysis, we often refer to fricatives with just the feature [+continuant].) Sometimes /l/ behaves as if it is [−continuant], but it most often patterns as [+continuant].

Affricates

Affricates are unclear. First, an affricate could be treated as a stop with tongue grooving (which leads to high-amplitude noise on release): [−continuant, +grooved]. No feature would represent the change during the segment from a stop-like articulation to a fricative-like articulation, but this fails for affricates such as [tθ], which are [−grooved] (and show up in the speech of some children as the realization of /ʧ/). Second, affricates might be specified as both [−continuant] (at the beginning) and [+continuant] (at the end), but this also has empirical difficulties. We think that different children may make use of different representations, but we favor the [−continuant,+continuant] analysis.

---

4. [+nasal]: A sound made with the velum lowered so that air moves through the nasal cavity.

- **+** Sounds are [+nasal] if air is vented only through the nasal cavity, as in nasal stops, or if air additionally is vented through the oral cavity, as in nasalized vowels, glides, and liquids.

- **−** All oral vowels, glides, liquids, and obstruents are [−nasal].

5. [+lateral]: A sound in which central airflow is blocked in the oral cavity but air is directed over at least one side of the tongue.

- **+** All *l*−type sounds are [+lateral].

- **−** All other sounds are [−lateral].

6. [+tense]: A sound produced with relatively greater "muscular tension."

- **+** [+tense]: [i], [e], [u], [o]

- **−** Lax [−tense] vowels: [ɪ], [ɛ], [ʊ], [ʌ], [ə] ([æ], [ɑ], [ɔ]?)

Note: The low vowels of English were historically lax but are phonetically fairly tense in most North American dialects. Voiceless obstruents are also redundantly [+tense] (to control the high intraoral air pressures involved), while voiced and devoiced obstruents are redundantly [−tense].

Vowels Versus Glides

Vowels are not distinguished from glides by features. Glides are nonsyllabic vowels: [w] is a nonsyllabic [u], [j] is a nonsyllabic [i], and [ɹ] is a nonsyllabic [ɝ]. They are distinguished by syllable position: vowels are in peaks (with V timing units), and glides are in onsets and codas (with C timing units). Syllabic consonants (V) are also distinguished from nonsyllabic consonants (C) by timing units and not by features. For convenience, we will sometimes use a pseudofeature, [+syllabic] for (syllabic) segments that have a V timing unit and [−syllabic] for (nonsyllabic) segments that have a C timing unit.

2.1.2. Laryngeal Features

1. [+voiced]: A sound produced with vocal fold vibration (e.g., [d], [i]).

+ Voiced segments (whether obstruents or sonorants) are [+voiced].

− Any segment in which the vocal folds are not vibrating is [−voiced].

2. [+spread glottis] ([s.g.]): A sound in which the vocal folds are spread wide, leading to low-amplitude noise at the glottis.

+ Voiceless aspirated stops are [+s.g.], as in English stops that are onsets to stressed syllables (*tip* [tʰɪp]; *racoon* [ræˈkʰūːn]). Generally, there must be at least 25 msec of voicelessness after release for a stop to be [+s.g.].

+ Voiceless sonorants are [+s.g.], as in [m̥] and [n̥] (which often occur in the speech of English-learning children).

+ Voiceless fricatives and [h] are also [+s.g.]. Voiceless fricatives are redundantly [+s.g.] so that high airflow leads to loud fricative noise. Young children may not be aware that a spread glottis is necessary for production of voiceless fricatives (or may have difficulty producing the voiceless glottal airflow) and may treat them as [−s.g.] (see the end of Section 5.4.2, and Section 7.1.9).

− All other segments are [−s.g.].

3. [+constricted glottis] ([c.g.]): A sound in which the vocal folds are pulled together tightly, so that regular periodic vibration is impossible.

+ All [+c.g.] segments are [−voiced], by definition. Glottal stop ([ʔ]) is [+c.g.].

− All other segments are [−c.g.].

In Table 2.1, voiceless stops are given as [+/−s.g.] and [+/−c.g.], because they can appear as aspirated, unaspirated, or with glottal constriction, in different environments.

Devoiced Obstruents

Devoiced obstruents (such as [b̥]) in English are usually treated as [+voiced], even though there is no voicing during closure. Devoiced obstruents might actually be [−voiced,−s.g.,−tense].

2.1.3. Place Features

The features that govern place of articulation are divided into two groups: the *articulator* features that determine which major articulator (the lips, the tongue tip, or the tongue body) is used, and the *subsidiary* features that fine-tune the information provided by the articulator features. The articulator features have only one feature value (i.e., they are not binary); this is reflected by capitalizing the first letter of their names and not using [+] or [−] signs (see below). The other features are binary. The subsidiary features are usually defined in such a way as to be *dependent* on the articulators with which they are associated. Thus subsidiary features can be present only if their associated articulator feature is present. For example, unless the lips are used ([Labial]), the feature [round] is irrelevant, since [round] requires use of the lips.

The Lips

1. [Labial]: A sound made with some involvement of one or both lips.

   + Bilabial ([p], [b], [ɸ], [β], [m]) and labiodental ([f], [v], [ɱ], [ʋ]) consonants are [Labial].

   + All rounded sounds—both vowels and consonants—are [Labial].

Note: If there is no involvement of the lips, the segment is *blank* for this feature because [Labial] is irrelevant. (See further discussion under Section 2.4 on feature geometry.)

/r/

We treat English /r/ (or /ɹ/) as [Labial], since /r/ is rounded in onsets (*red* [ɹ̹ɛd]) and when syllabic and stressed (*bird* [bɝːd]). However, /r/ is unrounded in codas after unrounded vowels (*fair* [fɛr]) and when syllabic and unstressed (*wicker* [wɪkɚ]). We believe that it should be treated as inherently rounded because it shows an affinity for rounding: for example, it is rounded in codas after rounded vowels (*four* [fɔɹ]). [Labial] is deleted in codas after unrounded vowels and in unstressed syllables.

---

2. [+round]: A sound involving protrusion of the lips with narrowing at the corners of the mouth.

   + All rounded vowels (e.g., [u]) and consonants (e.g., [w], [r]) are [+round].

− Simple bilabial and labiodental consonants are [−round].

3. [+labiodental]: A labial sound made with only one lip.

+ All labiodentals ([f], [v], [ɱ], [ʋ]) are [+labiodental].

− All bilabial consonants and rounded segments are [−labiodental].

The Tip of the Tongue

1. [Coronal]: A sound made by raising the tip or blade of the tongue.

+ [Coronal] includes alveolars ([t], [d], [n], [l], [s], [z]), interdentals (θ, ð), dentals (s̪, z̪), palatoalveolars ([ʃ], [ʒ], [tʃ], [dʒ]), alveopalatals ([ɕ], [ʑ], [tɕ], [dʑ]), palatals (e.g., [ç], [ʝ], [ɲ]), and retroflexes (such as [r]), plus the glide [j] and front vowels.

Note: All other places of articulation are unmarked for [Coronal]. Many English speakers produce [θ] and [ð] as dentals, not as true interdentals. For simplicity, we use the term *dental* in this book to include interdentals, and use *interdentals* when we need to be more specific.

2. [+anterior]: A coronal sound made at the alveolar ridge or farther forward.

+ Interdentals, dentals, and alveolars are [+anterior].

− Palatoalveolars, retroflexes, palatals, and front vowels are [−anterior].

Note: Noncoronal consonants are blank (not marked) for [anterior].

3. [+distributed]: A coronal sound made with a wide area of contact between the tip or blade of the tongue and the roof of the mouth or the teeth.

+ Interdentals, dentals, palatoalveolars, alveopalatals, and palatals are [+distributed].

− Only alveolars and retroflexes are [−distributed].

4. [+grooved]: A coronal sound made with a grooved tongue (a narrow channel at or near the midline). A grooved tongue channels the air and leads to high-amplitude noise. Only fricatives and affricates can be [+grooved].

+ Alveolar fricatives are [+grooved].

− Palatal fricatives and interdental fricatives are [−grooved] (as are lingual stops).

? Dental fricatives can be either [+grooved] ([s̪]) or [−grooved] ([θ, ð]) Children may use insufficient grooving even of alveolar fricatives, leading to a [−grooved] fricative.

The Tongue Body

These features refer to the exact position of the main body of the tongue, from palatal to uvular places of articulation, including height.

1. [Dorsal]: A sound made with the back of the tongue body.

   + The [Dorsal] consonants are palatals, velars, uvulars, and pharyngeals.

   + Vowels and glides are also [Dorsal].

   + [Dorsal] is also present in velarized consonants (such as English "dark" [ɫ]).

Other consonants are not marked for [Dorsal].

Velarized "dark" [ɫ]

We treat /l/ as inherently nonvelarized; it becomes velarized in codas, when syllabic, and in onsets before [+back] vowels (see below). However, some children may take the phoneme to be inherently velarized /ɫ/, and develarize it in onsets before front vowels. Substitutions for /l/ (particularly [w]) may reflect the velarized variant rather than the alveolar variant of /l/.

---

2. [+back]: A sound with the back of the tongue body raised or lowered.

   + Velar and uvular consonants are [+back], as are velarized consonants (including English "dark" [ɫ]).

   – The [−back] phones are the palatals, including front vowels and [j].

Note: Backness is not defined for labials, anterior coronals, palatoalveolars, pharyngeals, or glottals.

3. [+high]: A sound for which the tongue body is raised.

   + High vowels and glides, plus velar and palatal consonants are [+high].

   – Uvular and pharyngeal consonants and mid and low vowels are [−high].

4. [+low]: A sound for which the tongue body is lowered.

   + Only low vowels and pharyngeals are [+low].

   – Other dorsal segments are [−low].

/ɔ/

The symbol /ɔ/ is used ambiguously, to refer to a low vowel (as in North American *dog* [dɔːg]) or to a mid vowel (as in British *all* [ɔːl] or in the diphthong [ɔɪ], in North American *boy*).

 Exercises

1. List *all* the features that the following groups of sounds share.

   Suggestion: Just run down the features in Tables 2.1 and 2.2.
   Underline the features that are "most important" for characterizing the group.

   EXAMPLE: s v x   [−syl, +cons, −son, −nas, +cont, −lat, −c.g.]

   a. ʌ ɔ e æ   b. ʤ d ɬ ð   c. ʊ o w ɔ
   d. s β j o h   e. ɪ w g j u

2. In each of the following groups of sounds, one segment does not fit in because it does not share a certain feature with the other segments. Indicate the sound that does not fit in and one feature for that sound that is *not* shared with the rest of the sounds in the group. There may be more than one correct response. Try to find them all. *Note:* Sometimes a segment will be different because it *lacks* a major place feature.

   EXAMPLE: m d z n b [z] is [+continuant]

   a. æ ɛ ɔ u   b. i w e æ   c. u k b ɑ
   d. p t ʧ g   e. n l w ʐ r   f. m d v ʃ θ
   g. s e g m h

3. List *all* the features that would change if the first sound were changed into the second:

   EXAMPLE: p → b [+voiced] (and [−tense])

   a. v → z   b. u → ɑ   c. e → ẽ
   d. l → j   e. w → b   f. kʰ → h
   g. ʊ → u   h. s → θ   i. k → ŋ

4. Identify whether the following consonant-and-vowel pairs have any place or manner features in common, and if so, which:

   a. m u   b. t ɑ   c. k ɑ   d. s o
   e. n e   f. w u   g. g ʃ   h. v æ

2.2. Constraints and Repairs for Features and Feature Combinations

Table 2.3 shows constraints and repairs that affect features and feature combinations. There are two types of constraints.

- Individual feature constraints: A particular feature such as [Dorsal] or [+nasal] may be entirely impossible in the child's system.

- Feature combination constraints. Two features may be possible (e.g., [+voiced], [−continuant]) but not within a single segment. In that case, voiceless stops are possible, and voiced sonorants are possible, but voiced stops are not.

2.2.1. Single-Feature Constraints and Repairs

When there is a constraint against a specific feature, deletion occurs of either the feature itself or the segment containing the feature. If just the feature is deleted, and the rest of the segment remains, then another feature must be inserted to replace the deleted feature. Sometimes, additional features need to change to make the segment pronounceable. We address two examples. Consider the word *cow* /kaʊ/ when there is a constraint against velars (such that velar consonants cannot appear in the child's speech):

Constraint:	[Dorsal] is impossible	
Alternative Repairs:	a. Delete segment	[aʊ]
	b. Delete [Dorsal] and insert [Coronal]	[taʊ]

The segment /k/ can be deleted entirely, but that would include the deletion of other features that the child is capable of producing. A less radical solution is to delete just the feature [Dorsal] and then insert some other place feature; most often [Coronal] is inserted (see Section 2.2.2 below).

Table 2.3. Constraints and Repairs for Features and Feature Combinations

Child's Constraint	Target Word Challenge	Repair
Feature X prohibited	Impossible feature	• Delete feature X.
		1. Insert default.
		2. Spread other nondefault.
		• Delete segment containing feature.
Feature combination prohibited, e.g.:	Impossible feature combination	• Delete one feature.
− no coronal fricatives		1. Insert default.
		2. Spread feature to replace it.
− no labial nasals		• Delete segment containing feature.
− no voiced stops		• Move one feature elsewhere.

This leads us to a very important constraint:

▶ **FAITHFULNESS:** Pronounce words as much like the adult pronunciation as possible.

Speakers try to be faithful to a word's pronunciation, so that listeners can figure out which word was intended. Deleting a whole segment makes the pronunciation completely unfaithful to that segment. Retaining some features allows a *partial match* with the adult pronunciation, which is more faithful (and more intelligible).

Faithfulness is very useful in accounting for the types of substitutions that occur when a given feature is impossible. Consider /l/ and the word *low* /loʊ/:

Constraint:	[+lateral] is impossible	
Alternative Repairs:	a. Delete whole segment	[oʊ] (very unfaithful)
	b. Delete [+lateral], insert [−lateral], and change other features:	[joʊ]
		[woʊ]
		[doʊ]
		[ðoʊ]
		[noʊ]

Deletion of the whole /l/ is straightforward, although very unfaithful. Deletion of just [+lateral], with insertion of [−lateral], is problematic, because that would lead to the feature combination [+sonorant,+consonantal,+continuant,−lateral], which corresponds to a trilled [r], which does not occur in (most dialects of) adult English and is extremely unlikely for North American English-learning children. To yield a pronounceable consonant, some other feature must also change. The child can be unfaithful to particular features, and pronounceable segments result:

Faithful to	Unfaithful to	Results in	
+son,+cont	+cons	glide	
		j	(faithful to Coronal)
		w	(faithful to Dorsal in [ɫ])
+son,+cons	+cont	nasal	
+cons,+cont	+son	fricative	
+cons	+cont,+son	stop	

Different children take different options, depending on faithfulness to various features.

2.2.2. Feature Combination Constraints and Repairs

A similar choice about repairs arises whenever there is a constraint on combinations of features, as seen in the following example using the word *go* /goʊ/:

Constraint:	[Dorsal] and [+voiced] may not be combined	
Alternative Repair:	a. Delete whole segment	[oʊ]
	b. Delete [Dorsal] and insert [Coronal]	[doʊ]
	c. Delete [+voiced] and insert [−voiced]	[koʊ]

Because two features are involved, there are two options for deletion, one for each feature. A third option would be to move one of the features elsewhere. Consider the word *goat* /goʊt/:

Repair: Move (flop) [Dorsal] onto final consonant   [doʊk]

The features [Dorsal] and [+voiced] are both found in the child's pronunciation, just not in the same place they appear in the adult pronunciation of this word. The pronunciation [doʊk] does not violate the constraint against voiced velars but is unfaithful to the *location* of the features [Dorsal] and [Coronal] in the adult pronunciation.

There may be constraints against the combination of any two features, or even of combinations of three or four features. Repairs fall along the lines sketched here.

 Exercise

5. List the possible repairs for the following:

Constraint	Word
a. [+nasal] is impossible	no /noʊ/
b. [Labial] is impossible	foot /fʊt/
c. [Labial] & [+nasal] cannot be combined	mouse /maʊs/
d. [−cons] & [Labial] cannot be combined	why /waɪ/

2.3. Defaults: Not All Features Are Created Equal

Some features and feature values are treated in a special fashion that is distinct from the way other features and feature values are treated. These special features and feature values are referred to as *default* features and feature values (or sometimes as *unmarked* features and feature values). Generally, defaults are the most frequent features or feature values for a language (and the most frequent values are remarkably similar across adult languages and across children). Defaults are involved in two special (and opposite) patterns. In nonassimilatory patterns, they are commonly used as a substitute for other features; defaults replace other features. In assimilatory patterns, however, the opposite is true; *other features tend to replace defaults.*

The following appear to be the defaults for consonants in adult English, as well as for most English-learning children and most other adult languages. The default consonant (the one with the most default features) seems to be [t], with the following feature values being defaults:

Place defaults: Coronal, +anterior
Manner defaults: −sonorant, +consonantal, −continuant, −nasal, −lateral
Voicing defaults: −voiced

Vowels, in contrast, seem to vary. There is some evidence that the default vowel of adult English (in stressed syllables) is /ɛ/, but it is possible that /ə/ is the default for younger children. Whether /ɛ/ or /ə/ is the default, the following are default features:

Height: [−high], [−low]

It is unclear whether the default is [−back] ([Coronal]) (as for /ɛ/) or [+back] (as for /ə/).

Nondefaults have the value opposite to the above default value or, in the case of the consonant articulator features, will be all places but [Coronal, +anterior]. (See Tables 2.4 and 2.5 for a list of nondefaults for consonants and vowels, respectively.)

It is not certain that all speakers (especially children) have the same default features and feature values. For an occasional child, it is useful to assume that the default place of articulation is labial or dorsal, or that the default manner of articulation is a fricative.

Constraints and repairs relating to defaults and nondefaults are presented in Table 2.6, with discussion in the next few subsections.

Sometimes nondefault features are *redundant,* in that they are predictable from other features. For example, all velar ([Dorsal]) consonants are [+high], and all glides are [+continuant]. In phonological development, redundant nondefaults (such as [+continuant] in glides) often appear earlier than nonredundant nondefaults (such as [+continuant] in fricatives).

Table 2.4. Nondefault Consonant Features for Adult English (/t/ = default)

	p	t	tʃ	k	b	d	dʒ	g	f	θ	s	ʃ	v	ð	z	ʒ	m	n	ŋ	l	r	w	j	h	ʔ
consonantal																					−	−	−	−	−
continuant									+	+	+	+	+	+	+	+									
nasal																	+	+	+						
lateral																				+					
Laryngeal	✓	✓	✓	✓	✓	✓	✓	✓	✓	✓	✓	✓	✓	✓	✓	✓	✓	✓	✓	✓	✓	✓	✓	✓	✓
voiced					+	+	+	+					+	+	+	+									
spread glottis	(+)	(+)	(+)	(+)																				+	
Place	✓	✓	✓	✓	✓	✓	✓	✓	✓	✓	✓	✓	✓	✓	✓	✓	✓	✓	✓	✓	✓	✓	✓	✓	
Labial	✓				✓				✓				✓				✓				✓	✓			
Coronal			✓				✓			✓		✓		✓		✓					✓		✓		
anterior			−				−					−				−					−				
distributed										+				+											
grooved										−				−											
Dorsal				✓				✓												✓		✓	✓		

Note. Nondefaults in this table represent learned values for English but do not include *redundant nondefaults,* such as [+voiced] for [+sonorant] consonants.

Table 2.5. Nondefault Vowel Features for Adult English

	i	ɪ	e	ɛ	æ	u	ʊ	o	ɔ	ɨ	ə	ʌ	ɑ/a
Labial						✓	✓	✓	✓				
Coronal													
Dorsal	(✓)	(✓)	(✓)	(✓)	(✓)	(✓)	(✓)	(✓)	(✓)	(✓)	(✓)	(✓)	(✓)
back						+	+	+	+	+	+	+	+
high	+	+				+	+			+			
low					+				(+)				+

Notes. For adult English, /ɛ/ is considered the default vowel; in child speech, /ə/ may be the typical default vowel. Features for /ɛ/ and /ə/ are identical except in terms of backness; thus, for a child, [−back] or [+back] may be the nondefault value for [back].

Cells that are blank indicate that the given feature is irrelevant for that particular segment.

All vowels have [Dorsal] features. Because [back], [high], and [low] are dependent features of [Dorsal], [Dorsal] is included.

2.3.1. Defaults Substitute for Nondefaults

Two interactions occur between substitution processes and the default status of a feature:

- Defaults are often possible even when nondefaults are not.

- When nondefaults are impossible, the nondefault feature is often replaced by the default feature.

Typical examples follow.

Process	Nondefaults and Defaults	Example		
Fronting:	Nondefault [Dorsal] replaced by default [Coronal]	cow	/kɑʊ/	[taʊ]
	Nondefault [−anterior] replaced by default [+anterior]	shoe	/ʃuː/	[suː]
Backing:	Nondefault [Labial] replaced by default [Coronal]	cup	/kʌp/	[kʌt]

Table 2.6. Constraints and Repairs: Defaults and Nondefaults

Child's Constraint	Target Word Challenge	Repair
No nondefault features ■ anywhere ■ in codas ■ in unstressed σ ■ in initial unstressed σ	Nondefault feature impossible	• Delete nondefault feature. 1. Insert default. 2. Spread other nondefault. • Delete segment containing nondefault.

Stopping:	Nondefault [+continuant] replaced by default [−cont]	see	/si:/	[ti:]
	Nondefault [+nasal] replaced by default [−nasal]	comb	/koʊm/	[toʊb]
Devoicing:	Nondefault [+voiced] replaced by default [−voiced]	bed	/bɛd/	[bɛt]

This makes sense, in that the less frequent nondefault feature is replaced by the more common nondefault feature. It appears to be an effect of differences in practice between high-frequency and low-frequency features.

2.3.2. Nondefaults in Assimilations

In assimilations, as mentioned previously, there is a strong statistical tendency for nondefault features to replace default features. The following are common:

[Dorsal] vs. [Coronal]:	take	/teɪk/	[keɪk]
[Labial] vs. [Coronal]:	top	/tɑp/	[pɑp]
[+nasal] vs. [−nasal]:	time	/tɑɪm/	[nɑɪm]
[+cont] vs. [−cont]:	tease	/ti:z/	[si:z]

Although the opposite assimilations are possible, they are far less common. As a general rule of thumb, *if a feature replaces another in an assimilation, it is not a default feature.*

Assimilations may also take place between two nondefaults:

[Dorsal] vs. [Labial]:	cup	/kʌp/	[pʌp] OR [kʌk]
[+nasal] vs. [+continuant]:	mess	/mɛs/	[fɛs] OR [mɛn]

Although a given child may show assimilation of just one sort, across children both types of assimilation are equally common. Velars assimilate to labials as commonly as labials assimilate to velars. Nasals assimilate to fricatives as commonly as fricatives assimilate to nasals.

✎ Exercise

6. For all consonants: (a) identify whether the change is an assimilation or a substitution, (b) note which feature is involved, and (c) state whether the feature is a default or a nondefault. Depending on whether the feature is a default or a nondefault, state whether the process that occurred is expected.

a. calf	/kæf/	[tʰaf]	b. mud	/mʌd/	[bʌt]
c. pen	/pɛn/	[pɛt]	d. muddy	/mʌdi/	[mabi]
e. down	/dɑʊn/	[nan]	f. corn	/kɔrn/	[tʰoʊn]
g. fish	/fɪʃ/	[bɪt]	h. movie	/mu:vi/	[vu:vi]

The next two sections of the chapter (2.4 and 2.5) contain formalism and are background information relative to the analysis sections in Chapters 5–10. They explain relationships among features in nonlinear phonology and how repairs (processes) work in nonlinear theory. These sections are not directly applied in the analysis chapters but provide a foundation for them and can be read as such.

2.4. The Relationship Between Features: Feature Geometry

In early generative phonology, segments (phonemes) came to be viewed as groups of features. The prevailing view was that the features were unordered with respect to each other. Segments were just a bundle of simultaneously occurring features. This is no longer held to be true. Features are integrated into a hierarchical structure, such that there is one location for every feature and a feature can appear only in that location.

Every feature is independent of every other feature; we refer to this property as *feature autonomy*. Further, as we look across the different segments in a word, the same feature in each segment is found at the same location, so that all the tokens of that feature seem to create a line of their own. Each line is called a *tier*. We refer to each tier by using the name of the feature on that tier: the coronal tier, the continuant tier, the voicing tier, etc. This approach is known as *nonlinear* phonology.

It is not enough to have just the feature tiers. We also need to capture the notion of the segment: that features on different tiers occur at the same time. Simultaneous occurrence of elements on different tiers is expressed via the *association line:* a link between elements on two tiers. Association lines make explicit at what point in time an element occurs. Without an association line, there are no instructions for the element to be produced at any time, so it cannot be pronounced at all. Two elements are simultaneous if they are connected via an association line, or if they are linked to elements connected by an association line. For example, consider some tiers containing place features, as in Figure 2.A.

The features [anterior] and [Coronal] are simultaneous and, consequently, are linked. The same is true of [Coronal] and [distributed], and [Coronal] and [grooved]. However, there are no direct links between the dependent features [anterior], [distributed], and [grooved]; because the dependent features are all simultaneous with [Coronal], they are all simultaneous with each other.

Just as syllables are structured groupings of segments, segments are structured groupings of features. Segments have subgroupings, just as syllables do (onsets, peaks, etc.). All place features are grouped together under a Place node. All features affecting the larynx are grouped together under the Laryngeal node. All the features of the segment are grouped together under the Root node (which defines the segment). Manner features link directly to the Root node. Figure 2.B offers a common

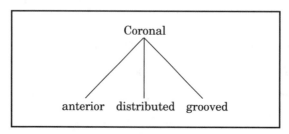

Figure 2.A. Associations of coronal features.

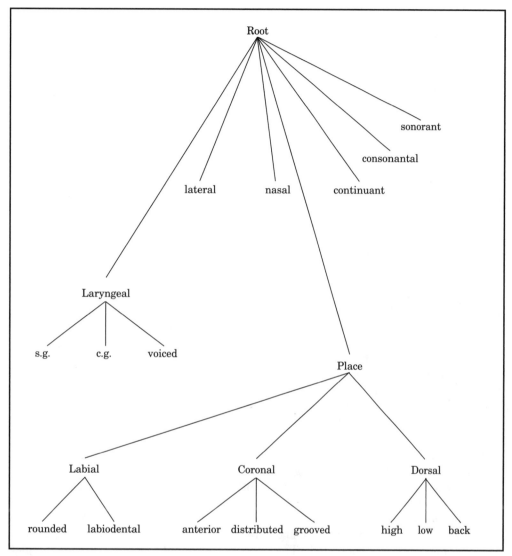

Figure 2.B. Feature geometry.

portrayal of feature geometry in recent theory. Note that the Place node links only to the articulator nodes, which in turn link only to the dependent features that are defined for each articulator. The Laryngeal node links directly to each laryngeal feature, with no further substructure.

One class of segments lacks a Place node: the glottals [h] and [ʔ]. These segments often behave as if they have no place features. This is reasonable phonetically, since glottals involve the larynx (just as all segments do), but what is going on above the larynx does not seem to be important: the supralaryngeal vocal tract takes on whatever configuration is needed for surrounding segments. For example, /h/ is a voiceless version of the vowel that follows the /h/: /hɪt/ [ɪ̥ɪt], /hæt/ [æ̥æːt], /huːt/ [u̥uːt], /hɑt/ [ɑ̥ɑːt]. The lack of a Place node gives glottals special properties.

Because elements on different tiers are independent of each other, there is no reason they must appear in a simple one-to-one relationship with each other. Both of the situations shown in Figure 2.C are possible. On the left, two consecutive

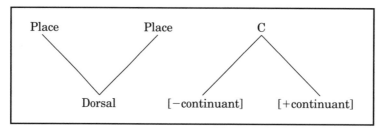

Figure 2.C. Multiple linkings of features.

segments share the same gesture for velar place of articulation, as is found in consonant clusters such as the /ŋk/ of *sink* /sɪŋk/. On the right, we have one possible representation for affricates: a consonant that begins as [−continuant] (a stop) and ends as [+continuant] (a fricative).

These representations entail something that has been stressed in phonetics for many years: It is impossible to slice speech into discrete, segment-sized units. Hockett (1955) noted that segments overlap; he provided the following analogy: The segments of phonological theory are like Easter eggs, each discrete and with a unique pattern, that pass through a machine that smashes them, after which it is difficult to tell which bit of yolk, egg white, and shell came from which egg. In nonlinear phonology, one cannot divide representations into discrete segments, because individual features can extend over a sequence of two or more segments.

Once we limit the number of association lines, we introduce a *dependency* relation between some features. Consider the feature links portrayed in Figure 2.D. Suppose we were to add a link between B and the second A. Automatically, C would become simultaneous with the second A, even though we did not overtly change the link between B and C. Similarly, if we were to delete B, C would no longer be linked, and it would also be deleted. By limiting the number of association lines between tiers, we introduce dependencies, whereby we predict that *groups* of features should behave as chunks, being deleted together, etc. This is the reason behind having structure in feature geometry: to allow groups of features to be easily deleted or assimilated as a group.

Deletion can provide evidence for feature groups. In the process known as *glottal replacement,* the entire Place node is deleted. (The double slash through the association line means that it is deleted.) The affected consonant thereby becomes the glottal [h] or [ʔ], neither of which has a Place node. (See Figure 2.E.)

Note: The glottal [h] tends to result from voiceless fricatives, because they are both [+continuant]. The glottal [h] also tends to result from aspirated stops, since they are [+s.g.]. From unaspirated stops, which are neither [+continuant] nor [+s.g.], the glottal [ʔ] tends to result.

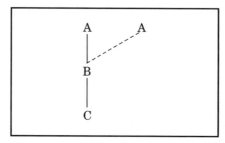

Figure 2.D. Feature dependencies.

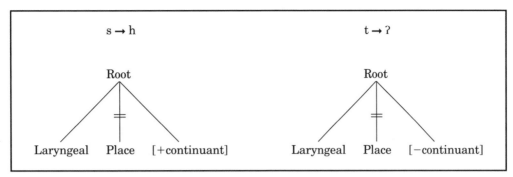

Figure 2.E. Delinking of Place in glottal replacement.

2.5. Basic Constraints and Processes: Spreading, Delinking, Deletion, Insertion

The examples above showed processes, rules, and repairs in nonlinear phonology. The types of processes that are used in nonlinear phonology reflect the differences in worldview from linear phonology. Since features are independent elements, nonlinear processes focus on features (and connected groups of features) rather than segments. There are only two possible (process) operations in nonlinear phonology: addition and deletion. The material that is added or deleted can be either a phonological element (a feature, node, timing unit, etc.) or an association line. Given these two operations (insertion and deletion) and the two objects on which these operations may be performed (elements and association lines), we have four different combinations:

1. Add an association line to an existing element (*spreading*).

2. Delete an association line from an existing element (*delinking*).

3. *Insert* an element that had not been there before and add an association line to it.

4. *Delete* an existing element (and its association lines).

There is no possibility of changing an element that is already present into something else. To change [−nasal] into [+nasal], we must break it down into two operations: delete [−nasal] and insert [+nasal]. Breaking down rules into components like this is advantageous. Rules that were feature changing in earlier phonology now involve one of two (automatic) situations: assimilation (the spreading of features) or replacement of a nondefault feature with a default feature.

2.5.1. Spreading

The operation that is *most prototypically nonlinear* (and that cannot be stated within linear theories) is the addition of association lines between two existing elements: *spreading*. The addition of the association line realigns two elements in time: Two elements that do not occur at the same time in the underlying representation are realigned so that they occur at the same time on the surface. *All assimilations are analyzed as spreading* (portrayed in Figure 2.F). This is a formal rule within nonlinear phonology. (We do not portray the formalism within our scan analysis presented in the second part of this book but demonstrate it here as background information.)

35

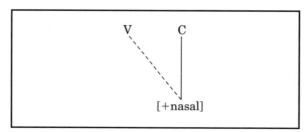

Figure 2.F. Spreading (assimilation) of [+nasal].

The solid lines denote existing association lines. The dashed line represents the addition of an association line; the dashes show what changes in the process. This "rule" adds an association line between the feature [+nasal] of the consonant and the preceding vowel; because the vowel thereby becomes simultaneous with the feature [+nasal], the vowel is now nasalized.

When elements spread, we need to consider the direction in which they spread. Spreading is *leftward* (or *right-to-left;* R-to-L) if the element is linked up so that it now begins earlier than it otherwise would have. Spreading is *rightward* (*left-to-right;* L-to-R) if the element ends later than it otherwise would have. In some processes, a feature might spread *bidirectionally:* both leftward and rightward. However, spreading is usually in just one direction.

Place features often spread together. For example, in English it is common to find colloquial pronunciations like the following:

nine pigeons   [nãɪ̃m pʰɪʤn̩z]

nine cuckoos   [nãɪ̃ŋ kʰuːkuːz]

nine thrushes   [nãɪ̃n̪ θrʌʃəz]

The final nasal of the word *nine* has three different pronunciations. In each case, the place of articulation assimilates from the following consonant. Because *every* place feature changes, it appears that the Place node itself is spreading, rather than individual features: Whatever the place of the second consonant, that will be the place of the nasal. (See Figure 2.G.) Note that all features that are dependent on the organizing node (in this case, the Place node) are "dragged along" when the organizing node spreads (as in the previous example of glottal replacement, Figure 2.E).

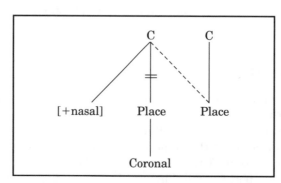

Figure 2.G. Place spreading (assimilation).

2.5.2. **Feature Linking**

Unlinked features are subject to three repair processes:

- The unlinked feature or node may simply be deleted (as in the Place delinking example, Figure 2.G).

- The unlinked feature can link up elsewhere. Consider a child's pronunciation of the word *smoke* /smoʊk/ as [fõʊ̃k]. In this case, the child's onsets could contain only one consonant, but the nondefault features [Labial], [+continuant], and [+nasal] had to link up somewhere (Figure 2.H). [Labial] of /m/ and [+continuant] of /s/ linked to the one available consonant. The nondefault [+nasal] linked to the vowel. This example showed *coalescence* (or *merger* or *fusion*) of [+continuant] and [Labial] (along with merger of their two timing units) and *migration* of [+nasal] to the vowel.

- A new segment can be inserted (*epenthesis*) in order to provide a place for the unlinked feature to attach. One real instance of this comes from a child who did not have rounded vowels:

| no | /noː/ | [nˠːm] |
| shoe | /ʃuː/ | [ɕɯːm] |

The [Labial] feature was delinked from the vowel (because all vowels had to be unrounded), and a nasal consonant was inserted after the vowel, to provide a segment in which the [Labial] feature could be pronounced.

In the *smoke* example, [+nasal] migrated to the neighboring segment (vowel). But a feature can *flop* (*migrate*) onto a segment that is farther away. In Chapter 8, we give an example (in Table 8.1) in which [Labial] migrated from the /r/ of the cluster /kr/ to the onset position of the second syllable, i.e., *crayon* as [keɪwʌ̃n]. Sometimes, the features of two segments will flop and interchange (*metathesize*), e.g., as in [pʌk] for *cup*.

2.6. **Consonants and Vowels: Next to Each Other but Apart**

In words, consonants and vowels are often next to each other. This neighborliness occurs at the level of timing units (the CV strings). In spite of their neighborliness and

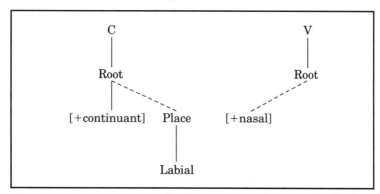

Figure 2.H. Fusion and migration. Example: *smoke* → [fõʊ̃k].

coarticulatory gestures, however, consonants and vowels are most often insulated from each other in phonological patterns. One way to explain this insulation is to assume that consonants and vowels are on different *planes* in the representation. This involves putting the Root nodes of consonants on a different tier than the Root nodes of vowels. For example, the word *ketchup* /kɛtʃəp/ would appear as in Figure 2.1.

The Root nodes of consonants, and all features under them, would be on a different (geometric) plane than the Root nodes (and all features) of vowels. As a result, there is a sense in which any two consecutive consonants are next to each other, even when a vowel "separates" them. Similarly, any two consecutive vowels are next to each other, even when "separated" by a consonant. It may seem odd to posit that consonants and vowels are on separate planes. We perceive them as occurring in a fixed order relative to each other, and it is natural to think of speech as a stream of segments: a single line of Root nodes. However, phonetic studies of speech production suggest that consonants and vowels are produced in separate "channels." Thus, consonants can be invisible to vowels, and vowels can be invisible to consonants. We have found this separation of consonants and vowels to be extremely useful for phonological development, particularly in cases of distant assimilation or migration, e.g., assimilations such as [keɪk] for *take.*

But we also have to account for those patterns in which (a) there are assimilations or dissimilations between consonants and vowels, e.g., spreading of [Labial] in words such as [bo] for *dough* (see Chapter 8), and (b) certain vowels or consonants appear to block spreading. Compare the following examples:

dog /dɑg/ [gɑg]   /g/ = [Dorsal] ([+back])   /ɑ/ = [Dorsal] ([+back])

tick /tɪk/ [tʰɪk]   /k/ = [Dorsal] ([+back])   /ɪ/ = [Coronal] ([−back])

[Dorsal] spreads leftward from the velar *only* if the vowel is also [Dorsal] and [+back], as in *dog.* However, if the vowel place feature is different from that of the final consonant, as in *tick* ([Coronal], or [−back]), spreading does not occur. If the place features of the rime segments are the same, assimilation can proceed. If the vowel feature is different, spreading of [Dorsal] from the /k/ is blocked by the different place feature of the vowel. In these examples (and in the case of [bo] for *dough*), place features of consonants and vowels seem to "see" each other. We could assume that, in such specific cases, C-place (the Place node of consonants) and V-place (the Place node of vowels) are on the same plane, unlike adult phonology. Alternatively (and this is our preferred analysis), we could assume that features can spread across the two distinct planes when the relevant level of interaction between consonants and vowels is at the level of timing units (where C and V are next to each other). If an interaction takes place at a "high" level in the phonological hierarchy, lower levels are often affected. (See Section 3.2 and Bernhardt and Stemberger, 1998, for more discussion of this issue.)

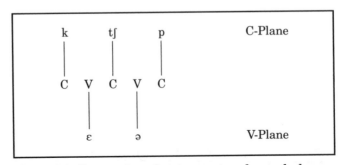

Figure 2.1. Separation of consonant and vowel planes.

2.7. Summary: Nonlinear Theories, Features, and Feature Combinations

- Features are the primary phonological elements.

- Segments are simultaneously occurring combinations of features.

- Features are autonomous but organized in hierarchical groups, under the Root node (manner features), the Laryngeal node, and the Place node.

- Subsidiary features are dependent on organizing higher-level features and structure for their existence and in terms of the phonological patterns that affect them.

- If a feature or feature combination is impossible, there are several possible repair processes to avoid using it: deletion of a feature or its segment, movement of the feature, or insertion of a different feature or of an intervening feature.

Chapter 3
Position in the Word, and Sequences

S o far, we have addressed features and segments in and of themselves. But there can be effects on the realization of a feature that are external to the segment. There are constraints on which features may appear in which position in the syllable or word. There are also constraints on the features that may appear in a sequence of consonants or vowels, such that one feature may not be next to another feature.

3.1. The Effects of Word Position on Features

A given segment might be treated differently in different words because of the effect of its position in the word or syllable. Features may be restricted to onsets, to codas, or to intervocalic position. There are three distinct patterns: (a) Nondefault features are impossible in "weak" positions in the word; they may be replaced by default features, or features from nearby "strong" positions may spread into the weak position via assimilation. (b) Vowel-like features are often predominant in codas. (c) Consonant-like features are often predominant in onsets.

3.1.1. Nondefault Features in Weak Positions

Several parts of a word can be identified as "weak" positions, in which constraints are often very strong:

- codas
- unstressed syllables in general
- word-initial unstressed syllables
- the second consonant in a word-initial consonant cluster

These weak positions often show a very limited set of possibilities. Even in adult English, codas in word-final unstressed syllables are more restricted than codas in word-final stressed syllables. As an exercise, the reader can try to generate as many words as possible ending in /p/ and /t/, in stressed versus unstressed syllables. Many words end in /t/ in both stressed and unstressed syllables (such as *sit* /sɪt/ and *bucket* /bʌkət/), and many end in /p/ in stressed syllables (such as *sip* /sɪp/). But few words end in /p/ in unstressed syllables (*ketchup* /kɛtʃəp/ being one).

Commonly, these weak positions tend not to allow nondefault features. Default features *may* be allowed to occur in weak positions. There is a tendency toward allowing voiceless stops and coronals, even if voiced stops, fricatives, labials, and velars are

Table 3.1. Constraints and Repairs Relating to Word Position

Child's Constraint	Target Word Challenge	Repair
Nondefault feature impossible in weak position ▬ no [Dorsal] ▬ no [Labial] ▬ no [+nasal] ▬ no [+cont] etc. SAME FEATURE IS POSSIBLE ELSEWHERE.	Feature impossible in weak position: • codas • unstressed syllables in general • word-initial unstressed syllables • second consonant in a cluster	• Delete segment. 1. Delete completely. 2. Spread in other segment. • Delete feature. 1. Insert default. 2. Spread other feature.

not possible. Constraints and repair processes relating to word position are listed in Table 3.1. A typical pattern would involve production of fricatives (nondefault [+continuant]) in word-initial stressed syllables but an absence of fricatives in codas and word-initial unstressed syllables:

sister	/sɪstɚ/	[sɪtɚ]
pass	/pæs/	[pæt]
support	/səpɔrt/	[təpɔrt]

Rather than insertion of the default feature, an assimilation could occur, of the whole segment or of the relevant feature:

sister	/sɪstɚ/	[sɪtɚ]
pass	/pæs/	[pæp]
support	/səpɔrt/	[pəpɔrt]

Note: Different weak positions may show different patterns. They do not have to be affected equally.

3.1.2. Feature Affinities

Syllables are a rhythmic alternation between a closed vocal tract and an open vocal tract. The optimal way to begin a syllable is with as closed a vocal tract as possible: with a voiceless stop. The features of voiceless stops (which are the default features for consonants) are often more prevalent in onsets in early acquisition.

Syllables should optimally end in an open position: a vowel. When the syllable ends in a consonant, it may optimally have a fairly open vocal tract. The consonant may share features with vowels. The following are often found only (or mostly) in codas in early acquisition: velar consonants (cf. adult [ŋ], which cannot occur word-initially), fricatives, liquids, and nasals. In many instances, especially with velars and fricatives, codas may be the only location in which the features ([Dorsal] and [+continuant]) may occur in consonants:

| cow | /kaʊ/ | [taʊ] | vs. | bike | /baɪk/ | [baɪk] |
| see | /siː/ | [tiː] | vs. | mouse | /maʊs/ | [maʊs] |

There are thus two opposite trends in codas. Because codas are a weak position, they may have more (or only) default features. Because they are at the end of a syllable, they may have more (or only) vowel-like features (which, for consonants, are the nondefaults). Most children show a mixture of these two trends. For example, the first consonants to appear in codas are often (default) voiceless stops, but the second consonants may be (nondefault, vowel-like) nasals. For a minority of children, one trend predominates to the exclusion of the other.

Intervocalic consonants may also show a predominance of vowel-type features. This can occur if they (a) are being treated as codas, or (b) assimilate features from the vowel on either side.

 ## Exercise

1. Given the constraint and the word that violates it, list as many different types of repairs as you can.

Constraint	Word
a. No (independent) [+voiced] in coda	/rʌb/
b. No (independent) [Place] in initial unstressed syllable	/dʒəˈræf/
c. No [−consonantal] in onset	/jɛs/
d. Onset must have [Place]	/hɛd/
e. No (independent) [Dorsal] in coda	/teɪk/

3.2. Segments or Features Occurring "Next to" Each Other

Constraints often affect two features or segments when they are "next to" each other. Note that there is more than one way in which two elements can be next to each other. Furthermore, different definitions of "next to" might be relevant for different children and different constraints and processes.

The usefulness of more than one definition of "next to" is clear, given an analogy with objects in the world. Consider a parking lot in which some spaces are filled with cars and some are empty. If two cars are in adjacent spaces, they are clearly next to each other for all purposes: it is impossible to put another car between them, and "assimilation" (for example, the door of one car banging into the other car) treats them as next to each other. If two cars are separated by an empty space, however, they are not next to each other for all purposes: another car can be placed between them, and they are too far apart for one car's door to bang the other car. However, an object thrown from one car may go through the intervening empty space and hit the other car, so the two cars are next to each other for that purpose. Whether we consider two cars separated by an empty space to be next to each other depends on our purpose, but two cars in adjacent spaces are next to each other for all purposes. Similarly, "next to" in phonology depends on the purpose.

The following are different ways of characterizing what "next to" means:

- The two segments have adjacent timing units (C's and V's are next to each other).

- The two segments have adjacent Root nodes on the consonant plane or the vowel plane (two consonants with no intervening consonants are next to each other).

- Two Place nodes are not separated by another Place node on the same plane but *may* be separated by a placeless consonant such as [ʔ] or [h].

- Two [Labial] nodes are not separated by another [Labial] node but could be separated by nonlabial consonants.

When two identical features are next to each other by any of these definitions, one might be deleted, or they might be merged into a single token linked to two segments (see Section 3.3). Features may spread to another location that is next to the feature that is spreading, by any of these definitions.

 Exercise

2. Identify whether two features are next to each other on the consonant plane and in general: (When we indicate sequences, we use a hyphen between the features and no intervening spaces. This differentiates sequences of consonants from simultaneous feature combinations, which are indicated by "&.")

   a. [Labial]-[Labial] in [biːheɪv]

   b. [Labial]-[Dorsal] in [pæk]

   c. [+nasal]-[+lateral] in [neɪzəl]

3.3. **Constraints on Sequences**

All languages prohibit some sequences of features. For example, in word-initial position, English allows /s/-[−continuant] clusters /sp, st, sk, sm, sn/ and [−sonorant]-[+sonorant] (&[−nasal]) clusters (clusters starting with a stop or fricative, followed by a non-nasal sonorant, i.e., a liquid or a glide). Other word-initial sequences, such as [+sonorant]-[−sonorant] (in, for example, */mt/) are impossible. Even within the allowed patterns, particular sequences are impossible:

[Coronal]-[+lateral]:	*/tl/
[−sonorant,+continuant,+voiced]-[+sonorant]:	*/vl/, */zw/

Thus, words such as /træp/ and /klæp/ can occur, but words such as */tlæp/ are impossible. Similarly, words such as /flæt/ and /swɑt/ can occur, but */vlæt/ and */zwɑt/ are impossible. In the middle and at the end of the word, /kt/ and /pt/ are possible, but */tp/, */tk/, and */pk/ are not:

[Dorsal]-[Coronal]:	/ækt/		*[Coronal]-[Dorsal]:	*/ætk/
[Labial]-[Coronal]:	/hɛləkɑptɚ/		*[Coronal]-[Labial]:	*/hɛləkɑtpɚ/
*[Dorsal]-[Labial]:	*/æpk/ */æpkɚ/			

In adult speech, such constraints on sequences are reflected by the absence of words with those sequences. In child phonology, there are often constraints on sequences that are possible in adult speech. Words with those sequences are then subject to a repair that deletes one or the other feature or separates them so that they are no longer next to each other. In our experience, sequence constraints are among the most difficult to detect. They often initially look like between-word variability: a segment such as word-initial /s/ is consistently pronounced one way in some words but a different way in other words. Before concluding that the words are just arbitrarily different, the environment needs to be examined. The pronunciation of the /s/ is often predictable from the particular consonants and vowels that are present in the word.

One common sequence constraint relates to place of articulation. It may be impossible to have sequences of consonants in which the first is alveolar and the second is velar. In adult English, this constraint holds only when there is no intervening vowel between the two consonants, e.g., */ætk/, but /tæk/. In child phonology, the constraint may hold between two consonants even if there is an intervening vowel. In that case, a repair process is needed to avoid the impossible sequence. (See Table 3.2.)

Consider possible repairs of the constraint that prevents the [Dorsal]-[Labial] sequence in *cup* /kʌp/:

Delete one feature:	[kʌt]	(fill in default [Coronal] to replace the deleted [Labial])
	[kʌk]	(spread [Dorsal] to replace the deleted [Labial])
Delete one segment:	[kʌ] *or* [ʌp]	
Re-order features:	[pʌk]	

Table 3.2. Constraints and Repairs for Sequences

Child's Constraint	Target Word Challenge	Repair

A sequence is impossible:
 	
▬ no [Coronal]-[Dorsal]
▬ no [+cont]-[−cont]
▬ no [−nasal]-[+nasal]
etc.
	Impossible sequence:
	
	• no intervening segment
	
	• separated by C or V
	
	• separated by nothing on the relevant tier
		• Delete one segment.
		
		• Delete one feature.
		  1. Insert default.
		  2. Spread other feature to replace it.
		
		• Separate features.

A feature may not be repeated: ▬ [+cont] may not appear twice ▬ [Dorsal] may not appear twice etc.		1. Insert segment between. 2. Move one or both features. • Reverse the order of the features. • Merge two identical features.

Separation is unlikely here, because the two consonants are already separated by a vowel. The only way to separate them would be to insert another consonant, and probably a vowel also, and that is unlikely: [kʌtəp]. Separation is a more likely repair when there is no intervening segment, such as with a prohibition against a fricative before a stop, as in the word *spot* /spɑt/:

Delete one segment: [pɑt] *or* [sɑt]

Re-order features: [psɑt]

Separate features: [səpɑt]

How do we know that there is a sequence constraint active here, and not just a constraint limiting onsets to a single consonant? If there are onsets with two consonants, such as in *break* /breɪk/ [bweɪt], then onsets are possible *as long as* they have certain sequences ([−son]-[+son], [−cont]-[+cont], etc.). In such cases, we can be more certain that sequence constraints are relevant. (See Section 8.1.)

Note that assimilation is a common repair for sequence constraints. In child phonology, the most common assimilations between distant segments involve place of articulation: Labial Harmony and Velar Harmony. In general, spreading is right-to-left, meaning that the prohibited sequences are *[Coronal]-[Dorsal] and *[Coronal-Labial]. Note that these are the same sequences that are absent in adult English if no vowel appears between the two consonants. Although there are other reasons that assimilations may occur, most often they are the result of constraints on sequences. Nasal assimilation is also common:

bean   /biːn/   [miːn]   (cf. adult [bīːn])

The lack of [−nasal]-[+nasal] sequences is also true of adult English: vowels become nasalized before nasal consonants, and sequences such as [pm] are basically absent within words (*[ʤʌpmi]). In contrast, [+nasal]-[−nasal] sequences are common: *need* /niːd/ [niːd], *jumpy* /ʤʌmpi/.

The above examples all showed sequences of *different* features. However, there can also be constraints on repetition of the *same* feature. The same kinds of repairs can occur to prohibit sequences of the same feature. For example, suppose that [Labial] may not appear twice, as it does in adult pop /pɑp/:

Delete one segment: [pɑ]   *or* [ɑp]

Delete one feature: [pɑt]   *or* [tɑp]

Reverse the order
of the features: not relevant, because the features are identical

Separate the two features: [pɑtəp]   (very unlikely)

There is an additional option, however: merge the two tokens of [Labial], creating a single [Labial] gesture that links to both Place nodes on the consonant plane, as shown in Figure 3.A.

This has the effect of *preserving* the labiality of the two consonants. How do we know when such an apparently invisible merger has occurred? When the phonological patterns show that the feature [Labial] is impossible *unless* there is another token of [Labial] next to it. It is relatively common for [Labial] to be impossible after a [Dorsal] or [Coronal] consonant but to be possible after a [Labial] consonant:

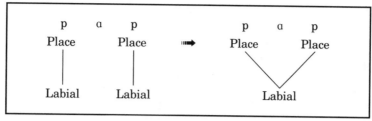

Figure 3.A. Merging of identical C-Place of two consonants.

top /tɑp/ [tɑt]

cup /kʌp/ [kʌt]

pop /pɑp/ [pɑp]

It appears that the shared [Labial] feature *helps* the child produce a labial consonant late in the word. Whenever a feature (or entire segment) is impossible in one part of a word, *unless* it is identical to another nearby feature (or segment), it is an indication that a merger has occurred. Because a single gesture extends over both segments, there is no repetition of the feature (which would involve two distinct tokens of the gesture) and thus no sequence problem.

 Exercise

3. Given the constraint and the word that violates it, list as many different types of repairs as you can:

Constraint	Word
a. No [Coronal]-[Dorsal] sequence	/teɪk/
b. No repetition of /i/	/jir/
c. No (independent) manner features between vowels	/bʌni/
d. No [Coronal]-[Labial] sequence	/twaɪs/

3.4. Summary: Word Position and Sequences

- Features can be subject to word-position restrictions; features can be restricted to onsets, to codas, or to intervocalic position.

- Nondefault features may be impossible in weak positions in the word.

- Vowel-like features may be predominant in codas, and/or consonant-like features may be predominant in onsets.

- There can be constraints on sequences of the same or different features.

- Sequence constraints in child phonology may reflect those of the target language or may be specific to a given child.

- Sequence constraints may affect features in segments that are fully next to each other or distant.

- Between-word variability, assimilations, and metatheses are often clues to sequence constraints in child phonology.

Part II
Scan Analysis Procedures (and Intervention Strategies)

Chapter 4
Introduction to Scan Analysis

The major purpose of the subsequent chapters (Chapters 5–10) is to take the reader through the components of a nonlinear scan analysis, a methodology that involves no (or minimal) counting. The final chapter of the book describes some intervention strategies and techniques. This introduction outlines the goal types based on the nonlinear analyses, gives suggestions for goal selection, and gives an overview of the scan itself. Before proceeding to analysis, it helps to know ahead of time what the intervention program might look like and why.

4.1. Goal Types

The purpose of the scan analysis is to derive an intervention plan for a child with a phonological disorder. The types of goals that the nonlinear methodology can lead to are represented in Table 4.1. There are two major dichotomies in goal types: (a) syllable and word structure versus segments and features, and (b) "new stuff" versus "old stuff" in new combinations or places. The first division is fairly straightforward and follows the discussions of syllables and words in Chapter 1 (word length, stress patterns, and word shapes) and of position and sequences in Chapter 3 versus that of segments and features in Chapter 2. The second division is less obvious and will, we hope, become clearer in Chapters 5–8. We give a basic introduction to those divisions here. Note that the goal types are numbered in terms of their order of analysis (not by any hierarchical division).

Table 4.1. Goals in a Nonlinear Phonological Intervention Plan

Phonological Level	Syllable & Word Structure	Segments & Features
Totally new stuff	Type 1	Type 2
	(Phrases) Word lengths Stress patterns Word shapes	Individual features (and related segments)
	Type 4	Type 3
Old stuff in new places *or* in new combinations	1. New word positions for old segments	New combinations of old features
	2. New sequences of segments	

4.1.1. New Elements ("New Stuff")

"New stuff" includes syllable and word structures *or* features that are missing (or very marginal) in the child's system.

Rule of thumb for intervention targets: Generally, when targeting the "new" element, it is effective to use some "old" element to support it, putting new features in existing word shapes or targeting new word shapes with old features and segments. This follows from the principle of incremental learning, using strengths to bolster needs. It also follows from the major division in the phonological hierarchy between prosodic (word/syllable) structure on the one hand and features on the other hand.

Goal type 1: New syllable and word structures. If a child has no word-initial clusters, CCV and CCVC are new word shapes. If a child has no codas (syllable-final consonants), CVC is a new word shape.

Goal type 2: New individual features and segments. If a child has no velars, [Dorsal] is a new feature. If a child has no fricatives, [+continuant] is a new feature.

4.1.2. Old Elements ("Old Stuff") in New Places or New Combinations

During phonological development, it is not uncommon for the members of a category to emerge one by one. In terms of *place of emergence,* velars may appear first in coda, and only later in onset (see Chapter 3). In terms of *simultaneous feature combinations,* labial stops and coronal fricatives may emerge before labiodental fricatives.

Goal type 3: New simultaneous combinations of "old" features. A child may be able to produce individual features but not in simultaneous combination with each other. For example, a child may produce labial stops [p] and [b] and coronal fricatives [s] and [z] but not labiodental fricatives [f] and [v]. Thus, the goal would be the simultaneous combination of [Labial] (from [p] and [b]) and [+continuant] (from [s] and [z]), i.e., a new "place" for old features.

Goal type 4: New places for old segments. In terms of syllable and word structure, targeting "old segments" in new places is similar to Goal Type 1 (targeting new word shapes with old features), in that (old) segments and features that are found in one word position or sequence are targeted in another (new) word position or sequence. In this case, however, it is not the word shape itself that is marginal. For example, although CVC may be fairly frequent in a child's system, one sound class may be missing in one word position or sequence. For example, (old) velars may appear in coda but not in onset (new place), or (old) nasals may precede non-nasals but not follow them (new place). Thus, the goal is to put the old elements in positions or sequences that are new for them.

4.2. Goal Selection

Many factors underlie goal selection within the goal types described. Some of these have to do with the phonological system itself; others have more to do with learning methods and social considerations.

4.2.1. Phonological Factors

The following phonological factors influence goal selection. They are not hard and fast rules but, rather, useful guidelines.

- *The four goal types:* To address needs for the whole phonological system, consider inclusion of a goal from each of the four goal categories discussed above.

- *Nondefault status:* In general, target the nondefault features. Children with phonological disorders often overuse default features. One goal is to circumscribe default use.

- *Phonetic tendencies:* Exploit phonetic tendencies when possible. Certain features ([Dorsal], [+sonorant], [+nasal], [+continuant], [−voiced]) are often "easier" in coda position, while others ([−continuant], [+voiced], and [Labial]) are often easier in onset positions. These factors can be relevant when choosing word positions for new features or when choosing features to use to promote new word shapes.

- *Generalization factors:* Choose targets that can stimulate generalization across a category. This may mean targeting more than one exemplar of a category (two fricatives, for example), while leaving some targets within the category as observation targets (to test whether generalization is occurring).

- *Developmental status:* This can be difficult to determine. Our knowledge about order and age of acquisition is minimal in many areas, particularly in word structure development, but also for segments, particularly vowels. Clearly, one would not start with multisyllabic words and complex clusters for a child with only CV's; an incremental approach to word shape development would make better sense. But specific developmental order of word shapes is not known. For consonants, it may seem logical to defer the later-developing segments (interdentals, liquids) as goals. But children with phonological disorders can have "chronological mismatch" (Grunwell, 1985). Thus, a child may be quite capable of learning /r/ when velars are still difficult. Developmental "norms," such as they are, are not necessarily best indicators for goal selection.

- *Intelligibility:* This is also difficult to determine for an individual. If it *is* possible to determine what might enhance intelligibility, this should enter into the process of goal selection.

4.2.2. Interaction with Other Linguistic Systems and Communicative Factors

Goal selection (and intervention strategies) can also be affected by other factors, such as communicative context, prosody, fluency, voice, morphology, syntax, oral mechanism, and perception. Communicative context may affect production, i.e., whether a word is pronounced on its own versus in a phrase, or in imitation versus spontaneously. Unusual rate, rhythm, or intonation may negatively influence intelligibility and may relate to word and syllable structure constraints. Dysfluency may be exacerbated by particular sounds or structures. Grammatical morphemes or phrasal combinations may be affected by phonological constraints (see Chapter 10). Oral mechanism or perceptual factors may affect a child's ability to produce or perceive certain targets. As part of the overall assessment, these factors need to be considered and, if any are a concern, integrated within the phonological intervention program.

4.2.3. Social Factors

Sometimes social factors overrule linguistic ones. A child may be very reticent, in which case it may be more facilitative to begin by targeting "old stuff" in new places or combinations. Starting with the familiar may help reduce anxiety and maximize opportunities for success. Or there may be a particular need within the family for production of certain elements (as in someone's name). Because there are often many goals, it is possible to accommodate those needs within the program.

4.3. The Scan

We now turn to a brief overview of the scan itself (Appendix D), the purpose of which is to help derive the goals for the intervention program.

4.3.1. Page-by-Page Breakdown

Page 1: *Cover Page.* Identifying information and summary of goals.

Page 2: *Bird's-Eye View.* A quick overview of the child's phonological system.

Page 3: *Syllable and Word Structure Analysis.* Word length, stress patterns, and word shapes.

Pages 4–5: *Consonant Analysis.* Manner, laryngeal, and place features across word positions, plus defaults.

Page 6: *Word Position and Sequence.* Segments in word positions and sequences.

Page 7: *Goal Summary.* Summary of the analysis, notation of other relevant factors such as social factors, interactions with other linguistic and communicative needs, goal selection and order, and intervention strategies.

Page 8: *Notes on Goal Selection.* Plus Vowel Features and Vowel Analysis Checklist.

4.3.2. The Analysis Chapters

Chapter 5 contains a full analysis for one child. Chapters 6–10 each focus on one part of the analysis.

Chapter 5, The Complete Scan Analysis: the analysis in overview.

Chapter 6, Syllable and Word Structure: page 3 of the scan.

Chapter 7, Consonant and Glide Analyses: pages 4–5 of the scan; word position effects, top of page 6 of the scan.

Chapter 8, Sequence: page 6 of the scan.

Chapter 9, Vowels.

Chapter 10, Interactions Between Phonology and Grammar.

In each chapter, in addition to the scan analysis, quantitative analyses are either demonstrated or described (depending on whether the data set is large enough for quantitative analysis).

In Chapters 5 and 7, data from one child are sufficient for illustrating the methodology. In Chapters 6, 8, 9, and 10, we present data from more than one child in order to illustrate the various analysis procedures. Different ways of organizing the data are presented as options. All of the data sets can of course be used in another section for practice. Four additional sets are given in Appendix C that are exemplary for the particular type of analysis.

The following tips may be helpful as you proceed through the analysis chapters:

- Have two parts of the blank scan sheet with you as a guide: the relevant page and the Goal Summary page.

- Read through our analyses first, then redo the data set yourself. You may come up with slightly different answers, something that is always possible in analysis. If your results look very different from ours, you may have observed something unique, or you may want to reread that section or the relevant theory sections in Chapters 1–3.

- Some readers may prefer to read the detailed and varying examples in Chapters 6–10 before going through the complete scan analysis in Chapter 5. Others may wish to skim Chapter 5 first, to have an overview of the whole process.

4.3.3. General Procedures

▶ **Step 1: Skim the data (Bird's-Eye View, page 2).**

Before proceeding carefully through the data, spend *5 minutes* maximum with a very quick skim of the data. This will help alert you to particular areas that will need more careful attention during the rest of the scan. This will be demonstrated in Chapter 5, with the full analysis.

▶ **Step 2: Code if needed.**

Each adult and child utterance may be coded for the particular analysis in question. *This is not a necessary step* in typical use of the scan form but may be helpful at the beginning if the reader is not used to doing a particular analysis. In typical use, your eyes skim over the data, looking for regularities and expected patterns and noting anything unusual as you go.

▶ **Step 3: Fill in the relevant scan sections.**

The relevant section is filled in page by page on the scan. A systematic step-by-step approach usually works best at first, with shortcuts being taken as one becomes familiar with the scan. Checks, circling, underlining, color coding, etc., are used rather than counting.

▶ **Step 4 (or 5): Summarize on the Goal Summary page.**

Page 7 of the scan summarizes strengths and needs for each part of the analysis and leads to goal selection. This can be done after each part of the analysis or at the end of the analysis.

▶ **Optional (alternative) step: Perform a quantitative analysis.**

If you decide that some type of counting should be done, either because the data are very variable or because you want to establish a baseline (or otherwise document efficacy), this is generally done before entering data on the Goal Summary page.

4.3.4. **Scan Glossary**

Definitions of terminology used in the scan and data protocols (that are not discussed above under goal selection) are given here for reference.

Basic inventory: The main forms a child uses for the particular analysis in question. They may or may not match the adult targets (*independent analyses,* i.e., what the child does independent of the adult targets).

Comparison with adult targets: On the Syllable and Word Structure Analysis page (page 3), typical patterns of difference between adult and child targets are indicated for underlining (or circling). On the Consonant Analysis page (page 4), the child's substitutions and missing forms are written in by hand (*relational analyses,* i.e., what the child does in relation to the adult targets).

Match: A "correct" production (*relational analysis*).

Maximum: The child's most advanced form for the particular analysis, *independent of the adult target.* For syllable and word structure this often is the longest word, but it may be a shorter word that has either infrequent or complex structures (clusters, codas, weak-Strong stress patterns, a specific rare segment). It informs about current potential.

Developing: What the child matches (has correct) some of the time (*a relational analysis*). Sometimes such forms become immediate goals, particularly for children who are reluctant to engage in the therapy process. Other times, these developing forms are baselines against which to measure progress. Developing forms are placed in parentheses.

Frequent: These forms are found frequently in the sample and are often the current optimal forms (defaults) for a child. They may or may not match adult targets. Frequent syllable shapes may be useful when targeting new segments. Frequent segments may be useful when targeting new forms.

Context differences: Sometimes context affects production. If the same words, structures, or segments have variable production, look to see whether there is any consistent difference based on elicitation context: spontaneous speech versus imitated production, production in single words versus in phrases.

Need to count, what? When data are variable and patterns difficult to determine, it is sometimes helpful to quantify patterns.

Needs: Forms that are missing, marginal, or developing in the sample, even when there is opportunity to produce them.

Strengths: What the child uses frequently and/or matches often.

Medial, syllable-final: The coda of a syllable within the word, e.g., the [p] of *captain.*

Medial, syllable-initial: The *identifiable* onset of a syllable within a word (syllable-initial-within-word), e.g., the /t/ of *captain* or the initial consonant(s) of the second syllable of a word with weak-Strong stress, e.g., the [tʰ] of *guitar* or the [m] of *tomato.*

Medial, intervocalic: A consonant between two vowels, where stress is on the first vowel and the onset or coda status of the consonant is ambiguous (ambisyllabic?), e.g., the [n] of *bunny*.

Syllable-initial/onset: Onsets of all syllables within the word (word-initial and syllable-initial-within-word), e.g., both the /k/ and the /t/ of *captain*.

Obstruent: A stop, affricate, or fricative.

Chapter 5
The Complete Scan Analysis

This chapter contains a complete scan analysis for one child, thereby providing an overview of the analysis methodology. Each section of the scan form (Appendix D) is replicated and preceded by a general explanation of that section and followed by summary notes for the particular analysis of that child's data. Because the intent of this chapter is to give an overview of the scan, only general commentary is provided. Subsequent chapters discuss each component of the scan in detail, using data from other children. For readers who prefer to see the whole picture before proceeding to details, it will be helpful to read this chapter first, possibly returning to it after going through the rest of the book. For readers who prefer to assemble a whole from parts, this chapter should probably be read after reading the detailed chapters.

5.1. The Child

Dylan: Age 4-7. Moderate phonological disorder.

Dylan's language comprehension skills were above average. To his speech–language pathologist, his language production skills appeared age-appropriate in terms of length and complexity of utterance. However, transcribers could decipher only 25% of the words of a conversational speech sample due to lack of intelligibility. He was starting to become embarrassed about his communication difficulties and was withdrawing in social situations. In terms of metaphonological awareness, he was able to segment sentences and words and knew some letters but could neither rhyme nor do alliteration. He was very motivated to learn, was amenable to a variety of activities, and had excellent home support. In Table 5.1 is a small subset of his assessment sample. (For additional words and an extended analysis, see Bernhardt and Stemberger, 1998, Chapter 8.)

The data in Table 5.1 are presented in columns, in a way that we find helpful for quick scanning. The columns allow for up to three syllables across the page. The column headings (C, V) help to speed up coding and analysis of word shapes. (If a sample contains longer, more complex words, a wider page with more columns can be used.) The forms given for the adult are for typical adult pronunciations in British Columbia, Canada. Coding conventions are as follows:

- If a word is between one and three syllables in length, the word-final consonant(s) is/are entered in the WF (word-final) consonant column(s) to allow for quick final consonant scanning.

- The following abbreviations are used: Ø = missing (deleted) consonant; I = imitated; C = connected speech; WI = word-initial; WF = word-final; SF = medial, syllable-final; SI = medial, syllable-initial.

Table 5.1. Dylan's Data

Word	Adult	Child	WI C1	WI C2	WI V	SF C	SI C1	SI C2	SI V	SI C	SI V	WF C1	WF C2	I/C
eleven	(ʔ)iːlevn̩	ʔiːlɛm	ʔ		iː		l		ɛ	ø		m̩		
money	mʌ̃ni	mʌi	m		ʌ		ø		i					
noisy	nɔizi	nɔiʔi	n		ɔɪ		ʔ		i					I
pink	pʰɪ̃ŋk	pʰɪ̃ŋ	pʰ		ɪ̃							ŋ	ø	
black	blæk	bwæɪ	b	w	æɪ							ø		
ten	tʰɛn	tʰɛ̃n	tʰ		ɛ̃							n		C
together	tʰəˈgɛðɚ	gɛdʊ[a]	ø		ø		g		ɛ	d	ʊ			
truck	tʰrʌk	twʌ	t	w	ʌ							ø		
tub	tʰʌb	pʰʌː	pʰ		ʌː							ø		
dolly	dɑli	dɑːʔi	d		ɑː		ʔ		i					
comb	kʰõʊm	kʰõʊm	kʰ		õʊ							m		
green	griːn	gwiːn	g	w	iː							n		
fish	fɪʃ	bɪʔ	b		ɪ							ʔ		
thumb	θʌ̃m	bʌ̃m	b		ʌ̃							m		
that	ðæt	dæ	d		æ							ø		C
sister	sɪstɚ	dɪʔɪ	d		ɪ		ʔ		ɪ					
sleep	sliːp	bwiː	b	w	iː							ø		
soapy	soupi	bouʔiː	b		oʊ		ʔ		iː					
stickerbook	stɪkɚbʊk	dɪʔoubʊ	ø	d	ɪ		ʔ		oʊ	b	ʊ	ø		C
zoo	zuː	duː	d		uː									
shoe	ʃuː	duː	d		uː									
chicken	tʃɪkn̩	tʰɪʔɪ̃n	tʰ		ɪ		ʔ		ɪ̃			n		C
jacket	dʒækət	dæʔɪʔ	d		æ		ʔ		ɪ			ʔ		C
radio	reɪdijoʊ	weɪjəʔou	w		eɪ		j		ə	ʔ	oʊ			
leaf	liːf	wiː	w		iː							ø		
look	lʊk	lʊː	l		ʊː							ø		C
hand	hænd	hæ̃n	h		æ̃							n	ø	
you	juː	juː	j		uː									C

aAlternate forms of *together:* [təgɛə], [tʊgɛdɪ]. The three tokens were uttered in sequence (self-repetition). *Note.* Throughout, the adult forms are the adult pronunciations, not the underlying adult representations.

- Long vowels are usually coded as Vː, while diphthongs are coded as VV, in order to distinguish them from each other.

- When children use a large number of glottal stops for consonants, word shapes can be coded with glottals, e.g., ʔV for CV, or ʔVʔ for CVC. Alternatively, G (glide) may be used instead of C if a child uses many glides ([w], [j], [h], [ʔ]). In this way, we indicate how the child is marking the consonant positions. The G and ʔ also indicate that [+consonantal] is not well established in a given word position. Progress can then be measured in terms of change from G or [ʔ] to C.

- Affricates are coded as C.

- Postvocalic and syllabic /r/ and /l/ may also be coded in some special way, particularly since children often treat them as vowels rather than consonants. A syllabic marker can be transcribed as a diacritic under the consonant to indicate the syllabic variant, e.g., [r̩].

5.2. Step 1: Bird's-Eye View

The purposes of the Bird's-Eye View (scan page 2) are as follows:

- to obtain an overall impression of the phonology
- to see which parts of the scan will be most relevant

Segments (Phonemes)

Consonant sound classes in sample: (Circle if present; use parentheses to indicate limited numbers)

(Stops,) (nasals) fricatives, (liquids,) (glides) (has [h], some [l]s)
(Labials,) (coronals) [dentals, (alveolars) palatoalveolars], (velars)
(Voiced/voiceless)

Missing sound classes from above: _Fricatives, dentals, palatoalveolars, /r/_

Major segmental substitution patterns: _Stops for fricatives; glide [w] for liquids; [ʔ] medially and finally_

Vowels _Generally accurate_

    Substitutions:

    Defaults:

    Diphthongs:

    Analysis needed: ☐ Yes ☑ No
    (See final page of scan)

Syllable and Word Structure

Syllables added to words: ☐ Yes ☑ No If yes, ☐ Often ☐ Seldom

Syllables missing from words: ☑ Yes ☐ No If yes, ☐ Often ☑ Seldom

Patterns specific to a given word position:

General omission:	☐ Initial ☑ Medial	☑ Final
Reduced clusters:	☑ Initial ☐ Medial	☑ Final
	↘/s/-clusters	
Position-based substitution pattern:	☐ Initial ☑ Medial	☑ Final [ʔ] medially (and word-finally)

Other General Observations

Unusual prosody: ☐ Yes ☑ No

Unusual oral–motor characteristics: ☐ Yes ☑ No

Variability

Same word:	☑ Yes ☐ No	If yes, ☐ Often ☑ Seldom
Same speech sounds:	☑ Yes ☐ No	If yes, ☑ Often ☐ Seldom

    Assimilation/metathesis (Possible sequence constraints): ☑ Yes ☐ No _Probably_

5.2.1. Summary Notes

Dylan had limitations in terms of segments, syllable and word structure, and sequences. The Bird's-Eye View began to define possible needs for intervention. For Dylan, these included fricatives, liquids, /s/-clusters, and word shapes with medial and final consonants other than [ʔ]. With a general overview of his phonology as a background, we could then proceed to find out more about each part of the phonology in order to determine specific goals and goal sequences.

5.3. Step 2: Syllable and Word Structure Analysis

The purposes of the Syllable and Word Structure Analysis (Scan Page 3) are as follows:

- To note general prosodic factors that may be impacting negatively on comprehensibility

- To analyze word length, stress patterns, and word shapes

Table 5.2 shows the Syllable and Word Structure Analysis of the scan form. Summaries follow for each column within the scan. (*Note:* In scans, where no data are available, a "data gap" is noted.)

5.3.1. Summary Notes

Unusual prosodic factors: In the assessment session, Dylan frequently used creaky voice, more likely indicating embarrassment in the testing situation than voice pathology.

Word Length (column 1): Dylan generally matched word length in terms of number of syllables per word (although there was occasional variability for three-syllable words, as in the word *together*). Words of four or more syllables were not included in the sample and could be collected in addition at a later point. However, word length did not appear to be a major need. Words with three or more syllables could be observed over time to ensure continued progress.

Stress Patterns (column 2): Dylan frequently used the typical English Sw stress pattern but also showed developing ability with the less common wSw patterns, as noted for the variable productions of *together*. (The weak syllable was omitted once. In the other productions, the segments produced differed on subsequent repetitions of the word, with different vowels, and with /ð/ missing or surfacing as [d].) More data could be collected, but needs in this area were probably minimal. His longer words could be monitored over time, to ensure development of the many stress patterns in English.

Word Shapes (column 3): Word shape needs were apparent in Dylan's sample. Dylan did use a variety of word shapes, up to a maximum of CVVCVʔVV, e.g., *radio* as [weɪjəʔoʊ]. However, the primary matching word shape was CV(V). All other basic forms were still developing, with some

Table 5.2. Dylan's Syllable and Word Structure Analysis, Scan Page 3

Unusual prosodic factors? (circle) pitch, (voice) resonance, duration, rate, rhythm, intonation, loudness
child has creaky voice

	Word Length	Stress Patterns	Word Shapes
Basic inventory	(1 syllable) (2 syllables) (3 syllables) 4 syllables Other: Data gap: 4+ syllables	(Sw) Ss Sww (Sws) Ssw wS (wSw) swS Other: Data gap: Ss, Sww, Ssw, wS, swS	V(V) ((C)V(V)CV(V)) V(V)C CV(V)CV(V)C (CV(V)) CV(V)CCV(V)C (CV(V)C) Other: cvvcv?vv (C)VCC C2, C3 = ? or (CCV(V)(C)) nasal glide
Matches by category	(1 syllable) (2 syllables) (3 syllables) 4 syllables Other: Data gap: 4+ syllables	(Sw) Ss Sww (Sws) Ssw wS (wSw) swS Other: Data gap: Ss, Sww, Ssw, wS, swS	V(V) ((C)V(V)CV(V)) V(V)C No CV(V)CV(V)C (CV(V)) CV(V)CCV(V)C (CV(V)C) Other: (C)VCC No C2, C3 = ? or (CCV(V)(C)) nasal glide
Child's maximum	3	wSw	CCVC or CVVCV?VV
Child's most frequent	1 2 (Both) Other:	(Sw) Other:	V(V) CVC (CV(V)) CVCV Other: CV(V)?V
Child's developing forms (some matches)	2 syllables (3 syllables) 4 syllables	wS Other: wSw	CV(V) (CVC) (CVCV) (CCV(V)) (C)VCC (CVCVC) Other:

Comparison with adult targets	Syllables missing?
	Rarely
	
	Syllables added?
	No
		Missing:
		  Weak syllables Yes
		  Strong syllables
		Stress shift?
		
		Equal stress?
		
		Segments differ on repetition
		of multisyllable words?
		  (Yes: wSw)
			Missing C's:
			(WF) WI (SIWW) (SFWW)
			(Clusters)——/s/-clusters
			[?] or Glide for C: Yes
			Missing V's: No
			  Diphthong
			  WF WI Medial
			Added C's: No, except ?
			Added V's: V > VV
			when WF C missing?

Context differences? Spontaneous vs. imitated Single word vs. phrases	Unknown	Unknown— Better in imitation?	Unknown
Need to count? What?	Variable? No	Variable? Yes, for wSw No need to count	Variable? Yes Count CVC, CVCV(C), CCV(V)
Other data needed? What?	(4+ syllables)	wS (Sww, Ssw, swS, Ss)	More /s/-clusters
Needs? (Add to Goal Summary page, Goal 1, page 7)	(Observe 3+)	(Observe wS(w))	CVC, CVCV, /s/-CV

Note. Only relevant data included in table. Parentheses indicate inconsistency in child production.

variability noted. CVCV and CVCVC tended to match the adult target if one of the C's (usually a noninitial C) was [?], e.g., *dolly* as [dɑʔiː], *chicken* as [tʰɪʔĩn]. Initial stop-glide clusters were common, but /s/-clusters were reduced, e.g., *black* as [bwæɪ], but *stickerbook* as [dɪʔoʊbʊ]. Word-final consonants were present but only if they were nasals or [?], e.g., *green* as [gwiːn] and *fish* as [bɪʔ]. When final consonants were missing, vowels were sometimes lengthened (*look* as [lʊː]) or diphthongized (*black* as [bwæɪ]), presumably to compensate for missing final consonants.

5.3.2. Optional Step: Quantitative Analysis

The scan analysis does not involve computation. Quantification can be useful, however,

- for clarifying goal selection when targets are highly variable, and

- for determining clinical effectiveness (comparing baseline and outcome measures).

As an example, baseline match proportions are presented in Table 5.3 for Dylan's CVC and CVCV word shapes. Glottal stop substitutions were noticeably more frequent for C2 of CVCV than for C2 of CVC. Matches and omissions were more common for CVC. (Note, however, that the higher proportion of CVC matches was biased by the high frequency of nasal coda targets in the CVC sample.)

5.3.3. Goal Summary

Strengths and needs for word structure are next entered on the scan's Goal Summary. (See Table 5.9 at the end of the chapter.) Strengths were CV(V) monosyllables and Sw disyllables. Other more complex structures were present but only infrequently or with limited segmental content (CVC, CVCV, CCV, CVCVC, wS patterns, multisyllabic words). We now have more detailed information about possible word and syllable structure needs than we had after the Bird's-Eye View: All but the most basic word shapes were needs and potential goals. We still are not sure which of the word shapes to choose for goals and which segments to use to target the word shapes. That will become clearer after doing the segment and feature analysis next.

5.4. Step 3: Consonant Analysis

The purposes of the Segment and Feature Analysis are as follows:

- To note general articulatory factors that may be influencing substitution patterns

- To compile a consonantal inventory and identify substitution patterns

- To analyze individual features, (simultaneous) combinations of features, and defaults

Table 5.3. Matches, Omissions, and Compensations for CVC and CVCV

Target	% Match for C2		% Omission of C2		% Use of [ʔ] for C2		Compensatory Vowel Lengthening	
C(C)VC[a]	4/12	(33.3%)	5/12	(41.7%)	1/12	(8.3%)	2/12	(16.7%)
CV(V)CV(C)[b]	0/6	(0%)	1/6	(16.7%)	5/6	(83.3%)	0/6	(0%)

[a]Target onsets with clusters included.

[b]For two-syllable CVVCV and CVCVC targets in the sample only, with focus on C2. Note that Dylan did produce C2 some of the time in three-syllable targets (as in *together, stickerbook*).

5.4.1. Phonetic Inventory

The first step in segmental and feature analysis is compiling the phonetic inventory by word position. The first two rows of page 4 of the scan are available for the inventory, which is subdivided into [+consonantal] (consonant) and [−consonantal] (glide) segments. (See Table 5.4.)

Dylan's word-initial inventory contained labials, coronals, and dorsals (velars), voiced and voiceless stops, nasals, glides, and (infrequently) /l/. Syllable-initial medial consonants inconsistently included the voiced stops, /l/ and [j], but the most frequent phone was [ʔ]. Word-finally, only nasals and [ʔ] appeared. No syllable-final medial consonants occurred in this sample (but there was only one target, in the word *sister*).

5.4.2. Substitution and Feature Analyses

The rest of page 4 of the scan and the first column on page 5 are used to indicate the *major* substitution patterns for segments by feature type. *A substitution is entered into a cell only if there is a problem for the feature that heads the row.* For example, if a child produces [t] for /k/, the manner and voice features are not in jeopardy; only the place feature is. Thus, the /k/ > [t] substitution is noted only in the place feature section of the scan (in the [Dorsal] row), not in the manner or laryngeal sections. (See Chapter 7 for more details on how to enter substitution patterns.)

Tables 5.5 and 5.6 and the Goal Summary in Table 5.9 show the feature analysis for Dylan. Summary notes below discuss manner, laryngeal, and place features in turn.

Part of the analysis involves determination of default features and feature values. The points below provide some guidance to that purpose.

Hints for Determining Defaults (see Chapters 3 and 4, also)

• Segments that appear frequently as substitutions often have default features. A number of repair processes may result in production of the same set of segments and features (e.g., velar fronting or stridency deletion can result in frequent use of [t]). Features of [t] are the adult defaults and may or may not be the default features for a child's system.

• In assimilations, the default feature usually succumbs to the nondefault features.

Summary Notes: Manner Features

The features used in this analysis are [+consonantal] (for true consonants), [−consonantal] (for glides), [+lateral] (for /l/), [+nasal] (for nasals), [−continuant] (for stops), [+continuant] (for fricatives), and [−continuant]-[+continuant] (for affricates). (See Chapter 3 for a review of these features.)

Table 5.4. Dylan's Consonant and Glide Inventory, Scan Page 4

Feature	Adult Targets	Word-Initial	Medial, Syllable-Final	Medial, Syllable-Initial	Word-Final
[+consonantal] inventory	All but glides below	m n pʰ **b** t tʰ **d** kʰ g (l)		b **d** g (l) ∅	m n ŋ ∅
[−consonantal] inventory	ʔ h w j r	ʔ h w j		ʔ j	ʔ

Note. Boldfaced segments match the adult targets *and* are also used as substitutions. Italics designate phones used as substitutions only. Otherwise, segments are used as matches (correct) only. Parentheses indicate consonants that match the adult target only some of the time.

Table 5.5. Dylan's Consonant Analysis, Scan Page 4

Overuse? (circle) (labial,) dental, alveolar, palatal, velar, lateral, nasal, uvular, pharyngeal, (glottal,) other

Phonetic inventory: First 2 rows. List non-English phones also. **Substitutions:** On row for the specific feature.

Feature	Adult Targets	Word-Initial	Medial, Syllable-Final	Medial, Syllable-Initial	Word-Final
[+consonantal] inventory	All but glides below	m n pʰ b t tʰ d kʰ g (l) (Bold = match + subst.)		b d g (l) ∅	m n ŋ ∅
[−consonantal] inventory	ʔ h w j r	ʔ h w j		ʔ j (Italic = sub only)	ʔ
[+lateral]	l	(l > w)		(l > ʔ)	
[+nasal]	m n ŋ			n > ∅	
[−continuant]	p t k b d g ʔ m n ŋ			ʔ (Feature ok)	∅
[+continuant] (&[−sonorant])	f v s z θ ð ʃ ʒ	Fricatives > stops; Cluster /s/ > ∅	st > ʔ	ð, v > ∅ ð > d (2)	f > ∅
[−continuant]- [+continuant]	tʃ dʒ	Affricates > stops			

Manner Default Summary: Expected: [−cont], [−nasal]; [−cons] for /l/ Other: Yes					

Feature	Adult Targets	Word-Initial	Medial, Syllable-Final	Medial, Syllable-Initial	Word-Final
[+voiced] obstruents	b d g v z ð ʒ dʒ				
[−voiced] obstruents	p t k f s θ ʃ tʃ	Vl. fric. > **vd.** stops		p > ʔ ([−voiced] ok)	ʃ > ʔ ([−voiced] ok)
[+spread glottis]	h; Asp. stops; (vl. fricatives)	Vl. fric. > **vd.** stops			

Laryngeal Default Summary: Expected: [−voiced] Other: [+voiced] for WI stop ʔ or h default: Medial, WF					

Feature	Adult Targets	Word-Initial	Medial, Syllable-Final	Medial, Syllable-Initial	Word-Final
Labial	p b m f v w			v > ∅, Lab > WF p > ʔ, Lab > WI	p, b, f > ∅ but Labial > onset
Coronal [+anterior]	t d n l s z θ ð	Cor > Lab if Lab in coda (seq. problem)	st > ʔ	n > ∅; d > j ð > d, ∅; z, (l) > ʔ	∅ (n > m - migration)
Coronal [−anterior]	ʃ ʒ tʃ dʒ j r	[−anterior] > [+anterior] except /j/		gap	ʃ > ʔ
Coronal [+grooved]	s z ʃ ʒ tʃ dʒ	All > [−grooved] stops			
Coronal [−grooved]	θ ð	θ > b; [−grooved] stops		ð > d, ∅	gap
Dorsal	k g ŋ (w) (j)			k > ʔ	k > ∅ g gap
Coronal & Labial	r	r > w			ɚ: oʊ, ɪ

Place Default Summary: Expected: Coronal [+anterior]; [+grooved] Other: Yes No frics.					

Variable? (circle) Spontaneous/imitated?   Connected/single words?   Same word?   (Same C?)

Count what? No   **Data needed?** See gaps noted above.

---

1. **[+consonantal], [−consonantal], [+lateral]** (consonants, glides, and /l/): In terms of substitutions, [−consonantal] [ʔ] was a frequent substitution for consonants in non-word-initial positions, particularly word-medially. Glides also replaced /l/ and /r/, e.g., [w] appeared word-initially ([wi] for *leaf*), and [ʔ] appeared word-medially (*dolly* as [dɑʔiː]).

Needs: • [+consonantal] word-medially and -finally, already identified as a Type 1 Word Shape need for C2 of CVC, CVCV(C).

• Consistent production of [+lateral] (Type 2 New Feature need).

Table 5.6. Dylan's Consonant Analysis: Summary, Scan Page 5

Feature	Summary of Substitutions (from page 4)	Goal Type 2: Feature Marginal or Not Used at All	Goal Type 3: Feature Marginal or Not Used in Specific Feature Combinations*
[+consonantal]	Medial and final C > ? or ø (l > glide)	[+consonantal] in medial and final positions	
[−consonantal]			
[+lateral]	(l > [−lateral] glide)	[+lateral]	
[+nasal]	Medial n > ø Other medials?		Medial /n/ (Cor & [+nas])
[−continuant]	(Medial: ?) Final: ø	Final [−continuant] (except nasals)	
[+continuant] (&[−sonorant])	Onsets > stops Final (med) > ø	[+continuant]	[−voiced] & [+continuant]?
[−continuant]-[+continuant]		[−continuant] [+continuant]	

Manner Defaults Needing Change: ([+cons] needed for /l/)

[+voiced] obstruents			
[−voiced] obstruents	WI Vl. fric. > vd. stops		[−voiced] & [+continuant]?
[+spread glottis]	WI Vl. fric. > vd. stops		[+sp. gl.] & [+continuant] & [−voiced]

Laryngeal Defaults Needing Change: Reduction of [+constricted glottis] use; Onset [+voiced]?

Labial	Labial survives (migration, assimilation)		
Coronal [+anterior]	Coronal > Labial if Labial somewhere in word Non-WI > ?, ø	Coronal... Labial sequences Non-WI: All except WF n	
Coronal [−anterior]	[−anterior] > [+anterior] (not [j])	[−anterior] (except /j/)	
Coronal [+grooved]	No fricatives	[+grooved] fricatives	
Coronal [−grooved]	No fricatives	[−grooved] fricatives	
Dorsal	Positional gaps	Dorsal non-WI except ŋ	
Coronal & Labial	Coronal missing		Coronal & Labial for /r/

Place Defaults Needing Change: No

*See box at top of page 6

---

2. **[−continuant] and [+nasal]** (stops and nasals): Nasals and oral stops were both established word-initially but had different patterns in non-word-initial positions. The [−continuant] feature of stops was maintained word-medially, even when there was a glottal stop substitution, as in [boʊʔi] for *soapy;* however, the [+nasal] /n/ was missing word-medially. Word-finally, stops were absent (as in *sleep* as [bwi:]), but nasals were consistently present.

Needs: • [−continuant] ([−nasal]) word-finally, already identified as a Type 1 Word Shape need for C2 of CVC, CVCV(C).

 • /n/ word-medially (Type 1 CVCV Word Shape or Type 4 Positional need; see below).

3. **[+continuant] ([−sonorant]):** Fricatives and affricates appeared as stops (*that* as [dæ], *chicken* as [tʰɪʔîn]). The stop substitutions had the same structural pattern as other stops; that is, they were always present word-initially and sometimes word-medially but were otherwise missing or had [ʔ] substitutions.

Needs: [+continuant] (−[sonorant]) was a need across word positions.

4. **Default manner features:** For Dylan, the default summary box shows typical defaults ([−nasal], [−continuant], [−consonantal]). However, the *high frequency* of [−consonantal] substitutions for [+consonantal] is *unexpected* and an indicator of severity.

5. **Feature combinations with manner?** The stop substitutions for fricatives showed a noteworthy pattern in terms of voicing: voiced ([−spread glottis]) stops appeared for *all* fricatives. Because laryngeal features were implicated in a pattern that concerned manner ("stopping" of fricatives), a feature combination difficulty was suspected. This will be discussed further under "Laryngeal Features."

Hint Regarding Feature Combinations

Differences within a feature category for the various segments that contain that feature may indicate difficulty with simultaneous combinations of certain features. For example, if [f] and [v] occur but not /s/ or /z/, then [Labial] and [+continuant] can combine but not [Coronal, +anterior] and [+continuant]. Or if /k/ occurs but not /g/ or /ŋ/, then [Dorsal] can combine with [−voiced] but not with [+voiced] or [+nasal]. Taking note of differences among segments within a feature category thus often helps to determine if they are feature combination needs. *Note:* The "&" designates a feature combination: [+voiced] & [+continuant] & [−sonorant] = voiced fricatives.

Summary of Manner Feature Needs

1. **[+consonantal], [−continuant], [+nasal]:** These features were present but not in all word positions. Their absence contributed to lack of well-established word shapes. Thus, they were potential features to use for Type 1 Word Shape goals CVC and CVCV.

2. **[+continuant] (& [−sonorant]):** Fricatives and affricates were not present in any word position. [+continuant] ([−sonorant]) was a need: New Feature Goal Type 2 (across word positions).

3. **[+lateral]:** This was a developing feature and therefore a continuing need: New Feature Goal Type 2 (across word positions).

Summary Notes: Laryngeal Features

The Bird's-Eye View showed presence of both [−voiced] and [+voiced] features. Voicing matched syllable-initially for stop realizations of stop targets. However, *fricatives* had a noteworthy substitution pattern: voiceless fricatives surfaced as voiced stops (e.g., *fish* as [bɪʔ]), even though aspirated word-initial voiceless stops were possible. (This was not true, however, for the affricate /ʧ/.) What could account for that pattern?

For both voiceless fricatives and aspirated stops in English, the [+spread glottis] feature is predictable but for different reasons: voiceless fricatives can *only* be produced with an open glottis, but stops are produced with aspiration just in word-initial position as a particular aspect of English phonology (i.e., aspiration is not a necessary aspect of stop production). Voiced segments, on the other hand, are [−spread glottis], because they are not produced easily with an open glottis. (See Section 2.1.2.) In Dylan's case, when [+continuant] was not produced for fricatives, the redundant [+spread glottis] feature was lost with it, possibly because the production of a redundant feature was dependent on production of the feature with which it is redundant (a type of "parasitic" loss). Without the [+spread glottis] feature, either an unaspirated voiceless stop or a voiced stop could occur. Since unaspirated stops do not appear word-initially in English, the voiced stops were perhaps the best option. (Note that this is not a *necessary* pattern; some children do maintain the [+spread glottis] feature in fricative substitution patterns, using either [h] or aspirated stops for fricatives.) The [+voiced] feature may have been a word-initial default, given the voiced stop substitutions for fricatives (although no such evidence was available from stops for stop targets). A frequent laryngeal default feature was [+constricted glottis] ([ʔ]).

Summary of Laryngeal Feature Needs

1. **[+continuant] & [−voiced] (& [+spread glottis]):** This need was not immediately obvious in the Bird's-Eye View but gives further information about choices for fricative goals, as we discuss in goal selection at the end of the chapter: Feature Combination Goal Type 3.

2. **Elimination of the [+constricted glottis] default:** The [+constricted glottis] ([ʔ]) needed to be eliminated word-medially (and -finally).

Summary Notes: Place Features

1. **Major place features:** The Bird's-Eye View revealed the presence of the three major place features [Labial], [Coronal], and [Dorsal]. Manner and laryngeal substitution patterns showed no variable patterns involving place, i.e., there were no obvious difficulties with combination of place and manner or place and laryngeal features. There was some variability with respect to production of labials and coronals, however. [Coronal] was vulnerable when there was a labial in the target, e.g., *dolly* as [dɑːʔiː], *sister* as [dɪʔɪ], but *tub* as [pʰʌː], *thumb* as [bʌ̃m]. [Labial] migrated to the coronal position in the word (as in *tub*) or assimilated if there was a nasal in coda (as in *thumb*). This suggests place sequence constraints and will be discussed further on page 6 of the scan. [Dorsal] was not subject to labial assimilation or migration, although dorsal stops appeared in word-initial position only, consistent with general stop production. The dorsal nasal, [ŋ], was produced word-finally, however.

2. **Other place features:** [grooved] and [−anterior] (except for [j]) were absent for fricatives (where they are nonredundant). Expected substitutions ([w] for /r/, alveolar stops for palatoalveolars and dentals) prevailed.

3. **Default place features:** Because [Coronal] was the target of assimilation, [Coronal] was the most likely place default. Use of alveolars in substitution patterns for coronals suggests that [+anterior] was the specific coronal default.

Summary of Place Feature Needs

Place feature needs, independent of sequence or word shape needs, are listed below:

- **[−anterior], [grooved]:** For fricatives (New Feature Goal Type 2).

- **Combination of [Coronal] & [Labial]:** For /r/ (Feature Combination Goal Type 3).

Summary Notes (bottom of scan page 4)

Variable? (circle) Spontaneous/imitated? Connected/single words? Same word? (Same C?) Coronals
Count what? *Not needed*   Data needed? *Some gaps but not significant*
                                                          for this analysis

5.4.3. Goal Summary

At this point, more information is added to the Goal Summary sheet (Table 5.9). Strengths and needs for (new) individual features and feature combinations are entered in accordance with the analysis on page 5 of the scan. (On page 5, "Feature Marginal or Not Used" is a feature that would be an "Individual Features" need in the Goal Summary. "Feature Marginal or Not Used in Specific Feature Combinations" is a feature to be entered in the "Feature Combinations" column in the Goal Summary.) Word shapes available for targeting new features were CV(V), CVC (where C2 = [+nasal]), and CCV (used in the sample in terms of stop-glide clusters).

The available segments for word shape development can be entered now or after the next analysis (see Section 5.6).

Hints Regarding Feature Strengths and Needs

• The "Strengths" cells for features and feature combinations list word position information where relevant. This helps determine available segments for syllable and word structure goals.

• The "Needs" cells list general new feature or new feature combination needs *only*, but *not* word position needs for particular features or segments (which are entered as Type 4 Word Position Goals).

5.5. Step 4: Word Position and Sequence Needs

On page 4 of the scan, we noted some effects of word position and sequence constraints on feature production but not in any detail. On page 6 of the scan there are two charts, the first dealing with word position, and the second with sequence constraints.

5.5.1. Word Position Strength

Word position constraints are defined as *partial* limitations on a word position (only *some* features or segments missing in that position). This is different from a word *shape* constraint, in which one word position (or more than one word position) is absent or marginal (has few or no segments). Copying a feature from one word position to another strengthens the target word position. The particular feature is also strengthened, but, because strategies for intervention often involve manipulation of structure (e.g., onset-rime techniques; see Chapter 11), this is considered primarily a word structure need.

To determine word position needs, enter on the chart those segments and features that are *present in some word positions but missing in partially established word positions*. For example, fricatives ([+continuant]) might be present in word-final position but absent in word-initial position, although word-initial position might have other types of segments, e.g., stops, nasals, and glides.

A table such as Table 5.7 generally lists sound classes and consonants that are missing in partially established word positions but found elsewhere.

For Dylan, general syllable structure constraints prohibited consonant production in C2 of CVC and CVCV. Furthermore, feature constraints appeared across word positions. Thus, he had no specific word position needs that were not subsumed under word shape needs.

5.5.2. Sequence Constraints

The second half of page 6 deals with sequences. Sequences also involve an interaction of position and segments or features. Segments may be pronounceable except in the context of some other segments.

The scan chart focuses on sequences that most commonly show difficulty:

- clusters (in any word position)

- consonants and vowels

- distant consonants separated by vowels (particularly those differing in place and feature [+nasal]).

(*Note:* Sequences also exist between distant vowels and at word boundaries, i.e., between words. These are not examined in the chart directly but can be noted if relevant.)

Hint for finding sequence constraints

• Where between-word variability exists, sequence constraints can sometimes be responsible. Assimilation or dissimilation, metathesis, coalescence, and epenthesis can suggest sequence constraints.

Table 5.8 shows sequence information for Dylan.

The feature analysis indicated possible place sequence constraints involving [Labial] and [Coronal]. Encouragingly, sequences with [Coronal] and [Labial] were not *im*possible, as the word *eleven* ([ʔiːlɛm̩]) shows, but they were rare. Most assimilations and feature migrations occurred for target [Coronal]-[Labial] sequences. Sequences of manner and voice showed no signs of assimilation or migration, suggesting that sequence constraints probably did not involve these features.

Other information from this chart was previously noted also: the absence of /s/-clusters and the presence of stop-glide clusters. The absence of word-final clusters

Table 5.7. Segments Missing in a Given Word Position (but occurring elsewhere), Scan Page 6

Word-Initial	Medial: Syllable-Initial	Medial: Syllable-Final	Word-Final
	All missing except some voiced stops and nasals	All missing except nasals	All missing except nasals

Note. Many medial and final consonants were omitted. Thus, CVC, CVCV, and CVCCV(C) were word structure needs.

Table 5.8. Sequences of Segments and Features, Scan Page 6

Consonant Assimilation (top > [pɑp]) **OR Dissimilation** (tot > [tɑp]) *Anticipatory Labial assimilation* *(with [m] coda)*	**Coalescence (fusion)** (/tr/ > [f])	**Epenthesis** (tray > [təweɪ])
		Metathesis (fish > [ʃɪf]) **OR Migration** (cup > [pʌ]) *Yes: Labial to Coronal target position*
	CV Assimilation (bee > [di]; do > [bu]) **OR Dissimilation** (boo > [du])	**Other Patterns** *Omission of /s/ in /s/C* *Omission of WM, WF C's*

Clusters Produced: (circle matches) [bw], [tw], [gw]

Missing Clusters: (compared with adult targets)* *All others*

Cross-V Sequences Produced: (Circle those produced. Put checkmarks over ones that match targets.)

(Lab-Lab,) (Cor-Cor,) Dors-Dors, (Lab-Cor,) Cor-Lab, (Lab-Dors,) (Dors-Lab,) (Cor-Dors,) (Dors-Cor,) (nonnasal-nasal;) other (*voice*)

Missing Cross-V Sequences: (compared with adult targets) (circle)

Lab-Lab, (Cor-Cor,) Dors-Dors, (Lab-Cor,) (Cor-Lab,) Lab-Dors, Dors-Lab, (Cor-Dors,) (Dors-Cor,) nonnasal-nasal; other

Context Differences for (A) or (B): Spontaneous/imitated? Connected/single word? For same word? For same C? *???*
Need to count? *Yes* **What?** *% Cor-Lab, Lab-Cor cross-V sequences*
Other data needed: *More examples with [Coronal]*

(e.g., *pink* as [pʰɪŋ]) is not unexpected, because non-nasal consonants were generally absent in coda position.

5.6. Step 5: Completing the Goal Summary

We can now go back to the Goal Summary (Table 5.9) and finalize the intervention plan. The top three rows summarize the analysis.

5.6.1. Immediate Intervention Goals and Strategies

In Table 5.9, the bottom five rows focus on the initial intervention plan: social and interaction factors, immediate goals, strategies, and order of goals in the program. Social and interaction factors are taken into account in both goal selection and sequence, and in strategy development. Dylan was sociable and amenable to a variety of activities, including those that required early literacy skills. When social factors are not an issue, goal selection and strategies can be based more on phonological needs than on social needs.

Immediate goals (in order) were determined to be:

1. word shapes CVC and CVCV (Goal Type 1)
2. fricatives /v/ in CV(V) and /s/ in /s/CV (Goal Types 2 and 3)
3. /r/ (and /l/) (Goal Types 2 and 3)

In the next section, we discuss the rationale for these choices and orders.

Table 5.9. Dylan's Goal Summary, Scan Page 7

Level	Syllable and Word Structure		Features and Segments	
Goal Type	**Goal Type 1** Structure	**Goal Type 4** Word Position and Sequences	**Goal Type 2** Individual Features	**Goal Type 3** Feature Combinations
Strengths	Word length 1, 2 syl. Stress patterns Sw Word shapes CV(V) CV [+nas] CGV	Segment and feature classes by word position Sequences Manner, Lab-Lab, Dors-Dors, Dors-Lab	[−consonantal] [+consonantal]: WI [+nasal] [−continuant] [+voiced] Labial: WI Dorsal: WI	Manner-Laryngeal [−cont]&[−voiced] &[+sp gl]: WI [−cont]&[+voiced], SI Manner-Place Place-Laryngeal
Needs	Word length 3? 4+? Stress patterns wS(w)? Word shapes CVC CVCV /s/CV	Word position Sequences With Coronal	[+lateral] [+continuant] [−anterior] [grooved]	Manner-Laryngeal [+cont]&[−voiced] &[+sp gl] Manner-Place Place-Laryngeal Place-Place Cor & Lab for /r/
Strengths To Use To Support Needs	Segments to use for structure goals	Segments to use for structure goals	Word shapes to use for feature goals	Word shapes to use for feature goals
	CVC, CVCV C1: m p b k g h w (no coronals) C2, CVC: pʰ b kʰ g C2, CVCV: m n p b k g (no [−cons])	Avoid coronals in C1	1. CV(V) or CV [+nas]; later, CVC, CVCV 2. [+cont] in /s/CV /s/CV: (not sn, st, i.e., no coronals)	1. CV(V) or CV [+nas] 2. Later, CVC, CVCV
Interactions (prosody, perception, morphology, motor)	None observed		No inflectional morphemes. Knows letters.	
Social Factors	Positive for intervention process			
Immediate Goals	CVC, CVCV	Place sequences with Coronal	[+continuant] fricatives, WI	1. WI /r/: Lab & Cor 2. [+continuant] & [−voiced] & [+sp gl]
Treatment Strategies	Mora, onset-rime, link C2 of both		/s/-CV; WI /v/ Awareness, motor	1. /r/: Oral-motor + contrast [w], [l] 2. [−vcd] fric: /s/CV
Goal # in Program (order)	1	Observation goal?	2	3

5.6.2. Rationale for Goal Order and Selection

1. **CVC, CVCV first:** *If CVC and CVCV are marginal or weak in a system, they are often first goals.* Without a good framework for the word, there is very little to "hang features on." Which segments should be used in those word shapes? The "Strengths" cells in the feature analysis list the available segments.

Hints for Choosing Segments for Word Shape Goals

• General rule of thumb: Choose well-established segments for new word shape goals. Children tend to do better when they do not have to learn too many new things at once.

• Take a child's phonetic tendencies into account. For example, velars and fricatives are often easier in non-word-initial positions at first. Voiceless segments are often easier word-finally, and voiced ones in non-word-final position. Some children do better at first when place of articulation is held constant across the word or between consonants.

• Choose more than one segment for establishment of a new word shape in order to promote focus on the word shape, not just the segment.

For Dylan, sequences of a coronal followed by a noncoronal would initially be avoided, because sequence constraints could interfere with word shape production.

For C1 of CVC and CVCV, then, labials and velars (dorsals) would be logical first choices. Continuing with C1, nasals, stops, and glides were available. Choices for C1, then, would be among [m], [pʰ], [b], [kʰ], [g], [h], and [w].

For C2, stops would be used primarily. Nasals already appeared in coda and thus would need to be targeted only medially in CVCV. For C2 of CVC, available segments would be [pʰ], [b], [kʰ], and [g]. For C2 of CVCV, choices would be among [m], [n], [p], [b], [k], and [g]. *Not all of the listed consonants would be used in treatment.* A balanced selection would be made (some labials, some dorsals, some glides, some nasals, some stops). Some segments would then be left as observation targets (to determine the extent of generalization).

2. **Fricatives next:** *In the first period of intervention, it is also useful to introduce a major feature category, even if only through awareness activities at first.* The rationale for the specific fricative choice (/v/ and /s/) is as follows. Because stop substitutions for fricatives word-initially were [+voiced], a voiced fricative might be more easily imitated word-initially than a voiceless one in a CVV word. Choices were /v/, /z/, and /ð/ or the affricate /ʤ/. Since all but /v/ were coronals (which were to be avoided in C1 because of sequence constraints), /v/ was the target of choice. But as a solitary exemplar of the fricative category, /v/ might not have had sufficient impact on the system. What other choices were available? The voiceless labial /f/ was a possibility, but Dylan appeared to have difficulty with the combination of [−voiced], [+continuant], and [+spread glottis] in word-initial position. He did use stop-glide clusters; i.e., he had the word shape CCV. With at least some /s/-clusters (/s/-stop clusters), /s/ can be considered "outside" the syllable (see Section 1.1) and perhaps therefore less subject to either the voicing combination difficulty (because it can be articulated independently) or the coronal-labial sequence constraint. To avoid having two coronals (as with /sn/, /sl/, or /st/), /sp/, /sk/, /sw/, and /sm/ would be the best choices.

3. **/r/ and (/l/):** After the two major initiatives, other goals can be addressed if needed, or the first two can be revisited in a cyclic fashion. For Dylan, other needs included coronal-labial and cluster sequences, and liquids /r/ and /l/. In "real life," the sequence constraints started to lessen after treatment of CVC and CVCV, but the liquids /l/ and /r/ remained marginal and thus became targets. The /l/ (already produced some of the time) was a relatively easy target in and of itself but was also useful as a contrast with the new segment /r/.

Comparing Goals from the Bird's-Eye View and the Full Scan Analysis

The Bird's-Eye View gives some ideas of what the needs will be for intervention, but not in detail. For Dylan, we knew that fricatives and /r/ would be goals, as would CVC, CVCV, and /s/-clusters.

What the deeper analysis provides is direction about specific targets, types of segments and sequences to use in word shapes, and goal sequence and strategies. For Dylan, this included the specific choice for fricatives (based on feature combination and sequence issues), the word shapes to use for fricatives, and the available segments and sequences to use for CVC and CVCV.

5.7. Dylan in "Real Life"

Dylan's program was basically as described above, with the exception that /r/ and /l/ were targeted with awareness activities only (because of the intervention study design). Dylan responded quickly to phonological intervention. At the end of the first 6-week period, he had sufficient use of CVC and CVCV that he could go on to other word structure goals, i.e., CVCC. The /s/-clusters and /v/ began to emerge, as did a number of other fricatives and affricates. The /l/ also became more consistent. In the second and third intervention periods, he gained competency with all fricatives, /r/, and clusters. At the end of the program (age 5-0), he had age-appropriate phonology: some inconsistency remained for liquid clusters, affricates, and interdentals. His alliteration skills improved, but he still could not rhyme. His confidence had returned completely in social situations. Interestingly, 2 years later he was tested and still had some inconsistency for liquid clusters and interdentals, showing that the intervention program had had a direct impact on his development; i.e., maturation was insufficient to account for change. A late-breaking report is that his speech has fully normalized. He is in a gifted program and is highly literate (at least 3 years beyond his age level for reading and writing).

5.8. Suggestions for Proceeding

At this point, you may proceed through the more detailed explanations in the following chapters, *or* do Dylan's analysis yourself as a self-testing practice, *or* take some data from a child you are working with and try to plug it into the scan (using the blank form in Appendix D). This may help highlight areas that you will want to focus on in the chapters that follow.

ℐ ∮ ω'
ℐ ϲ β ∘ ∮
λ ϲ ℼ β

Chapter 6
Syllable and Word Structure

Analyses in This Chapter
(pages 2, 3, and 7 of the scan)

- word length
- stress patterns
- subsyllabic content (CV shapes, moras, onset-rime)

6.1. Word Length

6.1.1. Expected Developmental Trends for Word Length

The lists below outline basic expectations for word-length development.

Age Expectations:

- Before age 3, children generally produce both one- and two-syllable words.

- By age 3, children tend to produce some multisyllabic words; the development of multisyllabic words continues gradually into adulthood.

- At all ages, monosyllabic words predominate in English speech.

Developmental Phonological Patterns:

- The most common developmental pattern with respect to word length is reduction of words (syllable deletion, as in [bʌk] for *bucket*).

- Less commonly, syllables may be added to a target word, either

    a. to rescue a final consonant that cannot be pronounced without a following vowel, or

    b. to fulfill minimum word-length constraints. (For example, a child might be able to produce *only* two-syllable words, such as [beɪbi] for *baby,* at some point in development. For monosyllabic targets, an extra syllable would have to be added, e.g., [dɑgə] for *dog*).

As noted in Chapter 4, Chapters 6–10 include data sets that are particularly illustrative for the analysis in question. In Sections 6.1.2–6.1.6, a word-length analysis is presented for a child for whom that was an identified need. Appendix C contains another data set for practice. (Refer also to Chapter 5 for terminology and form usage notes.)

6.1.2. Marnie's Data

Marnie: Age 3. Severe phonological disorder.

Marnie's language comprehension skills were in the borderline average range, and her language production was severely delayed. She had some difficulty with oral-motor movements. Her voice had a creaky quality, with use of hard glottal attack on vowel-initial words. Her older sister had a history of phonological disorder and intervention. A sample of Marnie's data is presented in Table 6.1.

6.1.3. Questions To Ask of the Sample

The following questions can be asked about word length. Some answers will be obvious and can be entered into the appropriate box on the scan form while transcribing or coding. Others will require word-by-word observation, especially when patterns are inconsistent.

- How long are words in the sample (basic inventory of length)—one syllable, two syllables, or three or more syllables?

- What word lengths match the adult target (match by category)—one-syllable, two-syllable, three-syllable, or longer words?

- What are the child's maximum, frequent, and developing word lengths?

Table 6.1. Word Length: Marnie's Data

Word	Adult		Child	
	Pronunciation	# of syllables	Pronunciation	# of syllables
apple	(ʔ)æpl̩	2	ʔɑː (I)	1
elephant	(ʔ)ɛləfn̩t	3	ʔʊʃʔə (I)	2
matches	mætʃəz	2	ʔjiʔʰ (I)	1
monkey	mʌ̃ŋki	2	ʔiː (I)	1
mom	mʌ̃m	1	mʌ̃m	1
more	mɔr	1	moʊjəʔ	2
knife	naɪf	1	wʊf (I)	1
no	noʊ	1	noʊ	1
bathtub	bæθtʰʌb	2	ʔaʔʌʔ (I)	2
bird	bɝd	1	boʊʔ (I)	1
balloons	bəlũːnz	2	buː (I)	1
toothbrush	tʰuːθbrʌʃ	2	ʔiʃʔʌʔ (I)	2
TV	tʰiːviː	2	ʔiəː (pause) ʔi (I)	2
daddy	dædi	2	diː	1
radio	reɪdioʊ	3	ʔoʊ	1

- In comparison with the adult target, are there missing or added syllables?

- Does context make a difference: Is there any difference between single words and connected speech, or between spontaneous and imitated productions?

- How variable are the data in general? Would counting help confirm patterns or set a baseline for determining effectiveness in treatment? What should be counted?

- Are more utterances needed to determine patterns for word length? What type?

- What are the child's needs in terms of word length?

6.1.4. Analysis Steps

For analysis of word length, the following steps are taken, starting with the scan's Bird's-Eye View. These procedures relate to the questions in the above section.

- **Step 1: Bird's-Eye View.** Look over the data quickly. Marnie's data show clear limitations on word length (see *daddy, TV,* and *balloons*). Note in the appropriate section of page 2 as follows:

  Syllables missing from words: ☑ Yes   ☐ No   If yes, ☑ Often ☐ Seldom

- **Step 2: Coding.** If patterns are not obvious, code word length (see Table 6.1).

- **Step 3: Scan section.** Fill in the word-length column on page 3 of the scan (see Table 6.2).

- **Step 4: Determination of needs and goals.** Enter information regarding word length into the Goal Summary on page 7 of the scan (at this point or after the entire syllable and word structure analysis). (See Table 6.3.)

6.1.5. Word-Length Scan for Marnie's Data

Tables 6.2 and 6.3 summarize the word-length analysis for Marnie's data. Words of one syllable were clearly a strength for Marnie. Longer words were usually reduced and therefore a need. Word-length constraints may also have affected phrase production; incorporation of syllables into prosodic contours may have been generally difficult. Because she could pronounce two-syllable words in imitation, the immediate goal was to stabilize two-syllable word production without adult models. This goal needed to be among the early goals in her program, because it severely limited word intelligibility and possibly even sentence production. Improvement in sentence length might be expected after she was able to produce two-syllable words spontaneously.

In terms of treatment, starting with reduplicated CVCV Strong-weak words (such as *Mimi, Deedee, Mumu,* etc.) would probably be facilitative. Tasks could begin with imitation of CV and then proceed to self-repetition of pronounceable CV's, with ever-shortening pauses between the CV's, until CVCV was produced spontaneously

Table 6.2. Marnie's Word Length Analysis, Scan Page 3

Unusual prosodic factors? (circle) pitch, (voice/resonance,) duration, rate, rhythm, intonation, loudness

creaky voice—hard glottal attack

	Word Length	Summary Notes
Basic inventory	(1 syllable) (2 syllables) 3 syllables 4 syllables Other:	→ *Sample contains:* 1-syllable and some 2-syllable words.
Matches by category	(1 syllable) (2 syllables) ((3 syllables)) 4 syllables Other:	→ *Impression of accuracy:* 1-syllable OK (can match 2- and 3-syllable words).
Child's maximum	2	→ *Longest word:* 2 syllables.
Child's most frequent	① 2 Both Other:	→ *Most frequent word length:* 1 syllable.
Child's developing forms (some matches)	(2 syllables) ((3 syllables)) 4 syllables	→ *Some matches for:* 2-syllable words.
Comparison with adult targets	Syllables missing? Yes Syllables added? Once	→ *Nonmatches have:* missing syllables.
Context differences? Spontaneous vs. imitated Single word vs. phrases	Yes: 2-syllable words in imitation	→ *Context difference:* 2-syllable words in imitation only (compare *daddy, elephant*).
Need to count? What?	Variable? 2-syl. Count 2-syllable words	→ % match for 2-syllable words (Table 6.5).
Other data needed? What?	Not at this point	→ No other data needed: patterns clear.
Needs? (Add to Goal Summary page, Goal 1, page 7)	2(+)-syllable words spontaneously	→ *Main need:* 2-syllable words spontaneously.

Note. Parentheses = inconsistency. Double parentheses = very marginal.

(me . . . . . me . . . me . . me > Mimi). There were also social factors to take into account for development of treatment strategies. Marnie preferred object-based tasks that changed frequently. The family was willing and able to carry on successful home practice activities.

In real life, Marnie's speech-language pathologist first targeted CV and CVC word shapes, thereby increasing the number of consonantal onsets and codas. Words with two syllables (CVCV) were the third goal in the first period of intervention. Marnie improved in all areas quickly, including sentence production (a happy ending!).

Table 6.3. Word Length: Marnie's Goal Summary, Scan Page 7

Level	Syllable and Word Structure	Summary Notes
Goal Type	**Goal Type 1** Structure	
Strengths	Word length 1 syllable Stress patterns Word shapes	→ *Strength for length:* 1-syllable words.
Needs	Word length 2+ syllables Stress patterns Word shapes	→ *Needs:* All other word lengths.
Strengths To Use To Support Needs	Segments to use for structure goals -	→ Need segmental analysis before filling in this box.
Interactions (prosody, perception, morphology, motor)	Sentence length constrained by word length limitations?	→ *Sentence production:* Limited by difficulty combining syllables into prosodic contours?
Social Factors	Attends for short periods. Prefers objects. Family familiar with speech therapy.	→ *Social factors:* Relevant for treatment strategies. (See below.)
Immediate Goals	2-syllable words produced spontaneously.	→ *Immediate goal:* Developing form (2 syllables) in *new context,* i.e., spontaneous speech.
Treatment Strategies	1. (C)VCV words with Sw, Ss stress patterns. 2. Start with reduplicative words (e.g., no-no, Mimi), using segments in inventory. 3. Tasks: Short, object-based. 4. Imitation at first. 5. Homework.	→ *Strategies:* Consider stimuli, methods, task types, home program.
Goal # in Program (order)	Early in program	→ *Goal order:* Severe limitation, therefore early goal.

6.1.6. Optional Step: Quantitative Analysis

Since two-syllable word production was inconsistent, quantification of that part of the analysis could be done to provide a baseline for treatment. Table 6.4 shows an independent analysis (what the child did on her own), and Table 6.5 shows a relational analysis (comparing the child's productions to the adult targets). Of the 15 words in the child's sample, Table 6.4 shows that 67% (10/15) were monosyllabic, and 33% were disyllabic. Table 6.5 shows a 46.7% (7/15) match for word length in the sample. For the nonmatching child productions, the predominant pattern involved syllable omission (7/8 of nonmatching forms), with only one word showing syllable addition (*more*).

Table 6.4. Marnie's Word Length: Independent Analysis

# of syllables	# of child productions	Proportion of total
1	10	10/15 (67%)
2	5	5/15 (33%)
3+	0	0/15 (0%)
TOTAL	15	

Table 6.5. Marnie's Word Length: Relational Analysis

# of syllables	# of adult targets	Matching child forms (%)	Syllables added	Syllables missing
1	5	4/5 (80.0%)	1/5 (20%)	
2	8	3/8 (37.5%)		5/8 (62.5%)
3+	2	0/2 (0.00%)		2/2 (100%)
TOTAL	15	7/15 (46.7%)	1/15 (6.7%)	7/15 (46.7%)

These proportions could be compared with similar counts after treatment to determine whether progress was being made. Because only two-syllable words were being targeted, three-syllable words would serve as baseline targets, to determine whether generalization was occurring.

6.2. Word Stress Patterns

6.2.1. Expected Developmental Trends for Word Stress

Development of stress patterns has not been sufficiently studied, although the following observations have been made.

Age Expectations:

In English, children can produce two-syllable words with initial stress (Sw) before they can accurately product two-syllable words with final stress (wS).

Developmental Phonological Patterns:

• The most common developmental patterns with respect to stress is omission of weak syllables, e.g., ['lũːn] for *balloon.*

• Less commonly, weak syllables may become strong, e.g., ['bʌˌlõn] for *balloon.*

Word stress analysis is shown for Barry in Sections 6.2.2–6.2.4. An extra data set is given in Appendix C.

6.2.2. Barry's Data

Barry: Age 12-1. Mild residual phonological disorder.

Barry had a general developmental delay and mild cerebral palsy, with specific delays in language development. He produced most English speech sounds (he also had Cantonese input) but was having difficulty with multisyllabic words and sentence production (data are in Table 6.6). He could read and spell at about a Grade-1 level. In terms of learning preferences, he was very visually oriented and liked music and rhythm activities. The family was familiar with home practice activities for speech and language.

6.2.3. Questions To Ask of the Sample

- What types of stress patterns are in the sample (basic inventory): Sw, wS, Sww, Sws, wSw, etc.?

- Which stress patterns match the adult targets (matches by category): Sw, wS, Sww, Sws, wSw, etc.?

- Is there a tendency for Strong-weak patterns?

- What are the child's maximum, frequent, and developing stress patterns?

Table 6.6. Word Stress: Barry's Data

Word	Adult		Child	
	Pronunciation	Stress	Pronunciation	Stress
alligator	ˈʔæləˌgeɪɾɚ	Swsw	ˈʔægərə	Sww
			ˈʔɛʊərə (I)	Sww
animal	ˈʔænəml̩	Sww	ˈʔænəməl	Sww
another	ʔəˈnʌðɚ	wSw	ˈnəðə (I)	Sw
awake	ʔəˈweɪk	wS	ʔəˈweɪk (I)	wS
balloon	bəˈlũːn	wS	ˈbolũːn	Sw
			bəˈlũːn (I)	wS
banana	bəˈnænə	wSw	ˈbənænə (I)	Sww
chicken	ˈtʃɪkn̩	Sw	ˈtʃʰɪkn̩	Sw
elephant	ˈʔɛləfn̩t	Sww	ˈʔɛfərə̃nt	Sww
			ˈʔɛləfn̩t (SC)	Sww
helicopter	ˈhɛləˌkʰɑptɚ	Swsw	ˈhaləˌkʰɑptɚ (I)	Swsw
living room	ˈlɪvĩŋˌrũːm	Sws	ˈlɪvĩŋˌrũːm	Sws
police	pʰəˈliːs	wS	ˈpoʊlis	Sw
potato chip	pʰəˈtʰeɪroʊˌtʃɪp	wSws	ˈpʰɪtʰoʊˌtʃɪp (I)	Sws
tomorrow	tʰəˈmɔroʊ	wSw	təˈmɔroʊ	wSw
vanilla	vəˈnɪlə	wSw	ˈvajə (I)	Sw
			ˈvænɪlə (I)	Sww
elevator	ˈʔɛləˌveɪɾɚ	Swsw	ˈʔɛvəˌlɔr (I)	Sws

- In comparison with the adult target, are strong or weak syllables missing, are there stress shifts, or do segments produced vary on repeated word productions?

- Does context make a difference: Is there any difference between single words and connected speech or between spontaneous and imitated productions?

- How variable are the data in general? Would counting help confirm patterns, or set a baseline for determining effectiveness in treatment? What should be counted?

- Are more utterances needed to determine patterns for stress patterns? What type?

- What are the child's needs in terms of stress patterns?

Reminder

The following examples review stress patterns:

Strong-weak (CANdle)
Strong-weak-weak (CAnada)
weak-Strong (baLLOON)
Strong-weak-strong (BUbbleGUM)
weak-Strong-weak (baNAna)

6.2.4. Stress Pattern Scan for Barry's Data

- **Step 1: Bird's-Eye View.** A quick look at the data showed that Barry's stress patterns were problematic at the time of assessment. No question on the scan form addresses that situation, so a note was added at the bottom of the form: "Stress difficulties noted."

- **Step 2: Coding.** Stress patterns were coded in the data table for purposes of illustration.

- **Step 3: Relevant scan section for stress patterns.** See Table 6.7.

- **Step 4: Goal Summary sheet of scan.** See Table 6.8.

- **Optional step: Quantitative analysis.** Additional counts of patterns are given in the following section.

Tables 6.7 and 6.8 summarize the stress pattern data for Barry. Barry sometimes produced the more marked weak-Strong(-weak) sequences in English, but he still needed assistance. A number of patterns accounted for differences between his productions and the adult targets: weak or strong syllable deletion, stress shift, and variable segment production. Barry's inability to produce wS sequences consistently may have had a negative influence on production of unstressed grammatical morphemes and, additionally, may have resulted in a somewhat unusual sentence intonation.

Table 6.7. Barry's Stress Analysis, Scan Page 3

Unusual prosodic factors? (circle) pitch, voice/resonance, duration, rate, (rhythm,) (intonation,) loudness

	Stress Patterns	Summary Notes
Basic inventory	(Sw) Ss (Sww) (Sws) Ssw (wS) (wSw) swS Other: (Swsw) Gaps: Ss, Ssw, swS	→ *Inventory and matches:* Words of up to 4 syllables (Swsw), but mostly Sw(w) stress patterns.
Matches by category	(Sw) Ss (Sww) (Sws) Ssw (wS) (wSw) swS Other: (Swsw) Gaps: Ss, Ssw, swS Nonmatch: Swsw, wSws	
Child's maximum	Swsw	
Child's most frequent	(Sw) Other: Sww	
Child's developing forms (some matches)	(wS) Other: wSw, Sws	→ *Developing:* wS(w) (*balloon, tomorrow*).

Comparison with adult targets	Missing:
	  Weak syllables Yes
	  Strong syllables Yes
	Stress shift? Yes
	
	Equal stress?
	
	Segments differ on repetition of multisyllable words? Yes
		→ *Comparison:* Variety of repairs: weak (*another*) and strong syllable deletion (*alligator*), stress shift (*balloon*), variable segments (*alligator*).

Context differences? Spontaneous vs. imitated Single word vs. phrases	Frequent words better? Imitated better?	→ *Context:* Better in imitation (*balloon*) & for frequent words (*tomorrow*).
Need to count? What?	Variable? wS Count wS, plus error patterns	→ *Count?* Quantify variable wS, error patterns.
Other data needed? What?	Ssw, Sws	→ *More data?* More 3-syllable patterns? Ssw, Sws.
Needs? (Add to Goal Summary page, Goal 1, page 7)	wS patterns, Ssw	→ *Most pressing needs:* wS(w), Sws(w).

Note. Parentheses = inconsistency.

Focusing on word stress also provided an opportunity for improving sentence intonation and production of unstressed elements in sentences.

Attention to weak-Strong(-weak) sequences was warranted. In order to facilitate production of stress, complex segmental sequences would be avoided at first. Visual stimuli (including print) and rhythm would be facilitative supports. Working on both words and short phrases would presumably stimulate both phonology and syntax.

Table 6.8. Word Stress: Barry's Goal Summary, Scan Page 7

Level	Syllable and Word Structure	Summary Notes
Goal Type	**Goal Type 1** Structure	
Strengths	Word length Stress patterns Sw, Sww Word shapes	→ *Strength:* Sw(w) patterns.
Needs	Word length Stress patterns wS(w), Sws(w) Word shapes	→ *Needs:* Primarily wS(w); also 4-syllable word patterns, starting with Swsw.
Strengths To Use To Support Needs	Segments to use for structure goals ------------------------------- Any	→ All segments available; watch sequences.
Interactions (prosody, perception, morphology, motor)	Related to omission of unstressed grammatical morphemes? Related to impression of unusual intonation?	→ *Interactions:* Grammatical morphemes omitted because unstressed? Intonation?
Social Factors	Attends for short periods. Can read at Grade-1 level. Very visually oriented. Likes music and rhythm tasks. Family supportive.	→ *Social factors:* Relevant for treatment strategies because of attention span and developmental delay. (See below.)
Immediate Goals	wS and wSw words in words and phrases	→ *Goal:* wS(w), in *both* words and sentences.
Treatment Strategies	1. Short drills with print and other visual support. 2. Rhythm support. 3. Link of wS sequences in words to grammatical morphemes in phrases. 4. Words without clusters and with minimal place changes at first.	→ *Strategies:* Consider social factors, interactions with morphology/syntax, and word complexity. Reduce sequence difficulty: same place consonants, no consonant clusters.
Goal # in Program (order)	Prior to further morphological and syntactic intervention	→ *Goal order:* Word stress prior to further work on morphology and syntax.

6.2.5. Optional Step: Quantitative Analysis

Match proportions for weak-Strong patterns would be a useful baseline for evaluating treatment effectiveness:

weak-Strong	2/4 matches	(50%)
weak-Strong-weak	1/5 matches	(20%)
total weak-Strong sequences	3/9 matches	(33.3%)

Knowing the relative proportions of the various repair processes might help clarify facilitative intervention strategies. Proportions of repairs affecting stress directly were as follows:

weak syllables missing	4/10 repairs (yielding Sw)
strong syllables missing	2/10 repairs (Swsw > Sww)
stress shift	4/10 repairs (yielding Sw, Sww)

Both syllable deletion and stress shift yielded Sw(w) patterns. However, identification of repair types was difficult for some items. For example, when *vaNIlla* is pronounced as ['vajə], a strong syllable is produced, but the segmental content of the target strong syllable is lost. The repair involves both stress shift *and* syllable deletion. Thus, repairs appeared to be less relevant than constraints on what could actually be produced. Intervention, therefore, might be less concerned with addressing repairs than with concentrating on the other stress patterns of English.

6.3. Subsyllabic Structure: Word Shapes

English has a great variety of word shapes in terms of CV configurations. For intervention purposes, usually only those in one- and two-syllable words are addressed, since they are most frequent and are also foundational for those in longer words. General trends are noted in Section 6.3.1 below.

6.3.1. Expected Developmental Trends for Word Shape

As noted above, English has a great variety of word shapes in terms of C and V configurations. However, for developmental analyses we generally focus on the most common word shapes, since they are the foundation for all of the more complex ones: CV(V), CVC, CCV(C), (C)VCC, CVCV, CVCVC, and CVCCV(C).

Age Expectations:

• Children under 2 generally produce CV(V) and CVCV words and are beginning to produce words with codas (CVC, VC). Some may produce more complex combinations of the above (CVCVC, CVCCV).

• By age 3, children generally produce some words with clusters, e.g., (C)VCC, or CCV(C). Cluster development then proceeds gradually until age 6 or 7.

Developmental Phonological Patterns:

• The most common developmental pattern with respect to word shapes is deletion of segments, particularly codas, or cluster elements.

• Less commonly, consonants or vowels may be added to words, either

  a. to rescue a consonant or vowel that cannot be pronounced otherwise, e.g., addition of a vowel to rescue a coda consonant, as in [bɛdə] for *bed;* or

  b. to fulfill syllable-length requirements, e.g., insertion of a glottal stop at the end of a vowel-final word when the long vowel or diphthong cannot be produced, as in [paʔ] for *pie.*

Sections 6.3.2–6.3.4 give a word shape analysis for one data set. Other useful word shape data sets are Marnie's (this chapter), Mandy's in Chapter 7, and Jeremy's in Appendix C.

6.3.2. Craig's Data

Craig: Age 3-1. Severe phonological disorder.

Craig had average language comprehension and a moderate delay in language production. He was a very active child who frequently used a loud voice. See Table 6.9 for a selected sample of his data.

6.3.3. Questions To Ask of the Sample

- What types of word shapes are in the sample (basic inventory): CV(V), CVC, CVCV, CCV, CVCC, CVCVC, etc.?

- Which word shapes match the adult targets (matches by category): CV(V), CVC, CVCV, CCV, CVCC, CVCVC, etc.?

Table 6.9. Word Shapes: Craig's Data

Word	Adult		Child	
	Pronunciation	Word Shape	Pronunciation	Word Shape
airplane	(ʔ)ɛrpʰlẽɪn	(ʔ)VC.CCVVC	beɪpeĩ	CVVCVV
mom	mãm	CVC	mʌ (I)	CV
mouth	mʌʊθ	CVVC	maʊ (I)	CVV
mouthy	mʌʊθi	CVVCV	mʌʔiː (I)	CVʔVː
noise	nɔɪz	CVVC	nɔɪ (I)	CVV
page	pʰeɪʤ	CVVC	pʰiː	CVː
piggy	pʰɪgi	CVCV	bɪʔi (I)	CVʔV
bee	biː	CVː	biː (I)	CVː
bib	bɪb	CVC	biː (I)	CVː
brush	brʌʃ	CCVC	beɪ	CVV
tub	tʰʌb	CVC	tʰæp (I)	CVC
candle	kʰændl̩	CVCCC̩	tʰæmoʊ	CVCVV
cook	kʰʊk	CVC	tʰʊʔ (I)	CVʔ
cooking	kʰʊkĩŋ	CVCVC	tʊʔi	CVʔVː
finger	fĩŋgɚ	CVCCC̩	pʰiːjə	CVGV
fish	fɪʃ	CVC	bɪ (I)	CV
fishing	fɪʃĩŋ	CVCVC	biːbi (I)	CVːCVː
spoon	spũːn	CCVːC	buː	CVː
sunglasses	sãnglæsəz	CVCCCVCVC	dʌʔtæʔiː (I)	CVʔCVʔVː

- What are the child's maximum, frequent, and developing word shapes?

- In comparison with the adult target, are consonants or vowels missing, is there syllable reduplication, evidence of vowel lengthening, or frequent use of glottal stops for consonants?

- Does context make a difference: Is there any difference between single words and connected speech or between spontaneous and imitated productions?

- How variable are the data in general? Would counting help confirm patterns or set a baseline for determining effectiveness in treatment? What should be counted?

- Are more utterances needed to determine patterns for word shapes? What type?

- What are the child's needs in terms of word shapes?

6.3.4. Word Shape Scan for Craig's Data

- **Step 1: Bird's-Eye View.** A quick look at the data shows that Craig had limited CV structure in words. Omission and reduction were frequent. Glottal stops appeared word-medially.

    Patterns specific to a given word position:

General omission:	☐ Initial	☑ Medial	☑ Final
Reduced clusters:	☑ Initial	☑ Medial	☑ Final
Position-based substitution pattern:	☐ Initial	☑ Medial ?	☐ Final

- **Step 2: Coding.** Comments in Chapter 5 about coding for Dylan's word shapes are relevant here.

- **Step 3: Relevant scan section for word shape.** See Table 6.10.

- **Step 4: Goal Summary page of scan.** See Table 6.11.

- **Optional step: Quantitative analysis.** Additional counts of patterns are given in the following section.

Craig had significant difficulty with word shape production. He used open CVV monosyllables most frequently (CVV = long vowel or diphthong). Word length was preserved, with long words having CV shapes similar to those of short words. (Compare *brush* as [beɪ] and *airplane* as [beɪpeɪ].) CVC and CVCV were beginning to develop (e.g., *tub* as [tʰæp], *candle* as [tʰæmoʊ]). Craig's delay in sentence production may have been related to his phonological delay (see Bopp, 1995).

Consonants were frequently omitted, but there were also several compensatory strategies for realization of consonants: (a) use of glottal stops word-medially and once word-finally, (b) reduplication of one of the syllables, and (c) compensatory vowel lengthening (short lax vowels becoming long tense vowels or diphthongs, as in *bib, fishing*). Quantification would clarify these observations. Further data would be needed to elucidate the patterns regarding vowel-initial words and compensatory vowel lengthening.

Table 6.10. Craig's Word Shape Analysis, Scan Page 3

Unusual prosodic factors? (circle) pitch, voice/resonance, duration, rate, rhythm, intonation, (loudness)

	Word Shapes		Summary Notes
Basic inventory	V(V) V(V)C (CV(V)) (CV(V)C) (C)VCC CCV(V)(C) CV:	((C)V(V)CV(V)) CV(V)CV(V)C CV(V)CCV(V)C Other: CV{G/ʔ}V(:) (CVʔCVʔV:) (CVʔ)	→ *Inventory, frequency, and matches:* Frequent open syllable CV(V), CVʔV; matches primarily for CV:.
Matches by category	V(V) V(V)C CV(V) ((CV(V)C)) (C)VCC CCV(V)(C)	(C)V(V)CV(V) CV(V)CV(V)C CV(V)CCV(V)C Other: CV:	
Child's maximum	CVʔCVʔV:		→ *Maximum:* 3 syllables with 2 C's, 2 [ʔ]s.
Child's most frequent	V(V) (CV(V)) Other: CV:, CVʔV	CVC CVCV	
Child's developing forms (some matches)	CV(V) (CVCV) (C)VCC Other:	(CVC) CCV(V) CVCVC	→ *Developing:* CVC (tʰæp), CVCV (tʰæmoʊ).
Comparison with adult targets	Missing C's: (WF) WI (SIWW) (SFWW) (Clusters) [ʔ] or Glide for C: Yes Missing V's: (VV) (Diphthong) WF WI Medial Added C's: (C for [ʔ] onset) Added V's: VV for VC?? Reduplication also		→ *Comparison:* Several repairs: Missing C (*spoon*); [ʔ] or glide (e.g., *cook, piggy*); compensatory vowel lengthening (*bib*); reduplication (*fishing, airplane*).
Context differences? Spontaneous vs. imitated Single word vs. phrases	Not apparent		
Need to count? What?	Variable? Yes Count CVC, CVCV, repairs		→ *Count where variable:* CVC, CVCV, and error patterns (repairs).
Other data needed? What?	1. CVC, lax V's 2. V-initial words		→ *More data?* CVC with lax V's to check compensatory lengthening; V-initial words.
Needs? (Add to Goal Summary page, Goal 1, page 7)	All word shapes except CV(V)		→ *Needs: Severe limitation:* All but CV(V).

Note. Parentheses = inconsistency.

All word shapes except CV(V) were needs. As noted for Marnie, the particular segments to use could be determined only after doing a segmental analysis (see Chapters 5 and 7).

The compensatory lengthening repair (vowel extension when consonants were missing) suggested that Craig was possibly aware of subsyllabic structure (and weight of subsyllabic elements, i.e., moras). Thus, intervention strategies that differentiated between long (tense or diphthongal) and short (lax) vowels might be facilitative. Starting with easily pronounceable words (such as reduplicative CVCV words) would most likely result in early success and would thereby help to engage him in the process. Once reduplicative words were more common, a link could be established

Table 6.11. Word Shapes: Craig's Goal Summary, Scan Page 7

Level	Syllable and Word Structure	Summary Notes
Goal Type	**Goal Type 1** Structure	
Strengths	Word length Stress patterns Word shapes CV(V)	→ *Strength:* Basic open syllable CV(V), CV:.
Needs	Word length Stress patterns Word shapes All but CV(V)	→ *Needs:* All other word shapes.
Strengths To Use To Support Needs	Segments to use for structure goals - - - - - - - - - - - - - - - - - - - Not yet known	→ Need segmental analysis before filling in this box.
Interactions (prosody, perception, morphology, motor)	Delay in language production related to phonological delay?	→ *Interactions:* Severe word shape difficulty related to language production delay?
Social Factors	Attends for short periods only. Play oriented.	→ *Social factors:* Need short, fun activities.
Immediate Goals	Basic word shapes: CVC, CVCV, V-initial words	→ *Goals:* Basic shapes: (C)VC, (C)VCV.
Treatment Strategies	1. Use segments in inventory. 2. Use reduplicated words with V: or VV first, then words with different C's. 3. Next draw links between CVC & CVCV, using lax V's in V1; rhythm support for C2.	→ *Strategies:* See Chapter 11 for discussion of CVC, CVCV intervention.
Goal # in Program (order)	Early in program	→ *Goal order:* Severe limitation, therefore early goal.

between CVC and CVCV, lax vowels being used in the first syllable ("pen-penny," "hip-hippy"). Rhythmic support to emphasize the C2 of CVC would probably also be facilitative (see Bernhardt, 1994b, and Chapter 11 for further suggestions). Short active games would be most likely to engage his interest and enthusiasm for intervention.

6.3.5. Optional Step: Quantitative Analysis

A quantitative analysis of the developing forms CVC and CVCV would provide a baseline for efficacy purposes. There were 10 CV(V)C targets, enough to calculate a match proportion:

CV(V)C match (counting [?] as a C): 2/10 (20%)

There were insufficient CV(V)CV targets in the sample to calculate a match proportion. However, CVCV could be examined in terms of his own (relatively frequent) two-syllable productions (even if they derived from more complex CV structures). Frequency of the various repair strategies, i.e., reduplication and glottal and glide replacement, could be examined in order to determine how often true consonants showed up in C2 in comparison with glides and glottals. One measure of treatment effectiveness would be an increase in consonant production versus glide or glottal replacement.

CVCV (with true C in C2, nonreduplicative):	1/7 (14.3%)
CVCV (with true C in C2, reduplicative):	2/7 (28.5%)
CVCV (with glide in C2):	1/7 (14.3%)
CVCV (with [ʔ] in C2):	3/7 (42.8%)

The other major repairs involved compensations relative to subsyllabic weight (vowel lengthening, diphthongization, or glottal stop replacement). There were 12 adult monosyllabic targets (each of which has two moras per syllable, as discussed in Section 1.4).

Proportion of monosyllabic words with adult syllable weight (two moras):	10/12 (83.3%)

Only *mom* and *fish* (as words with lax vowels) failed to show compensation for the missing coda. Quantitative analysis thus appears to confirm strong weight constraints on syllable production; compensatory strategies were used to satisfy moraic requirements when codas could not be produced. If Craig was already aware of the subsyllabic structure, more attention could be focused on production than awareness in treatment.

6.4. Final Comments

Children with phonological disorders often have deficits at some level of syllable and word structure: word length, stress patterns, and/or subsyllabic structure (word shapes, moras, onsets, rimes). Even if not problematic, certain aspects of a child's word and syllable structure may be exploited when targeting other parts of the phonology. Thus, we have found that it is worth taking the time to do these analyses, even when there do not appear to be any overt difficulties or current priorities for treatment. (Word shape analysis is the most time consuming for this section of the scan, but overall page 3 proceeds quickly during scanning.)

Chapter 7

Consonant and Glide Analyses

**Analyses in This Chapter
(pages 4, 5, 6, 7 of the scan)**

- phonetic inventory and substitution patterns
- manner, laryngeal, and place features
- feature combinations
- segments by word position
- choosing segments for word shape goals

This chapter demonstrates feature analyses for consonants and glides (pages 4 and 5 of the scan) and word position effects (top of page 6 of the scan). In the top two rows of page 4 of the scan is listed the child's phonetic inventory (segments used) in each word position. The rest of the feature chart summarizes major substitution patterns within and across word positions.

7.1. Trends for Consonant and Glide Development

Trends for consonant and glide development are noted in Section 7.1.1. (For a general review, see also Stoel-Gammon & Dunn, 1985, or Bernthal & Bankson, 1998. For an examination of developmental patterns in nonlinear frameworks, see Bernhardt & Stemberger, 1998, Chapter 5.)

7.1.1. Expected Developmental Trends for Consonants and Glides

Although there is no fixed order of acquisition of segments, the following general trends have been observed.

Age Expectations:

- The earliest nonsyllabic segments include stops, nasals, and glides with labial or coronal place of articulation.

- The liquids /l/ and /r/ and certain fricatives may not develop until age 8 or 9, although some children acquire them much earlier.

Developmental Phonological Patterns:

- The most common developmental patterns with respect to consonants are deletion and substitution. Deletion tends to occur most often because of syllable or word structure constraints but can occur when a segment cannot be pronounced. Early developing segments such as stops and glides tend to be used as substitutes for later-developing segments (such as fricatives, velars, /l/, and /r/).

- Less common repairs for unpronounceable segments might involve assimilation or additions of consonants or vowels. If /s/ is impossible, assimilation might result in [naɪn] for *sign*. If voiced stops are impossible in final position, [bɛdn̩] or [bɛdə] might occur for *bed*.

- With respect to word position, word-initial position often has a bigger variety of segments. However, some sound classes tend to develop word-finally or word-medially first, e.g., fricatives and velars. Further, word position effects are often noted for voicing: devoicing of final obstruents, and voicing or deaspiration of word-initial stops.

7.1.2. Mandy's Data

Mandy: Age 4-2. Severe phonological disorder.

Mandy had age-appropriate language comprehension but a mild delay in morphosyntactic production. She was not able to perform metaphonological tasks of rhyming, alliteration, or segmentation. There was a family history of language delay (her father and a younger sibling). Mandy was somewhat reluctant to participate in drill-like speech activities. Table 7.1 shows a portion of her speech sample data.

7.1.3. Questions To Ask of the Sample

- What is the child's inventory by word position, i.e., what consonants and glides are actually produced in word-initial, -medial, and -final positions, whether or not they match the adult target?

- What are the established, developing, and missing features by word position and by major feature types (manner, laryngeal, and place features)?

- What are the substitution patterns for consonants and glides?

- Which speech sounds are used frequently as substitutions and/or matches?

- What are the probable default features in the system?

- Are those defaults expected (given the target adult language) or unique to the child?

- Are there inconsistencies within sound classes, suggesting there might be particular difficulty with certain feature combinations (e.g., coronal fricatives [s] and [z] but not labiodental fricatives [f] or [v], velar stops [k] and [g] but no velar nasal [ŋ])?

- Does context make a difference: Is there any difference between single words and connected speech or between spontaneous and imitated productions?

- How variable are the data overall? Would counting help confirm patterns or set a baseline for determining effectiveness in treatment? What should be counted? (*Note:* Between-word variability may indicate sequence constraints, which are discussed in the next chapter.)

- Are more utterances needed of any type? What type?

Table 7.1. Mandy's Data

Word	Adult	Child	WI C1	WI C2	WI V	SF C	SI C1	SI C2	SI V	SI C	SI V	WF C1	WF C2	I/C
ice cubes	(ʔ)ʌɪskjuːbz	ʔʌguː	ʔ		ʌ	ø	g	ø	uː			ø	ø	I
mommy	mʌmi	mʌmi	m		ʌ		m		i					
nine	nãɪn	naɪ	n		aɪ							ø		I
puzzle	pʰʌzl̩	bʌjoʊ	b		ʌ		j		oʊ					I
bathtub	bæθtʰʌb	bæːdʌː	b		æː	ø	d		ʌː			ø		
tubby	tʰʌbi	dʌˤbi	d		ʌˤ		b		i					
dolly	dɑːli	dɑːɹi	d		ɑː		ɹ̥		i					
cake	kʰeɪk	geɪʔ	g		eɪ							ʔ		I
glove	glʌv	gwʌʊ	g	w	ʌʊ							ø		
feather	fɛðɚ	feɪɚ	f		eɪ		ø		ɚ					I
van	vãn	v̥æ̃ː	v̥		æ̃ː							ø		I
thumb	θʌ̃m	dʌ̃m	d		ʌ̃							m		
that	ðæt	dæ	d		æ							ø		C
smooth	smuːð	mũː	ø	m	ũː							ø		I
soap	soʊp	doʊpʰ	d		oʊ							pʰ		I
zipper	zɪpɚ	deɪɚ	d		eɪ		ø				ɚ			I
cherries	tʃɛriz	deɚ-iː	d		ɛ				ɚ		iː	ø		I
jumping	dʒʌ̃mpĩŋ	dʌ̃miː	d		ʌ̃	>[a]	m		iː			ø		
laughing	læfĩŋ	wæ̃iː	w		æ̃		ø		ĩː			ø		
roar	rɔr	wɔr	w		ɔ							r		I
watch	wɑːtʃ	wɑː	w		ɑː							ø		
your	jɔr	jɔr	j		ɔ							r		C
house	haʊs	haʊ	h		aʊ							ø		

[a]Generally, intervocalic consonants are considered to be in the SI columns (onsets). Here, the [m] of the child's *jumping* is entered in the SI column since the child produces only the [m] of the /mp/ target.

7.1.4. Analysis Procedures

For analysis of consonants and glides, the following steps are taken. These analyses are more detailed than analysis of word structure and thus generally take longer (depending on how many segments are in the child's inventory and degree of variability).

- **Step 1: Bird's-Eye View.** See Section 7.1.5.

- **Step 2: Inventory.** Basic to the feature analysis is the notation of the child's consonant inventory, both within and across word positions. The inventory is a list of the speech sounds that the child produces, whether or not they match the adult targets. The consonantal inventory by word position is entered into the top two rows of page 4 of the scan, with the true consonants ([+consonantal]) separated from the glides ([−consonantal]). Inventory segments may be coded (with color, circling, etc.) to indicate frequency and/or usage (i.e., as matches with adult targets, matches *and* substitutions, or substitutions *only*). Coding makes it easier to identify established, developing, and default features.

- **Step 3: Substitutions.** The remainder of page 4 and the summary column on page 5 are used to list substitution patterns for manner, laryngeal, and place features. The substitution patterns show the speech sounds that the child substitutes and omits in comparison with the adult targets. When there is a high proportion of omissions in some word position, the ∅ character is often used to indicate missing consonants. More detail on procedures is noted in Section 7.1.7.

- **Optional step: Quantitative analysis.** For a more precise determination of needs and/or to assess treatment efficacy later, it may be necessary to calculate percentage match for certain features.

- **Step 4: Determination of needs.** In the final two columns of page 5, needs for features are listed by row. If a feature is rarely or never produced, the feature itself is considered a need, and that is noted in the next to last column. If a feature is produced in some feature combinations but not in others, *the needed combinations are listed in the final column.* The strengths and needs for features and feature combinations are then entered on the Goal Summary sheet. At this point, the segments and features that are available for word shape goals are also listed on the Goal Summary sheet.

7.1.5. Bird's-Eye View

A quick look at Mandy's segments shows use of consonants in all sound classes but with inconsistencies across word positions and within sound classes. Word-medial and -final positions had many omissions.

Segments (Phonemes)

Consonant sound classes in sample: (Circle if present; use parentheses to indicate limited numbers)

(Stops,) (nasals,) fricatives, liquids, (glides) *(some f, v, r)*

(Labials,) (coronals) [dentals, (alveolars,) palatoalveolars], (velars)

(Voiced/voiceless)

Missing sound classes from above: _Coronal fricatives, /l/, /r/ in some word positions_

Major segmental substitution patterns: _Stops for some fricatives; glide [w] for /l/, (/r/); [j] medially_

Vowels *Generally accurate*

Substitutions:

Defaults:

Diphthongs:

Analysis needed: ☐ Yes ☑ No
(See final page of scan)

Syllable and Word Structure

Syllables added to words: ☐ Yes ☑ No If yes, ☐ Often ☐ Seldom

Syllables missing from words: ☐ Yes ☑ No If yes, ☐ Often ☐ Seldom

Patterns specific to a given word position:

General omission:	☐ Initial	☑ Medial	☑ Final
Reduced clusters:	(☑ Initial)	☑ Medial	☑ Final
Position-based substitution pattern:	☐ Initial	☑ Medial	☐ Final
		Glides word-medially	

7.1.6. Inventory

Mandy's inventory is shown in Table 7.2. All major places and manners of articulation were represented in the inventory. This was a positive aspect of Mandy's speech development. To determine needs, however, it is also important to know what is missing from an inventory. In her case, consonant omission was common word-medially and -finally, implying strong syllable and word structure constraints. Furthermore, fricatives were restricted (no sibilants or voiced fricatives), there was no /l/, and there were positional restrictions on /r/ and voicing. Stops were frequent, as expected in early development.

7.1.7. Substitution Analysis

Tables 7.3 and 7.4 show the complete consonant and glide feature analysis for Mandy (pages 4 and 5 of the scan).

More detail about substitution analysis procedures is presented in the list below.

1. Substitution patterns are identified by scanning individual word position columns, looking at patterns within individual words. When one or two instances of a pattern are observed, this is noted in the appropriate box on page 4, and then other patterns are looked for. *The idea is to identify major patterns* rather than note every substitution occurring in every word. Use general statements as much as possible: "Fric(ative)s > stops," or "All > [ʔ]." *Less is more!*

2. For each row (i.e., feature), *list a substitution only if the segment in question is missing that particular feature.* This helps later, when determining feature needs. For example, when target /s/ appears as [t], the feature [continuant] is a mismatch. Thus, /s/ > [t] is entered into the [+continuant] row. However, when /s/ is produced as [f], the mismatch concerns coronal [+anterior] *place* of articulation, not [+continuant]. Thus, /s/ > [f] is entered into the coronal [+anterior] row only.

3. Substitutions for [+consonantal] and [−consonantal] segments are entered in the "Summary" column, page 5 (because their page 4 rows are used for inventory).

Table 7.2. Mandy's Consonant and Glide Inventory, Scan Page 4

Feature	Adult Targets	Word-Initial	Medial, Syllable-Final	Medial, Syllable-Initial	Word-Final
[+consonantal] inventory	All but glides below	m n **b d g** f v̥	Ø	m **b d g** Ø	m pʰ Ø
[−consonantal] inventory	ʔ h w j r	ʔ h **w** j		*j ɾ*ᵃ	r (ɚᵃ)

Note. Boldfaced segments match the adult targets *and* are also used as substitutions. Italics designate phones used as substitutions only. Otherwise, segments are used as matches (correct) only. Parentheses indicate consonants that match the adult target only some of the time.

ᵃɚ designates an unstressed syllabic /r̩/. It also appeared as a syllabic substitution for syllable-initial /r/ (e.g., *cherries* as [dɛɚi:]).

Table 7.3. Mandy's Consonant Analysis, Scan Page 4

Feature	Adult Targets	Word-Initial	Medial, Syllable-Final	Medial, Syllable-Initial	Word-Final
[+consonantal] inventory	All but glides below	m n **b d** **g** f ɣ̥	∅	m b **d** g ∅	m pʰ ? ∅
[−consonantal] inventory	? h w j r	? h **w** j		j, ɾ	r (ɚ)
[+lateral]	l	l > w		l > ɾ	l > oʊ
[+nasal]	m n ŋ		∅		n, ŋ > ∅
[−continuant]	p t k b d g ? m n ŋ			p, (d) > ∅	All > ∅ except m, p
[+continuant] (&[−sonorant])	f v s z θ ð ʃ ʒ	s, z > d	∅	ð > ∅ / v, z > j	∅
[−continuant]-[+continuant]	tʃ dʒ	tʃ, dʒ > d			tʃ > ∅

Manner Default Summary: Expected: [−cont], [−nasal]; [−cons] for /l/   Other: Yes

Feature	Adult Targets	Word-Initial	Medial, Syllable-Final	Medial, Syllable-Initial	Word-Final
[+voiced] obstruents	b d g / v z ð ʒ dʒ	Stops ok / v > v̥ but z > d		(d), ð > ∅; b, g ok / z, v > j	∅
[−voiced] obstruents	p t k / f s θ ʃ tʃ	Stops > [+voiced] / s, θ, tʃ > d	∅	p > ∅ t k > d g / f > ∅	k > ? ∅, others > ∅ except 1 p match
[+spread glottis]	h; Asp. stops; (vl. fricatives)	Vl. stops voiced	No frics		No frics

Laryngeal Default Summary: Expected: [−voiced]   Other: [+voiced]   ? or h default: / WF?   WI, SI   WF k > ? (once)

Feature	Adult Targets	Word-Initial	Medial, Syllable-Final	Medial, Syllable-Initial	Word-Final
Labial	p b m f v w			Voiceless > ∅ / v > j; (b ok)	∅ except p once
Coronal [+anterior]	t d n l s z θ ð	l > w		l > ɾ / (d), ð > ∅	l > oʊ / All others > ∅
Coronal [−anterior]	ʃ ʒ tʃ dʒ j r	tʃ dʒ > d			tʃ > ∅
Coronal [+grooved]	s z ʃ ʒ tʃ dʒ	(no fricatives)			
Coronal [−grooved]	θ ð	(stops)		ð > ∅	
Dorsal	k g ŋ (w) (j)				All > ∅
Coronal & Labial	r	r > w			

Place Default Summary: Expected: Coronal [+anterior]; [+grooved]   Other: Labial   No

Note. For inventory, boldfaced items are both substitutions and matches. Italicized items are substitutions only.

4. Summarize the substitution patterns with general statements on page 5, including word position information where relevant. Word position information will be useful when (a) determining word position goals (Goal Type 4), and (b) when choosing segments for new word shapes (Goal Type 1).

The rest of Section 7.1 summarizes data from pages 4 and 5 in terms of manner, laryngeal, and place features. The detail contained in the feature chart can be daunting at first. The reader may find it helpful to fill out a blank chart row by row, comparing it bit by bit to the one in this chapter, and/or to make summary notes for each major section of Tables 7.3 and 7.4, comparing them to the following. Photocopying the tables and having them at hand while reading the text may also help.

To supplement the summaries, reviews of developmental trends, hints on analysis procedures, and selected sections from Table 7.4 are presented throughout.

Table 7.4. Mandy's Consonant Analysis: Summary, Scan Page 5

Feature	Summary of Substitutions (from page 4)	Goal Type 2: Feature Marginal or Not Used at All	Goal Type 3: Feature Marginal or Not Used in Specific Feature Combinations*
[+consonantal]	(Medial) and final C's > Ø or ([−cons] glides) /l/ > glide or vowel ([−cons])	[+cons]: Medial, final (*word struc.*)	
[−consonantal]			
[+lateral]	l > glide or vowel ([−lateral])	[+lateral]	
[+nasal]	WF n, ŋ > Ø		[+nas] & Dors or Cor: WF
[−continuant]	[−cont]: Some > Ø in WM, WF		[−continuant] & Dorsal or Coronal: WM, WF
[+continuant] (&[−sonorant])	WI Coronal > stop Medial, SI v, z > j Otherwise Ø (N.B. WI f, v OK)	[+continuant]: Medial, final (*word structure*)	[+cont] (& [−son]) & Cor (*sibilants*) [+cont] (& [−son]) & [+vcd]
[−continuant]- [+continuant]	WI > Stop Otherwise, Ø	[−cont]-[+cont] (*affricates*)	

Manner Defaults Needing Change: /l/ > [+consonantal]

Feature	Summary of Substitutions (from page 4)	Goal Type 2: Feature Marginal or Not Used at All	Goal Type 3: Feature Marginal or Not Used in Specific Feature Combinations*
[+voiced] obstruents	/v/ devoiced WI; Non-WI > Ø, except [+voiced] maintained when z, v > j		[+voiced] & [+cont] & [−son] (*voiced fricatives*)
[−voiced] obstruents	[−vcd] > [+vcd] in WI, medial (*except WI f*) [−vcd] > Ø in WF except for 1 [p] match	[−voiced] (*except WI f, WF p*)	
[+spread glottis]	/h/ OK; asp. [−cont] stops > voiced stops WI [f] only [+s.g.] fricative		[+s.g.] & [−son] & [−vcd], with [−cont] (and [+cont])

Laryngeal Defaults Needing Change: [+voiced] > [−voiced] WI?

Feature	Summary of Substitutions (from page 4)	Goal Type 2: Feature Marginal or Not Used at All	Goal Type 3: Feature Marginal or Not Used in Specific Feature Combinations*
Labial	Strong word initially Variable elsewhere; Medial > j, Ø although m, b OK; WF > Ø although m, p OK		[+cont] & Lab & [−son]: WM, WF, f, v; [−cont] & Lab: SI p; WF, b
Coronal [+anterior]	/l/ > Labial Most non-word-initial > Ø	Cor: /l/ Cor: Non-WI, all	[−cont] & Cor: WF [+cont] & Cor & [−son]
Coronal [−anterior]	No coronal fricatives; /j/ OK	[−ant] (not j, SF r)	[+cont] & Cor & [−son]
Coronal [+grooved]	No coronal fricatives	[+grooved]	[+cont] & Cor & [−son]
Coronal [−grooved]	No coronal fricatives	[−grooved]	[+cont] & Cor & [−son]
Dorsal	Final > Ø	Dorsal: Syl-final	[−cont] & Dors: WF
Coronal & Labial	Only WI /r/ > w		Cor [−ant] & Lab: WI /r/

Place Defaults Needing Change: Labial > Coronal?

7.1.8. Manner Features

The following general trends might be expected in manner feature development.

Age Expectations:

• the following early default manner features: [+consonantal] in onsets and codas, [−continuant] (stops), [−nasal] (oral airflow), [−lateral] (central airflow)

• the following early nondefault manner features: [−consonantal] and [+continuant] (glides), [+nasal]

Developmental Phonological Patterns:

• substitution of default manner features for nondefault targets

- appearance of consonants with default vowel features ([+continuant], [+sonorant]) in the rime (just after the vowel) or between vowels (i.e., fricatives, nasals, /l/, glides)

- limitations on syllable or word edges to [−continuant] stops or nasals

For Mandy's data, manner feature analysis showed the following, feature by feature (row by row).

1. **[+consonantal] and [−consonantal]:** Both consonants and glides were in the sample. Glides sometimes substituted for consonants word-medially or -finally. For these features, we note the following (see Table 7.5, an extract of the "Summary of Substitutions" column in Table 7.4).

Table 7.5. [+consonantal] Substitutions

Summary of Substitutions
(Medial) and final C's > Ø or glides ([−consonantal])
/l/ > glide (G) or vowel (V) ([−consonantal])

Many consonants were absent word-finally. In such cases, all features, including [+consonantal] were missing, e.g., *that* as [dæ], *laughing* as [wæ̃ɪ̃:]. As the example *laughing* shows, consonants were also missing sometimes word-medially. Sometimes [−consonantal] glides replaced consonants, e.g., [j], *puzzle* as [bʌjoʊ], and [ʔ], *cake* as [geɪʔ]. For /l/, a [−consonantal] glide or vowel appeared across word positions, e.g., *laughing* as [wæ̃ɪ̃:], dolly as [dɑːɹ̩i], *puzzle* as [bʌjoʊ].

In contrast, [−consonantal] targets surfaced as such, even if a different glide was produced, for example, when /r/ surfaced as [w] word-initially (e.g., *roar* as [wɔr]); hence, in the chart, no substitutions or needs are noted for the feature [−consonantal].

Needs: Because a *variety* of consonants lost the [+consonantal] feature, the feature itself (as opposed to the feature in combination) was a need, as we note in the next to last column ("Feature marginal or not used") in Table 7.4, here shown as an extract in Table 7.6.

Table 7.6. Individual Feature Need: [+consonantal]

Goal Type 2: Feature Marginal or Not Used at All
[+consonantal]: Medial, final (*word structure constraints*)

The need for [+consonantal] in these word positions is, furthermore, subsumed under general word structure constraints, as has been previously noted.

2. **[+lateral]:** The [+lateral] feature was not in the inventory. The following is noted in the "Summary of Substitutions" column in Table 7.4 (extracted here in Table 7.7).

Table 7.7. [+lateral] Substitutions

Summary of Substitutions
l > glide or vowel ([−lateral])

Need: Because /l/ was never produced, [+lateral] is identified as a specific feature need in the "Feature marginal or not used" column in Table 7.4, shown here as an extract in Table 7.8.

Table 7.8. Individual Feature Need: [+lateral]

Goal Type 2: Feature Marginal or Not Used at All
[+lateral]

3. **[+nasal] and [−continuant]** (nasals and stops): Nasals and stops were treated similarly in Mandy's system. Word-initially, there were no substitutions involving manner for either stops or nasals. Word-medially, they were sometimes missing, e.g., *tubby* as [dʌˀbi], but *zipper* as [deɪɚ]. Word-finally, only the labials [p] and [m] appeared, e.g., *soap* as [doʊpʰ], *thumb* as [dʌ̃m]. This is shown in the "Summary of substitutions" column (Table 7.4), shown here as an extract in Table 7.9.

Table 7.9. [+nasal] and [−continuant] Substitutions

Feature	Summary of Substitutions
[+nasal]	WF, n, ŋ > ∅
[−continuant]	[−continuant]: Some > ∅ in word-medial, word-final

Needs: The loss of [−continuant] and [+nasal] word-medially and/or -finally was similar to the loss of [+consonantal] in those word positions and a further indication of word structure constraints. However, limitations on [−continuant] and [+nasal] also appeared to reflect constraints against certain feature *combinations* in these positions. Labial stops and nasals were present (word-final [p] and [m] and word-medial [b] and [m]), but coronal and dorsal stops and nasals were missing. This suggests constraints against combination of [−continuant] or [+nasal] with [Coronal] or [Dorsal]. Combination needs for [−continuant] and [+nasal] are listed as such in the last column of Table 7.4, shown here as an extract in Table 7.10.

Table 7.10. Feature Combination Needs: [−continuant], [+nasal]

Feature	Goal Type 3: Feature Marginal or Not Used in Specific Feature Combinations
[+nasal]	[+nasal] & Dorsal; [+nasal] & Coronal: Word-final
[−continuant]	[−cont] & Dorsal; [−cont] & Coronal: Word-medial, word-final

4. **[+continuant] (& [−sonorant])** (fricatives and affricates): Fricatives and affricates are analyzed together for Mandy's data, because they had similar patterns. In word-initial position, the labiodental fricatives [f] and [v] were often present; however, singleton coronal fricatives and affricates surfaced as stops (see *soap* and *zipper* above). Elsewhere, a pattern of omission occurred, e.g., *smooth* as [mũː], *laughing* as [wæ̃ĩ]. Sometimes the glide [j] appeared for *voiced* fricatives /v/ or /z/ word-medially, e.g., *puzzle* as [bʌjoʊ], *screwdriver* as [guːdɑɪjɚ]. Table 7.11 shows the relevant section from page 5 of the scan form in Appendix D.

Table 7.11. Fricative and Affricate Substitutions

Feature	Summary of Substitutions
[+continuant] & [−sonorant] (*fricatives*)	WI *coronal fricative* > Stop Medial SI v, z > j Otherwise ∅ (N.B. WI f, v OK)
[−continuant]-[+continuant] (*affricates*)	WI *affricate* > Stop Otherwise ∅

Needs: There were two major differences within the fricative class: (1) Labiodentals [f] and [v] were present in word-initial position, but coronal fricatives were absent everywhere. (2) Different substitution patterns occurred for voiced versus voiceless fricatives word-medially. These differences suggest a variety of complex needs for fricatives and affricates. In terms of individual features (the next to last column in Table 7.4) there was (a) a general need for fricatives in medial and final positions (because of word structure limitations, as already noted for other consonants), and (b) a specific need for affricates everywhere. See Table 7.12 below.

Table 7.12. Fricatives and Affricates: Individual Feature Needs

Feature	Goal Type 2: Feature Marginal or Not Used at All
[+continuant] (& [−sonorant]) (*fricatives*)	Word-medial, word-final (*word structure*)
[−continuant]-[+continuant] (*affricates*)	[−continuant]-[+continuant]

There were also feature combination needs for [+continuant] and [Coronal] (as shown in the final column of Table 7.4 and extracted in Table 7.13) and voiced fricatives (relisted under laryngeal and place features).

Table 7.13. Feature Combination Needs: Fricatives

**Goal Type 3:
Feature Marginal or Not Used
in Specific Feature Combinations**

[+continuant] (& [−sonorant]) & Coronal (*sibilants*)

[+continuant] (& [−sonorant]) & [+voiced] (*voiced fricatives*)

---

5. **Default manner features:** *In nonlinear phonological intervention, feature goals are often the nondefault features.* Therefore, determining defaults is a step on the way to setting goals. See the list below for hints on determining defaults.

- Segments that appear frequently as substitutions often have default features. A number of repair processes may result in production of the same set of segments and features (e.g., velar fronting or stridency deletion can result in frequent use of [t]). Features of [t] are often the default features for the system.

- Default features generally succumb to nondefault features in assimilations (e.g., in *take* as [keɪk], the [Dorsal] feature takes over the default [Coronal]).

- An important aspect of default analysis is noting whether the child's defaults are the same as the adult defaults. Unusual defaults can impact negatively on intelligibility, and, thus, they are often a focus of treatment.

In the scan, expected defaults for adult English are listed on the form (and can be circled or underlined if applicable). In Mandy's case, the expected defaults prevailed. (See Table 7.3.) Stops replaced fricatives, showing an expected [−continuant] default; nasals appeared only where they should have (showing that [+nasal] was not a substitution or default), and the [+consonantal] /l/ surfaced as a [−consonantal] glide.

The manner features in Mandy's data can be summarized as follows (see also the Goal Summary sheet in Table 7.17):

1. Mandy's inventory and substitution patterns were fairly typical of early development. Stops, nasals, and glides were frequent, and fricatives and liquids were developing. Expected defaults prevailed, with some use of [−continuant] stops for fricatives and some use of [−consonantal] glides or vowels for /l/.

2. Word structure constraints severely limited production of features and segments word-medially and -finally.

3. Realization of manner features was sometimes affected by feature combination constraints. The feature [continuant] appeared more often in combination with [Labial] than with other place features. The feature combination of [−voiced] and [+continuant] appeared to be particularly problematic word-medially. More detail is given under laryngeal and place feature discussions.

We now proceed to a detailed analysis of laryngeal features.

7.1.9. Individual Laryngeal Features

The following laryngeal features are included in the analysis: [+voiced] and [−voiced] for stops and fricatives (for which voicing is a contrastive feature) and [+spread glottis] for /h/ and word-initial aspirated stops (and, as a redundant feature, for voiceless fricatives). When glottal stops are frequent substitutions for other segments, [+constricted glottis] is sometimes included.

The following trends can be expected developmentally for consonant laryngeal features.

Age Expectations:

- early default laryngeal features: [−voiced], [−spread glottis] for WI stops, [+constricted glottis] for [ʔ]

- early nondefault laryngeal features: [+voiced] (stops), [+spread glottis] for /h/

Developmental Phonological Patterns:

- Voicing develops gradually; prevocalic obstruents are commonly unaspirated or voiced, and postvocalic obstruents are commonly devoiced or voiceless in early development.

The following was observed about Mandy's production of laryngeal features.

1. **[+voiced] for stops, fricatives, and affricates:** In Mandy's speech, [+voiced] was generally preserved syllable-initially, even when there were substitutions for fricatives (/z/, /v/ > [j] word-medially; /z/ > [d] word-initially). The only exception was for /v/, which was partially devoiced in word-initial position (*van* as [v̥æː]). (See the "Summary of Substitutions" column, Table 7.4.)
Need: The sample had voiced stops and voiced sonorants. However, voiced fricatives did not occur. Thus, the feature combination of [+voiced], [+continuant], and [−sonorant] was a need, as shown in the last column of Table 7.4 and in Table 7.13.

2. **[−voiced]:** The only voiceless syllable-initial obstruent was word-initial [f], e.g., *feather* as [feɪɚ], but *thumb* as [dʌ̃m], *puzzle* as [bʌjoʊ], *zipper* as [deɪɚ]. The voiceless labial [p] appeared once word-finally, suggesting voiceless obstruents might be easier to produce in that position, e.g., *soap* as [doʊpʰ]. (See the "Summary of Substitutions" column, Table 7.4, and further detail in Section 7.3 on word position.)
Needs: [−voiced] was marginal overall. The variable patterns suggested a possible interaction of word position and feature combination constraints (voiceless fricatives in onset, voiceless stops in coda). Such interactions are taken into account during intervention planning (see Sections 7.3 and 7.4). However, because few voiceless segments appeared, the feature itself could also be designated as a need, as noted in the extract from Table 7.4 below, Table 7.14.

Table 7.14. Individual Feature Need: [−voiced]

Goal Type 2: Feature Marginal or Not Used at All
[−voiced] (*except* WI f, WF p)

3. **[+spread glottis] for /h/ and word-initial aspirated stops:** The feature [+spread glottis] is a *nondefault, nonredundant* feature for /h/, an *allophonic* feature for word-initial voiceless aspirated stops, and a *redundant* feature for voiceless fricatives (see Section 2.3). Mandy used [h] and word-initial [f] but had no aspirated stops (e.g., *cake* as [geɪʔ]) or other voiceless fricatives. This variability suggests constraints on (and needs for) specific feature combinations, particularly with [−continuant] for aspirated stops, but in general with [−sonorant] consonants. In Table 7.4, needs for [+spread glottis] are listed under the last column, shown here in Table 7.15.

Table 7.15. Feature Combination Need: [+spread glottis]

Goal Type 3: Feature Marginal or Not Used in Specific Feature Combinations

[+spread glottis] & [−sonorant] & [−voiced]

1. with [−continuant] (*for word-initial aspirated stops*), and also

2. with [+continuant] (*for voiceless fricatives*)

4. **Default laryngeal features:** Defaults appeared to be positional: [+voiced] syllable-initially and [−voiced] syllable-finally. (See Dinnsen, 1996.)
Need: The word-initial default needed to change to the [−voiced] value.

The laryngeal features in Mandy's data can be summarized as follows (see also the Goal Summary in Table 7.17).

1. Voiceless obstruents were generally infrequent, indicating an overall need for [−voiced]. However, feature combination and word position needs were also suggested: [−voiced] for stops in onset, [−voiced] for fricatives in non-word-initial positions, and [+voiced] in coda.
2. [+spread glottis] was a need for voiceless aspirated stops and voiceless fricatives.
3. The combination [+voiced] & [+continuant] & [−sonorant] for voiced fricatives was also a need.

7.1.10. Individual Place Features

The following list shows developmental trends for consonant place features [Labial], [Coronal], and [Dorsal]. (See Bernhardt & Stemberger, 1998, Chapter 5.)

Age Expectations:

• Early default place feature: [Coronal, +anterior]
• Early nondefault place feature: [Labial]

Developmental Phonological Patterns:

• Child-specific place defaults: [Labial] and [Dorsal] instead of [Coronal]; [−grooved] (flat, dental) instead of [+grooved] (for coronal fricatives and affricates)

• [Dorsal] (velars) in coda earlier than in onset, because of constraints promoting default vowel features in the rime

The summary of place features for Mandy's data follows.

1. **[Labial]:** [Labial] was fairly well established, appearing in more combinations, positions, and substitutions than other place features. Variability across word positions suggests feature combination and positional constraints, as shown in the extract from the "Summary of Substitutions" in Table 7.16. Voiced and voiceless labials had different patterns of realization. The (voiced) nasal [m] occurred in all word

positions (e.g., in *mommy* and *thumb*), and the voiced labial stop [b] occurred in all but word-final position (e.g., *bathtub* as [bæːdʌ̞], *tubby* as [dʌʰbi]). However, voiceless labials had different patterns of realization depending on manner and word position: [p] occurred word-finally (*soap*), and [f] and devoiced [v] word-initially (*feather, van*). No voiceless labials appeared word-medially (*zipper* as [deɪɚ], *laughing* as [wæiː]). (See also Section 7.1.11.) The extract from Table 7.4 for [Labial] is shown here in Table 7.16.

Table 7.16. [Labial] Substitutions

Summary of Substitutions

Strong word-initially
Variable elsewhere: Medial > j, Ø although m, b OK;
WF > Ø although m, p OK

Needs: Overall, [Labial] was a strong place feature, appearing in more combinations and positions than other place features. Restrictions reflected constraints on word structure or positional constraints on voicing.

2. **[Coronal] and [Dorsal]:** [Coronal] and [Dorsal] had similar patterns in terms of word position. [Dorsal] occurred word-initially and -medially but not word-finally (see the discussion on constraints against combination with [−continuant] word-finally above). Coronal targets were also absent word-finally, except for the [−anterior] [r] (see the discussion on constraints against combination with [−continuant] word-finally above).

Among the anterior coronals, only syllable-initial /l/ showed place substitutions, i.e., the labial [w] or [ɹ] for /l/. The [−anterior] targets had more substitutions: obstruents surfaced as [+anterior] stops (e.g., the palatoalveolar [ʧ] of *cherries* as [dɛɚiː]), and word-initial /r/ surfaced as the labial [w] (e.g., *roar* as [wɔr]). As noted above, there was a general constraint against combination of [Coronal] and [+continuant] for sibilants.

Needs: Needs relative to place were already mentioned under manner features because of feature combination issues. These can be reiterated in the place section of page 5 of the scan, as we have done for completeness, or a reference can be made to manner features above. To repeat, both [Dorsal] and [Coronal] features were absent word-finally in combination with [−continuant]. There was a general constraint against the combination of [Coronal], [−sonorant], and [+continuant] (sibilants), which affected both [+anterior] and [−anterior] fricatives.

3. **Default place features:** For coronals, [+anterior] segments substituted for [−anterior] targets, suggesting that the expected [Coronal, +anterior] default prevailed. However, labials were more prevalent than coronals in the system, appearing across word positions and with a variety of manners: stop, nasal, fricative, and glide categories. Thus, for Mandy, [Labial] may have been a child-specific place default.

The place features in Mandy's data can be summarized as follows. Basic place categories were established: [Labial], [Coronal, +anterior], and [Dorsal]. [Labial] appeared in more combinations, positions, and substitutions than other place features, suggesting that [Labial] may have been Mandy's place default. (See also Bernhardt & Stemberger, 1998, Chapter 5, for more detail on her use of place features.)

At this point, information is entered onto the Goal Summary sheet for each of the feature sections. Before discussing that here, however, additional commentary is given on feature combinations, one of the salient issues in Mandy's feature data.

7.1.11. Feature Combinations

The issue of feature combinations in phonological development has been minimally researched, with some observed trends noted in the list below. (See Bernhardt & Stemberger, 1998, Chapter 5.)

Age Expectations:

• One-by-one acquisition of fricatives and liquids (Ingram et al., 1980; Smit et al., 1990) over a protracted period, i.e., asynchronous development of feature combinations.

Developmental Phonological Patterns:

• Possible cyclicity in development, by which place, manner, and voice features alternate in acquisition, resulting in asynchrony of development for related segments (see Gierut, 1996). For example, a child might acquire a voicing contrast in stops, then acquire voiceless fricatives, then acquire voiced fricatives.

• Earlier development of default feature combinations than combinations with one or more nondefaults, e.g., [−nasal] and [Coronal] (/t/) before [+nasal] and [Coronal] (/n/), or [+continuant] and [Labial] (/f/).

• Word position effects on feature combination development (e.g., Dinnsen, 1996; Edwards, 1996; Bernhardt & Stemberger, 1998). Weak syllable positions might only allow default feature combinations (e.g., [t] in coda).

There are a multiplicity of combinations for a given language or inventory. For scan procedures, therefore, we note only the ones that seem most important for a given child's phonological development, focusing on contrasts between default and nondefault combinations. Selected combinations of manner and place features, manner and laryngeal features, and place and laryngeal features are examined (and sometimes place, manner, and laryngeal features together).

Above, we discussed several feature combination issues for Mandy. Occurring and needed feature combinations are reviewed below. Word position constraints are also indicated here. Just as with individual features, simultaneous feature combinations may vary with position in the word.

Manner and place: [Labial] combined with all target manner features, although there were particular word position constraints for specific segments. Coronal fricatives were absent.

▶ *Occurring:* [Labial] & [+continuant], WI position: labiodental fricatives, [w]

[Labial] & [−continuant] & [+voiced], all positions (except no word-final /b/)

[Labial] & [−continuant] & [−voiced] (/p/) except word-medially

▶ *Needs:* [Coronal] & [+continuant] & [−sonorant]: coronal fricatives

Word-medial /p/, word-final /b/

Manner and voice: Voiceless fricatives were present word-initially, but voiced fricatives were a need. Except for word-final [p], voiceless stops did not occur.

▶ *Occurring:* [−voiced] & [+continuant] & [−sonorant], WI position: voiceless fricatives

([−voiced] & [−continuant], WF position, marginally: voiceless stops)

▶ *Need:* [+voiced] & [+continuant] & [−sonorant]

Summary: Overall, [Labial] combined more frequently with other features than [Coronal] or [Dorsal], although there were positional restrictions in terms of voicing ([p] word-finally, [b] medially), and manner ([f] only word-initially). Coronal fricatives were a specific manner-place need. Voiced fricatives were a specific manner-laryngeal need ([+continuant], [−sonorant], and [+voiced]). Word position may have affected combinations of [voiced] with other features: [+voiced] combined more easily with [−continuant] in word-initial position, but [−voiced] combined more easily with [+continuant] (and [−sonorant]) in word-initial position.

7.1.12. Optional Step: Quantitative Analysis

Variable patterns are often illuminated through quantitative analysis. Given such a small data sample, quantification would not be particularly illuminating here. The patterns have been identified above on the basis of single tokens in many cases. However, if this sample were larger, the following measures would provide useful baselines:

• The degree of establishment (% match) or proportion of use (independent analysis) of any of the developing features or segments, *both across and within word positions,* e.g., [−voiced], [Labial] versus [Coronal], the variable individual segments such as /d/, /r/, etc.

• The relative degree of establishment (% match) of various feature combinations in contrast with each other, e.g., [−voiced] & Labial versus [+voiced] & [Labial].

These are not necessary measures for determining goals or analyzing patterns but can provide baseline records for specific targets in the child's system.

The next section of this chapter discusses goal selection and treatment planning.

7.2. Intervention Planning for Feature Development

The Goal Summary for Mandy is shown in Table 7.17. The last two columns in Table 7.4 list the missing features and feature combinations. These are transferred as needs into the Goal Summary sheet. In addition, the Goal Summary sheet lists strengths (determined by examining the phonetic inventory). Strengths identify features and segments that can be used (a) for word shape goals, (b) as targets to contrast with new feature and segment targets, and (sometimes) (c) as starting points to approach new articulations (see Section 7.2.4).

Table 7.17. Mandy's Goal Summary, Scan Page 7

Level	Features and Segments	
Goal Type	**Goal Type 2** Individual Features	**Goal Type 3** Feature Combinations
Strengths	[−consonantal] [+nasal] ([+consonantal]): WI only ([−continuant]): Positional and combination restrictions Labial (Coronal, +anterior): WI only (Dorsal): Syllable-initial only	**Manner-Laryngeal** [−cont] & [+voiced]: SI ([+cont] & [−voiced]: WI) **Manner-Place** Labial & all others, except as positionally restricted (see text) **Place-Laryngeal**
Needs	[+lateral] [−continuant]-[+continuant] ([−voiced]): Positional and combinatorial? [−anterior] (for fricatives) [grooved]	**Manner-Laryngeal** [cont] & [−voiced] (& [+sp gl]) [+cont] & [+voiced] **Manner-Place** [+cont] & [Coronal] **Place-Laryngeal** **Place-Place** Coronal & Labial for WI /r/
Strengths To Use To Support Needs	Word shapes to use for feature goals CV(V), CV(V)p, CV(V)m, CV(V)r When established: CVC, CVCV	
Interactions (prosody, perception, morphology, motor)	No inflectional morphemes Minimal metaphonological skills	
Social Factors	Use play-oriented activities	
Immediate Goals	[+lateral]	1. [+cont]&[Cor]&[−son]: first /s/; then /tʃ/, /ʃ/, or /θ/? 2. [+voiced]&[+continuant]: first /v/; then /z/, /ð/, /dʒ/?
Treatment Strategies	1. Awareness, contrast with [w], [r] 2. Oral-motor facilitation	1. Successive approximation from similar segments: [f] > [s]; [w] > [v] 2. Awareness, contrast 3. Later: /s/, /z/ plurals, possessive
Goal # in Program (order)	After word shape goals	After word shape goals

7.2.1. Review of Feature Strengths and Needs

Mandy's strong features across word positions were [−consonantal], [+nasal], and [Labial]. (See Table 7.17.) Other features were restricted in terms of word position or feature combinations. The features [−continuant] and [Dorsal] were strong in syllable-initial positions, and the features [Coronal] and [+consonantal] were strong word-initially only. (See Section 7.3 for more detail on positional restrictions.) As a redundant feature (of glides and vowels), [+continuant] was strong, but in combination with [−sonorant] (for fricatives) [+continuant] was strong only with [Labial] ([f] and [v]). As a nondefault feature, [+voiced] was strong when combined with [−continuant] in syllable-initial position (voiced stops). (It was also an expected redundant feature of glides and vowels.) The feature [−voiced] was developing (a) in word-final position in combination with [−continuant] (voiceless stops), and (b) in word-initial position with [+continuant] ([f]).

Needs for individual features were:

1. [+lateral]: /l/
2. [−continuant]-[+continuant]: /ʧ/, /ʤ/
3. [−voiced]
4. [−anterior]: /ʃ/, /ʒ/, /ʧ/, /ʤ/, word-initial /r/
5. [+grooved]: /s/, /z/, /ʃ/, /ʒ/, /ʧ/, /ʤ/
6. [−grooved] (for the interdental fricatives): /θ/, /ð/

The features [−anterior], [grooved], and [−continuant]-[+continuant] are subsumed under the feature combination [Coronal] and [+continuant], listed next. The feature [−voiced] is also considered a positional and feature combination need (see Sections 7.1.11 and 7.3).

Needs for feature combinations were:

1. [Coronal] & [+continuant]: Coronal fricatives and affricates
2. [+voiced] & [+continuant]: Voiced fricatives and affricates

Additional needs reflected word structure and positional constraints. Positional needs are discussed in Section 7.3.

7.2.2. Choosing Word Shapes for Feature Goals

In terms of available word shapes for feature goals, there were few choices. The only strong word shapes were CV(V) and CVC with word-final [m], [p], and [r]. Keeping to the principle of independent targeting of features and word shapes, CV(V) or CVC with the above-mentioned final consonants were the only available word shapes to use for new features. Once CVC and CVCV word shapes were more fully developed, a greater variety of word shapes would be available for new features and combinations. (Thus, ordering CVC and CVCV before feature goals might be advisable.)

7.2.3. Choosing Immediate Feature Goals

New Individual Feature

New features are those that do not occur in the sample or occur only marginally. In Mandy's case, these included [+lateral], features for coronal fricatives (e.g., [grooved], [−anterior]), and [−voiced]. The coronal fricative features could be subsumed under the feature combination goals (which include [+continuant] & [Coronal]); [−voiced] could be considered a combination and positional goal. Thus, the new feature choice was [+lateral]. The /l/ would be targeted first in word-initial position and then medially, after CVCV was better established.

New Feature Combinations

There were potentially many new combinations to target. The most important for this sample (in terms of frequency in English) was extension of the fricative category through combination of the occurring features [+continuant], [Coronal], and [−sonorant]. Voiced fricatives were a separate feature combination goal. Voiceless fricatives could be targeted first, following up on Mandy's success with /f/. Therapy could begin with the most frequent [Coronal, +anterior] /s/ or on the often later developing /θ/ or /ʃ/ (both of which have nondefault coronal features).

7.2.4. Treatment Strategies

Many treatment strategies have been developed over the years for introduction of new segments into a child's repertoire (see Bernthal & Bankson, 1998). Because it is not clear at the outset which strategies will be best for an individual, it is generally advisable to include a number of treatment methods in early parts of the intervention program, in order to find out what best suits the particular individual. Developing a child's awareness of the new targets and contrasting that child's similarities and differences with segments already in the repertoire can be useful. Similarly, techniques that focus on the actual production (oral-motor facilitation, prompts, imitation) can also be useful.

In Mandy's case, it would probably be advantageous to contrast /l/ with /w/ and /r/, which she uses in place of /l/. It would probably also be advantageous to contrast labial and coronal fricatives, and voiceless and voiced stops and fricatives. Contrasts might help establish new feature categories and show the differences between feature combinations.

Mandy might learn to articulate the new segments through successive approximation, starting with segments she could produce already and gradually changing articulatory gestures, to derive /l/ from /r/, or /s/ from /f/. Successive approximations use strengths to support needs and actively focus on differences between various feature combinations.

In the last two sections of the chapter, we show extensions of the feature analysis to other parts of the scan analysis.

7.3. Word Position Goals (Type 4)

Positional constraints are defined as *partial* limitations on a word position. These are examined at the top of page 6 on the scan. In the system we are presenting in this book, positional needs are considered to be different than general feature or word structure needs. Features and segments may be present in the inventory but not in certain word positions. A certain word position may be reasonably well established but not with all segments in the inventory. For example, a child may use stops, nasals, and fricatives in word-initial position, but use only stops and nasals in word-final position. Because fricatives do occur somewhere in the inventory, [+continuant] is active and is therefore not a general feature goal. Because codas are produced, CVC is not a word structure goal. Fricatives are needed in word-final position, that is, [+continuant] is *a specific word position goal*.

In Mandy's speech, C2 was generally missing in CV<u>C</u> and CV<u>C</u>V. Thus, for her, CVC and CVCV were *word structure needs*. She had *too few* consonants in C2 to consider the limitation to be on a few specific segment types in medial and final positions.

She did have some specific positional needs, however, as we noticed in the feature analysis (see Table 7.4):

1. word-initial [r]

2. [−voiced] word-medially and, for stops, word-initially

3. [+voiced] word-finally for [−sonorant] consonants (obstruents)

4. combinations of [−continuant] and [Coronal] or [Dorsal] in noninitial positions

5. minor need for varied specific combinations with [Labial] (see Section 7.1.11)

Either word structure or feature combination constraints or both were particularly implicated in numbers 4 and 5 above for place features. The feature [voiced] was also affected by feature or word structure constraints. However, there was a general sense that word position had a specifically limited effect on [voiced] because of the consistent differences in realization of [voiced] across word positions. Thus, Table 7.18 focuses on [voiced] and /r/ only, the feature and segment most affected by positional constraints. Positional needs are also entered into the Goal Summary sheet (see Table 7.19).

Mandy had a number of major needs in terms of word structure and feature development. Consequently, in early phases of intervention, positional goals would be of low priority in terms of her overall phonological system. (However, positional goals can be an "easy" place to start, because a child can at least articulate the target segments and can produce at least some segments in the targeted word position. If a positional goal were to be included for Mandy in early phases of intervention, this would necessarily involve word-initial position, because medial and final positions were structurally weak. The choices for word-initial position would be /r/ or the feature combination [−voiced] & [−continuant]. The only voiceless stop in the inventory was [pʰ], which occurred word-finally. Targeting voiceless stops might prove to be somewhat challenging at first, because it would also involve a relatively new feature, [−voiced], and a new feature combination: [−voiced], [+spread glottis], and [−continuant] (for aspirated stops). If early success was important, a short diagnostic probe could compare her relative stimulability for word-initial /r/ versus word-initial [pʰ], with the more stimulable one then being chosen for immediate intervention.)

For either /r/ or [pʰ], onset-rime techniques (see Chapter 11) might be useful treatment strategies. For example, increasingly faster repetitions of the word *or* ([ɔr ɔr ɔrɔr]) can result in pronunciation of *roar* as [rɔr]. Similarly, repetitions of *up* with heavy aspiration as [ʌpʰ ʌpʰ ʌpʰ ʌpʰʌpʰ] can lead to pronunciation of *pup* as [pʰʌpʰ].

7.4. Choosing Segments and Features for Word Shape Goals

Another offshoot of the segmental analysis is the selection of segments and features for word shape goals. Generally, "strong" segments and features are used for word shape goals. Children tend to do better when they do not have to learn too many new things at once. Mandy's well-established segments are entered into the Goal Summary sheet in the column pertaining to word shape development (Table 7.20). Not all of these would be used in treatment, but the option is there to use all or some. (By using only some, others remain as observation targets to determine whether generalization is occurring.)

Table 7.18 Segments or Features Missing in a Given Word Position (but occurring elsewhere), Scan Page 6

Word-Initial	Medial: Syllable-Initial	Medial: Syllable-Final	Word-Final
[−voiced] (&[−cont]) /r/	[−voiced]		[+voiced] (&[−sonorant])

Note. Many medial and final consonants were omitted. Thus, CVC, CVCV, and CVCCV(C) were word structure needs.

Table 7.19. Goal Summary Section:
Segment and Feature Classes by Word Position, Scan Page 7

Level	Syllable and Word Structure
Goal Type	**Goal Type 4** Word Position and Sequences
Strengths	Segment and feature classes by word position Word-initial: Strongest position (all but /r/, [−voiced] &[−continuant]) Word-medial: [+voiced], [Labial], [Dorsal] Word-final: [−consonantal], [+nasal], [Labial], ([−continuant]), ([−voiced]) Sequences
Needs	Word position Word-initial: /r/, [−voiced] & [−continuant] Word-medial, syllable-initial: [−voiced] Word-final: [+voiced] & [−sonorant] Sequences
Strengths To Use To Support Needs	Segments to use for structure goals Word-final: /r/, /p/
Interactions (prosody, perception, morphology, motor)	
Social Factors	
Immediate Goals	Word-initial: /r/, [−voiced] & [−continuant] (& [+spread glottis])
Treatment Strategies	Onset-rime alternations: e.g., [ɔr ɔr] > [rɔr]; [ʌpʰ ʌpʰ] > [pʰʌpʰ] (Chapter 11)
Goal # in Program (order)	First if early success is important, otherwise as a break between difficult goals

Mandy's strong word-initial consonants were voiced stops, nasals and glides, and [f]. Word-medially, she used voiced stops, [m], and glides. Segments available to strengthen medial position (C2) in CVCV and CVC were [n], [f], and the voiceless stops. The [n] and [f] would probably be easier first targets word-medially, because voiceless stops were generally difficult prevocalically. For C2 of CVC (an even weaker position than medial), it might be useful to review and practice with the already occurring [m], [p], and [r] before introducing the C2 targets ([n], [f], and the voiceless stops [t] and [k]).

In terms of intervention strategies, it is often useful to target the CVC and CVCV in the same time period, focusing attention on the need for C2 in both word shapes (see Chapter 11 for suggestions). Using similar vowels and C2's for both CVC and CVCV can often be mutually reinforcing, e.g., *pen, penny,* or *Mick, Mickey,* etc.

Table 7.20. Segments and Features for Word Shape Goals, Scan Page 7

Level	Syllable and Word Structure	
Goal Type	**Goal Type 1** Structure	**Goal Type 4** Word Position and Sequences
Strengths To Use To Support Needs	Segments to use for structure goals C1 of CVC, CVCV: m n b d g f h w j C2, CVC: n, t, k, f (m, p, r as initial review?) C2, CVCV: n; later, p, k, f (m, voiced; stops, glides as initial review?)	Segments to use for structure goals C1: r, pʰ C2: r, pʰ, (m)
Immediate Goals	CVC, CVCV	Word-initial /r/, pʰ

7.5. A Note on Mandy's Intervention Program in "Real Life"

Mandy was involved in a 16-week nonlinear phonological intervention study. Goals for Mandy included CVC, CVCV, [+lateral] ([l]), and [Coronal] & [+continuant] (fricatives and affricates [s], [ʤ], [θ], and [ʃ]). Each goal was targeted in three cycles (10 sessions for each goal in total) in a cycles approach over a 16-week period (48 total sessions). Different strategies were employed for the different goals (because of intervention study design factors). Oral-motor facilitation and elicited imitation were used for /l/, whereas awareness and perceptual contrast activities were used for fricatives (with no expectation of imitation). A variety of syllable structure elicitation techniques (as described in Chapter 11) were used for the word structure goals. By the end of the 16-week study, voiceless fricatives /s/, /ʃ/, and /θ/ were developing across word positions in conversation, although no voiced fricatives were yet present. Word structure showed significant improvement also. She was using /l/ in therapy activities but not yet in conversation.

7.6. Final Comments

- Children with phonological disorders typically have deficits in feature development, whether for individual features, particular feature combinations, or positional use.

- Strengths in the feature system can be exploited when targeting new feature combinations, new positional distributions of features, or new word shapes.

- Sometimes it is difficult to distinguish goal types, because they can overlap. A feature may be absent everywhere, only in specific feature combinations, only in certain word positions, or because of word structure constraints. Or all of the above may be true. For example, in Mandy's data, [−voiced] was generally weak but was also positionally affected, limited in certain combinations, and subject to word structure constraints. Such overlap can be noted in the analysis summary. Sometimes, during the intervention process, the stronger restrictions on that feature will become clearer. More important than the label in this case is the observation of overlap.

- The feature analysis can be time consuming at first. Readers are encouraged to develop individual shortcuts and shorthand to increase efficiency.

ᴂ φ ω'
ᴂ ᵖ ∘ f
λ ᶜ ᵖ ɳ β

Chapter 8
Sequence Constraints

Analyses in This Chapter
(pages 6, 7 of scan)

- consonant cluster sequences
- consonants separated by vowels
- CV sequences
- vowels separated by consonants

In previous chapters, we addressed segments as a function of their features or of their position in the syllable or word. Putting segments into sequences leads to additional difficulties. A child may be able to produce a particular phoneme, but not in sequence with some other phoneme. This leads to variability across words, since the phoneme is correct in some words but not in others. This chapter is devoted to exploration of such variability.

8.1. Consonant Cluster Sequences

Consonant cluster sequences are examined by word position and in terms of the segments they contain. Word-medially a consonant sequence may be in the same syllable (e.g., the coda cluster /mp/ of *jump rope*) or in two different syllables (e.g., the coda /k/ versus the onset /t/ of *doctor*). In English it is not always possible to determine whether a medial consonant is an onset or a coda. For example, in the word *monkey*, /ŋ/ may be analyzed as the coda of the first syllable and /k/ as the onset of the second, or both may be considered a coda cluster /ŋk/. In either case, they are a consonant sequence and can be examined as such.

Repair patterns that most often indicate sequence constraints are *assimilation* and *flop* (metathesis or migration). Assimilation avoids a prohibited sequence by making two elements the same. Flop avoids a prohibited sequence by changing the order of elements. Deletion and coalescence (fusion of elements) may also resolve sequence constraints, but, because they commonly arise as repairs for syllable structure constraints, they are not clear indicators of sequence constraints. (See Chapter 3.)

8.1.1. Expected Developmental Trends for Consonant Clusters

Developmental patterns for clusters appear to be fairly variable across children, although research is insufficient on this topic, particularly regarding medial and final clusters. The following general trends have been noted (see also Bernhardt & Stemberger, 1998, Chapters 6 and 7).

Age Expectations:

• First clusters tend to emerge between ages 2 and 3, with development occurring over a protracted period of time (until as late as age 8 or 9 for some children).

• Earliest clusters tend to be word-initial obstruent-glide clusters and/or word-medial or word-final nasal-stop clusters.

• Later-emerging clusters tend to be three-element word-initial clusters and word-final stop-stop clusters.

Developmental Phonological Patterns:

• The most common early pattern is reduction of clusters. Generally, the liquid, glide, or fricative is omitted (or, rarely, the entire cluster).

• Later, common patterns involve substitution for one element (e.g., /bl/ > [bj]), and/or assimilation (e.g., /tr/ > [fw]).

• Flop (e.g., /sp/ > [ps]), coalescence or fusion (e.g., /sp/ > [f]), and vowel epenthesis (e.g., /tr/ > [tər]) also occur but infrequently.

To illustrate cluster analysis, we will look at data for CC sequences in word-initial position. Similar procedures apply for clusters elsewhere in the word. All of the repair patterns described above are observable in the data of one child, Charles. Because certain clusters were possible for him, but other clusters were not, this was not simply a problem with syllable structure. For cluster data sets for other word positions, see Bernhardt and Stemberger (1998), Chapter 7. An additional data set for word-initial clusters is provided in Appendix C for practice.

8.1.2. Charles's Data

Charles: Age 5-10 (Bernhardt, 1992).

Charles had a moderate phonological disorder, with a noticeable tongue thrust during speaking and swallowing. (See Table 8.1.) His language comprehension and production skills were above average, and he was beginning to read and spell at the time of assessment.

8.1.3. Questions To Ask of the Sample

• What types of clusters are in the inventory, and which show matches with the adult targets—stop + glide, /s/-clusters, obstruent-liquid, etc.?

• Is there a general match between adult and child clusters?

• What are the child's frequent, developing, and missing or marginal clusters?

• In comparison with the adult targets, do clusters have missing consonants, or added consonants or vowels (epenthesis), or segmental substitution patterns (default substitutions, assimilation, metathesis, or coalescence)? What is the most common pattern?

• Does context make a difference, i.e., is there any difference between single words and connected speech, or between spontaneous and imitated productions?

Table 8.1. Charles's Data

CC	Target	Adult Pronunciation	Child Productions			
			Substitution	Omission	Assimilation	Epenthesis; Flop
br	bread	brɛd	bwʌdᵊ (C)			
	brush	brʌʃ			vwʌθ	
tr	trailer	tʰreɪl{ɚ/ə}ᵃ			vweɪjə (C)	
	train	tʰrẽɪn				dəweɪnᵊ
dr	dressed	drɛst			vwʌθt̪	
kr	crayon(s)	kʰreɪj{ɑ:/ɔ̃}n(z)ᵃ			fweɪjɔ̃nð	kəwejɔᵊn, keɪwʌ̃n
gr	gray	greɪ				gəweɪjᵊ
fr	friends	frẽndz	fwẽndð			
	front	frʌ̃nt		fʌ̃ᵊnt		
θr	three	θri:	fwi:			
pl	plum	pʰlʌ̃m		pʌ̃m		
bl	black	blæk		bæk		
kl	clean	kʰli:n		kʰĩ:n		
gl	glove	glʌv			vwʌbᵊ (C)	
fl	flower	flaʊ{ɚ/ə}ᵃ		fawɔᵊ		
mj	music	mju:zɪk		muðɪk		
tw	twenty	tʰwẽn(tʰ)i:ᵃ		wẽnt̪i:	fwẽnti: (C)	
kw	quiet	kʰwaɪ(j)ət		waijət (C)	fwaɪjɛt (C)	
sm	smooth	smu:ð		mu:v		
sn	snake	sneɪk	θn:eɪk			
	snowman	snoʊmæn		noᵊ mãnᵊ		
sp	spoon	spũ:n		pũ:mᵊ		
st	star	star		θauʷᵊ		
sw	sweater	swɛ{tʰ/ɾ}{ɚ/ə}ᵃ			fwʌdɔ	
sl	sleep	sli:p			fwi:p	
	Total child forms: 29	Match for CC slots: 11/29 (37.9%)	4/29 (13.8%)	12/29 (41.4%)	9/29 (31%)	4/29 (13.8%)

ᵃDialect exposure: British English (mother), Australian (father, residence), Canadian (residence).

- How consistent or variable are the data? If variable, do you need to count anything (and what) to be sure of patterns, or for efficacy purposes?

- Are more utterances needed of any type? What type?

8.1.4. Analysis Procedures

- **Step 1: Bird's-Eye View.** A quick look at the data shows that Charles had variable realizations of cluster targets word-initially. Some were reduced, and others had a variety of repair patterns.

- **Step 2 (and 4): Coding (and quantitative analysis).** In Table 8.1, data are organized in a way that facilitates observation of variable cluster patterns. This data chart is similar to phonological process charts. It allows for relatively quick quantitative analysis, comparing frequency of repair types and match for CC slots, as the numbers at the bottom of the table show. Charles had many ways of solving constraints against consonant sequences, and so for him, it was useful to set up a specific chart for clusters.

- **Step 3: Cluster analysis.** The relevant section of the scan is shown in Table 8.2 for Charles's cluster analysis (page 6, bottom). On the generic scan form, the same section is available for analysis of both clusters and cross-vowel sequences. This, of course, limits the space for each analysis. However, children often do not produce clusters at the same time as they show strong sequence constraints for consonants separated by vowels. Thus, this space is usually sufficient. *Note that for Charles, the form in Table 8.2 is slightly different from the generic scan in the appendix. As mentioned in the introduction, the scan form is only a guideline and can be adapted to fit the situation.*

Charles had no exact word-initial cluster matches with the adult target, although he did mark the two consonant slots over half of the time. His most prevalent repair pattern was omission (e.g., *plum* as pʌm]), but assimilation and segmental substitutions were also common (e.g., *brush* as [vwʌθ], bread as [bwʌdᵊ]). Other less frequent repair patterns were epenthesis (e.g., *crayon* as [kəwejɔˀn]) and, least frequently, flop of the glide to later in the word (e.g., *crayon* as [keɪwʌ̃n]). Usually the [+continuant] element (glide, liquid, fricative) was omitted from the cluster, but in the case of /st/, the [+continuant] fricative ([θ]) remained (*star* as [θauʷᵊ]). For those clusters that did occur, both segments had the same place of articulation: [Coronal], as in *snake* [θn:eɪk], or [Labial], as in *bread* [bwʌdᵊ]. They often had the same manner and/or voicing also, as in [vwʌbᵊ] for *glove* ([+continuant], [+voiced]). Such patterns indicate constraints against sequences of different features.

Table 8.2. Charles's Consonant Sequences, Scan Page 6

Consonant Assimilation (top > [pɑp]) OR Dissimilation (tot > [tɑp]) Assimilation: [fw], [vw]	Coalescence (fusion) (/tr/ > [f])		Epenthesis (tray > [təweɪ]) YES: [dəw], [gəw], [kəw]
			Metathesis (fish > [ʃɪf]) OR Migration (cup > [pʌ]) (YES: [k–w])
	CV Assimilation (bee > [di]; do > [bu]) OR Dissimilation (boo > [du])		Other Patterns Omission of one C

Clusters Produced: (circle matches) [fw], [bw], [vw], [θn] (all nonmatches)
Missing Clusters: (compared with adult targets)* All others (no stop-liq., fric.-stop, fric.-liq., nasal-glide)

| **WI Cluster Sequences Produced:** (Circle those produced. Put checkmarks over ones that match targets.)
    ✓
  (Lab-Lab) (Cor-Cor,) Dors-Dors, Lab-Cor, Cor-Lab, (Lab-Dors) Dors-Lab, Cor-Dors, Dors-Cor; nonnasal-nasal; other
       stop-glide, fricative-glide, (fric.-nasal)
Missing Cluster Sequences: (compared with adult targets) (circle)

Lab-Lab, (Cor-Cor) Dors-Dors, Lab-Cor, (Cor-Lab) Lab-Dors (Dors-Lab) (Cor-Dors) Dors-Cor, nonnasal-nasal; other (see above) |

| **Context Differences for (A) or (B):** Spontaneous/imitated? (Connected/single word?) For same word? For same C?
Need to count? Yes   **What?** Variable repair processes; % match for CC slots ——More assim.
Other data needed: No   in connected |

Note. Parentheses = inconsistent.

- **Step 4 (or 5): Goal summary.** Goals for Charles are worked out in the Goal Summary, Table 8.3. As observed already, labial clusters and [θn] were the only possible clusters at the time, leaving the rest as targets. Word shapes were varied; hence, any word shape starting with a cluster was usable in treatment. However, there were segmental limitations, because [s], [l], and [r] were not in the inventory, nor were they stimulable within clusters. That left only the stops and glides [w] and [j], and clusters /tw/, /kw/, /fj/, /mj/, and /pj/. Although those clusters are infrequent in English, Charles could pronounce their individual segments without difficulty. By targeting such clusters, he would be able to pronounce sequences with different place and manner more easily. Clusters such as /tw/ and /kw/ (as in *twin* or *quit*) would furthermore give practice with sequences he was likely to produce through substitution of [w] for /r/, once there was less

Table 8.3. Goal Summary: Charles's Word-Initial Clusters, Scan Page 7

Level	Syllable and Word Structure
Goal Type	**Goal Type 4** Word Position and Sequences
Strengths	Segment and feature classes found by word position Sequences Identical feature sequences in WI clusters: Labial-Labial, (Coronal-Coronal), Labial-Dorsal (where [w] = Dors) ([+continuant]-[+continuant])
Needs	Word position Sequences All other clusters
Strengths To Use To Support Needs	Segments to use for structure goals - C1: All stops, f ([s] not stimulable) C2: Glides (neither /l/ nor /r/ stimulable in clusters)
Interactions (prosody, perception, morphology, motor)	More assimilation in connected speech
Social Factors	Very participatory; early literacy skills
Immediate Goals	Stop-glide clusters: /tw/, /kw/, /fj/, /mj/, /pj/, /bj/
Treatment Strategies	1. Glide prolongation (onset-rime division), as in *too-in > twin* 2. Alternation of CVC to produce CCVC (*wick wickwick > quick*) 3. Use of letter knowledge to increase awareness of cluster elements
Goal # in Program (order)	1. Before learning /s/, /l/, and /r/, to stimulate CC production without sequence constraints. 2. After /s/, /l/, /r/ singleton establishment, to establish more frequent clusters.

frequent omission or assimilation (e.g., [kwaɪ] instead of the less intelligible [fwaɪ] for *cry*).

A number of strategies could help facilitate cluster production (see also Chapter 11):

- glide prolongation, dividing the word at the onset-rime boundary and gradually increasing speed, e.g., *to eat > to-eat > tweet,* or *two in > two-in > twin*

- alternation of CVC to produce CCVC (*wick wick > wickwick > quick*)

- adding a consonant to a syllable, e.g., *f + you > few*

- use of letter knowledge to increase awareness of cluster elements

In nine treatment sessions over a 3-week period, Charles (Bernhardt, 1992) showed a marked increase in cluster production, with virtual elimination of the assimilation repair. The CVC alternation and the glide prolongation (onset-rime division) were equally facilitative in treatment sessions. Both stop-glide and /s/-clusters (with [θ] for /s/) became frequent. At first he showed an increase in vowel epenthesis in stop-glide (and then in stop-liquid) clusters. Over time, the duration of the vowel gradually decreased, until epenthesis disappeared.

8.2. Consonants Separated by Vowels

At early stages of development, children may also (infrequently) show sequence constraints between consonants separated by vowels (*noncontiguous sequences*). Studies of this type of sequence constraint are fairly limited, but see Ingram (1974), Menn (1975), Stoel-Gammon and Stemberger (1994), Stemberger and Bernhardt (1997), Bernhardt and Stemberger (1998). A summary of trends follows in Section 8.2.1.

8.2.1. Expected Developmental Trends for Cross-Vowel Consonant Sequences

Age Expectations:

In normal development, cross-vowel (noncontiguous) consonant sequence constraints are relatively infrequent and tend to occur only in early acquisition.

Developmental Phonological Patterns:

- Variability between words with the same target consonant can indicate cross-vowel consonant sequence constraints (e.g., *toe* as [tʰoʊ] but *top* as [bap]). Clues are often assimilation (consonant harmony) or flop (metathesis or migration), the most common repair of sequence constraints.

- The most commonly affected features are place features, particularly [Coronal]-[Labial] and [Coronal]-[Dorsal] sequences (e.g., in *top* > [bat] or *dog* > [gag]).

- Less common repair patterns involve deletion, default consonant insertion (e.g., glottal stop), or dissimilation (e.g., *bit* as [bɪt] but *bib* also as [bɪt]). (Note, however, that deletion and default insertion are often a result of syllable structure constraints.)

Two data sets are provided for analysis practice, one for Roland in Sections 8.2.2–8.2.4 and one for Livia in Appendix C. Roland's phonology is discussed again in

Chapter 9, because there were strong interactions between phonological sequence constraints and syntactic development.

8.2.2. Roland's Data

Roland: Age 2-1

Roland was a typically developing late talker. He used word combinations rarely at age 2 (see Chapter 10). His parents had requested suggestions for language stimulation.

8.2.3. Questions Regarding Sequence Constraints

- Are there several examples of distant assimilation, metathesis, or consonant feature migration in the sample?

- What noncontiguous consonant sequences are present and absent in the sample in terms of place, manner, and voice features?

- Does context make a difference, i.e., is there any difference between single words and connected speech, or spontaneous and imitated productions?

- How consistent or variable are the data? If variable, do you need to count anything (and what) to be sure of patterns, or for efficacy purposes?

- Are more utterances needed of any type? What type?

8.2.4. Analysis Procedures

- **Step 1: Bird's-Eye View.** A quick look at the data shows that Roland had age-appropriate use of English phones (no interdentals, palatoalveolars, or [r]) and word structures (as complex as CCVCVC). However, the between-word variability for many of the segments suggested constraints on place and manner.

- **Step 2 (and 4): Coding (and quantitative analysis).** The sample is organized in Table 8.4 in a way to facilitate observation of the variable sequence patterns.

- **Step 3: Consonant sequences.** Roland's sequences are analyzed in Table 8.5. In terms of cross-vowel sequences, CVC words with the same place of articulation matched the adult target, e.g., *bib* as [bɪb]. Also matching (although not shown in the data set given) were words with glottal [h] and any following consonant, as in *head* as [hɛd] or *ham* as [hæm]. (Glottals are considered placeless in the feature specifications in this book, and thus place sequences are not involved with /h/ or [ʔ].) Across vowels, there was one matching [Labial]-[Coronal] sequence, i.e., *please* as [piːs]. This may have reflected a practice effect for a socially encouraged word. The only other noncontiguous sequences not involving a cluster were [Dorsal]-[Labial], e.g., *bagel* as [gɛbgɛ] and [Coronal]-[Labial], in *vitamins* [mlɛmlɛ]. A variety of repair patterns across words accommodated cross-vowel place sequence constraints. The most frequent were omission with glottal stop insertion (e.g., *boat* as [ʔoʊt]) and assimilation (e.g., *Casey* as [geɪki]), although flop and [l] epenthesis (forming onset clusters) also occurred (e.g., *vitamins* as [mlɛmlɛ]). Most sequences of voicing features appeared; there was possibly a

Table 8.4. Roland's Data

Adult Sequence	Word	Adult Pronunciation	Child Production				
			Sequence match	Omission or [ʔ]	Assim.	[l] Epen.	Flop
Lab-Lab	bib	bɪb	bɪb				
	poof	pʰuːf	pʰuːf				
Cor-Cor	night	nʌɪt	nʌt				
	lots	lɑːts	lɑs				
Dor-Dor	cookie	kʰʊki	kʊki				
Lab-Cor	please	pʰliːz	piːs				
	boots	buːts			blɪps		blɪps
(2 L-C)	<u>vi</u>ta<u>min</u>s	vʌɪɾəmn̩z			mlɛmlɛ		
	man	mæn				mlæn	
	boat	boʊt		ʔoʊt			
Cor-Lab	vi<u>tam</u>ins	vʌɪɾəmn̩z			mlɛmlɛ		
	number	nʌ̃mbɚ		bə			
Lab-Dor	bagel	beɪgl̩			gɛbgɛ		gɛbgɛ[a]
	milk	mɪlk		ʔɔk			
Dor-Lab	cup	kʰʌp			gʌpk[a]		
	come	kʰʌ̃m		ʔʌ̃m			
Cor-Dor	truck	tʰrʌk		ʔʌk			
Dor-Cor[b]	Casey	kʰeɪsi			geɪki		
Different Place	14 total		2/14 (14.3% match)	6/14 (42.9% of repairs)	6/14 (42.9% of repairs)	2/14 (14.3% of repairs)	3/14 (21.4% of repairs)

[a] A dorsal-labial sequence appeared in the child forms, although in *cup* there was not an exact match. Forms with [l] clusters also showed some place changes between labial and coronal.

[b] *Bagel* has a dorsal-coronal (g-l) sequence, but word-final /l/ did not appear in any contexts, and so this is ignored.

restriction on [−voiced]-[+voiced] sequences (*please* as [piːs]), but this may instead have derived from a tendency for word-final devoicing rather than from a sequence constraint. Manner sequences were reasonably flexible, although there were possible restrictions on nonnasal-nasal sequences (leading to the metathesis for *vitamins*).

A note on Roland's contiguous cluster sequences is also relevant here. Roland had some unusual (nonmatching) [bl] and [ml] cluster sequences in word-initial position, in addition to some nontarget word-final clusters [ps] and [pk]. His only word-medial consonant sequence was [b.g] in his production [gɛb.gɛ] of *bagel*. Interestingly, all of these clusters began with a labial, and most had a coronal in second position. Thus, in a neighboring consonant sequence (a cluster), he appeared to have better success with a [Labial]-[Coronal] sequence than when a vowel intervened.

Table 8.5. Roland's Cross-Vowel Sequences, Scan Page 6

Consonant Assimilation (top > [pɑp]) **OR Dissimilation** (tot > [tɑp]) YES: Dorsal; Labial	Coalescence (fusion) (/tr/ > [f])		Epenthesis (tray > [təweɪ]) YES: [l] in C[l], [ʔ]
			Metathesis (fish > [ʃɪf]) **OR Migration** (cup > [pʌ]) YES: /b-g/ > [g-b]; m > Onset
	CV Assimilation (bee > [di]; do > [bu]) **OR Dissimilation** (boo > [du])		**Other Patterns** Omission of WI C([ʔ])

Clusters Produced: (circle matches) WI *bl, ml,* WM *bg,* WF *ps, pk* (all as substitutions) N.B. All Labial-Other
Missing Clusters: (compared with adult targets) WI *pl, tr,* WM *mb,* WF *nz, ts*
Cross-V Sequences Produced: (Circle those produced. Put checkmarks over ones that match targets.) ✓   ✓   ✓   ✓   ✓ (Lab-Lab)(Cor-Cor)(Dors-Dors,)(Lab-Cor,)(Cor-Lab,)Lab-Dors,(Dors-Lab,)Cor-Dors, Dors-Cor; nonnasal-nasal; other [a]
Missing Cross-V Sequences: (compared with adult targets) (circle) Lab-Lab, Cor-Cor, Dors-Dors,(Lab-Cor,)(Cor-Lab)(Lab-Dors)(Dors-Lab)(Cor-Dors)(Dors-Cor)(nonnasal-nasal)other [−vcd]-[+vcd]

Context Differences for (A) or (B): Spontaneous/imitated? Connected/single word? For same word? For same C? [b] **Need to count?** Maybe   **What?** Types of repair patterns? N.B. Some words show unusual combinations of repair **Other data needed:** patterns that are hard to quantify. Perhaps more manner sequences, specifically nonnasal-nasal, fricative-other?

Note. [a]Roland had glottal-oral place sequences, as in [hæm] for *ham,* and [hɛd] for *head.*

[b]The few word combinations produced matched word-based sequence constraints. Match for *please* because a practiced word?

In the last part of Table 8.5, note is made of a significant interaction between phonology and syntax (see Chapter 10). In terms of sampling, more data would be needed to evaluate manner sequences. In terms of quantification, it might be useful to quantify repair processes for later comparison (as done in Table 8.4), although inventories of possible and impossible sequences might be more useful in terms of choosing intervention goals (in order to evaluate strengths and needs, and also because the unusual combination of processes in some words make quantification difficult).

• **Step 4 (or 5): Goal summary.** Roland did not have a phonological disorder, but he was a late talker, and it was considered appropriate to begin focused language stimulation. The Goal Summary (Table 8.6) summarizes his data for that purpose.

Although there were some initial attempts at [Labial]-[Coronal], [Coronal]-[Labial], and [Dorsal]-[Labial] sequences, different place sequences were rare outside of the unusual [Labial]-[Coronal] clusters. Nonnasal-nasal and fricative–first manner sequences were also possible needs, as was [−voiced]-[+voiced]. A variety of phones were available in all word positions, with the exception of final [l], possible restrictions on word-initial fricatives, and nonnasal-nasal sequences. Because Roland was a late talker, language stimulation aimed at new place and manner sequences in words and phrases was initiated in the home environment. Different activities around the house (including book reading, singing, and playing with favorite toys) afforded opportunities for stimulation, first of [Labial]-[Coronal] sequences in words and phrases and then of others.

Table 8.6. Goal Summary: Roland's Cross-Vowel Sequences, Scan Page 7

Level	Syllable and Word Structure
Goal Type	**Goal Type 4** Word Position and Sequences
Strengths	Segment and feature classes by word positions Identical place sequences Most voice and manner sequences Labial-coronal sequences in clusters Sequences
Needs	Word position Different place sequences across V's [−voiced]-[+voiced]? Nonnasal-nasal? Fricative-other? Sequences
Strengths To Use To Support Needs	Segments to use for structure goals C1: All stops and glides; m, n; l, possibly fricatives although there may be a fricative onset restriction. C2: Stops, fricatives [f], [s]; preferably [−voiced] WF obstruents (nasals if there are also nasals in C1 and the goal is place sequence).
Interactions (prosody, perception, morphology, motor)	Sequence constraints in phonology affecting syntactic development? (See Chapter 10.)
Social Factors	Very bright and active; excellent home environment
Immediate Goals	Different place sequence across vowels (Single words and word combinations; see Chapter 10)
Treatment Strategies	1. Awareness and production activities in daily routines, with CV separated from the final C, e.g., bu - bu - bu - bu—s, in familiar and motivating words. 2. Lab-Cor in single words, then combinations > Dors-Lab > others.
Goal # in Program (order)	N/A

Roland started producing many more [Labial]-[Coronal] sequences within a week or two of the onset of focused stimulation. Word combinations also appeared (see Chapter 10 for more details).

8.3. Consonant-Vowel Sequences

Consonants and vowels may show interactive phonological patterns in early development. (See Sections 2.6 and 3.2.) Observed patterns are shown in Section 8.3.1.

8.3.1. Expected Developmental Trends for Consonant-Vowel Sequences

Age Expectations:

• Assimilatory or dissimilatory effects on consonants preceding or between vowels or fricatives, e.g., intervocalic voicing, spirantization ("fricativization"), are relatively common in the first 3–4 years (particularly effects on voicing).

• In normal development, however, consonant-vowel place sequence constraints are relatively infrequent and tend to occur only in early acquisition.

Developmental Phonological Patterns:

• Word position differences for the features [voiced] and [continuant] can indicate consonant-vowel sequence constraints relative to those features.

• Variability between words that begin with the same consonant but have different vowels can indicate consonant-vowel place sequence constraints. A clue is often place assimilation between the vowel and the consonant (e.g., *do* and *boo* as [bu] but *day* and *bay* as [deɪ], with spread of [Labial] or [Coronal] from the vowel to the consonant).

• Less common patterns involve dissimilation (e.g., /bu/ > [du]), vowel height (see the example of Livia in Appendix C), or tenseness effects on consonant place.

8.3.2. Consonant-Vowel Interactions: General Notes

The scan form has one small box at the bottom of page 6 for making note of any consonant-vowel interactions. (See Table 8.5.) If they are a significant part of the phonological system, extra sheets can be used for analysis.

When patterns involving CV interactions are noted, CV sequences may become intervention targets and/or words may be chosen for other goals that avoid the CV constraints. Thus, on the Goal Summary sheet, CV sequences may show up in the "Needs," "Immediate Goals," or "Treatment Strategies" row. To show the types of possible patterns, we give three very short data sets illustrating the various types of patterns rather than giving one longer data set for a single child (because individual children usually tend to have only one of the possible patterns). A larger practice data set is in Appendix C (Livia's, which also includes distant consonant sequence constraints).

8.3.3. [Labial] and [Coronal] CV Interactions

Marnie (Chapter 6) had difficulty producing word-initial stops. The only (and fairly rare) occurrences of the word-initial labial stop [b] were with round vowels [oʊ] or [uː] (*bird* or *balloons*). (* = nonmatch)

Word	Adult Target	Child Form	Child Sequence
bird	bɝd	boʊʔ	C-Labial, V-Labial
balloons	bəlũːnz	buː	C-Labial, V-Labial
(tooth)brush	(tʰuːθ)brʌʃ	(ʔiʃ)ʔʌʔ	*Glottal (target C-Labial), V-Dorsal

In contrast, (the rare) word-initial [d] occurred only with [i], a high front (Coronal) vowel.

daddy	dædi	diː	C-Coronal, V-Coronal

Note also the production of *tooth* (*teeth*?) above, in which the [−anterior] coronal [ʃ] appeared after [i]. In these cases, the consonant appeared only when the C-place feature was identical to the V-place feature. Nasals were less affected, although there were still some indications of CV interaction.

mom	mʌ̃m	mʌ̃m	C-Labial, V-Dorsal, C-Labial
more	mɔr	moʊjə?	C-Labial, V-Labial (C-Coronal, V-Dorsal)
knife	naɪf	wʊf (I)	*C-Labial, *V-Labial (Coronal targets), C-Labial
no	noʊ	noʊ	C-Coronal, V-Labial

The highly practiced words *mom* and *no* matched the adult targets and did not show place assimilation. However, *knife* ([wʊf]) shows only one place feature ([Labial]) in the word. [Labial] spread from the coda consonant /f/ through the vowel to the onset.

Consonant-vowel interactions were only one of many patterns in Marnie's speech. Although *more consonant and vowel place feature sequences* were a *need* for her phonology, CV sequences were not a *goal* in the first cycle of therapy. Rather, initial consonant production was a major goal. However, observing the CV interaction pattern allowed the clinician to construct word sets that maximized probability of initial consonant production (i.e., using vowels and stops with the same place feature but allowing more variety for nasal onsets). Using *identical* place sequences between C and V was thus a *strategy* for intervention, rather than *different CV sequences* being an immediate goal.

As Marnie began to produce a variety of stop onsets consistently (after 8 weeks), the CV sequence constraints relaxed naturally (allowing any vowel to follow). Interestingly, she began to show noncontiguous consonant sequence constraints, with assimilation patterns across vowels in CVC and CVCV.

8.3.4. [Dorsal] CV Interactions

Some children master velars first with back vowels (see Williams & Dinnsen, 1987; Davis & MacNeilage, 1990). In clinical situations, Bernhardt has often found velars to be facilitated in elicitation through use of back vowels (in "words" such as *awk, caw, cocoa,* and *cuckoo*).

Sometimes a child produces *only* velars with back vowels (*comb* and *tooth* below) and *only* coronals with front vowels (*dress* and *cage* below, both from a child's data in Gierut, Cho, & Dinnsen, 1993).

Word	Adult Target	Child Form	Child Sequence
comb	kʰoʊm	ko	C-Dorsal, V-Dorsal
tooth	tʰuːθ	guʰ	*C-Dorsal (target C-Coronal), V-Dorsal
dress	drɛs	dɛ	C-Coronal, V-Coronal
cage	kʰeɪdʒ	tɛ	*C-Coronal (target C-Dorsal), V-Coronal

8.3.5. **Other CV Interactions: Height, Tenseness**

The examples we gave above showed place feature interactions. Vowel height can also be involved in CV interactions. Edwards (1995) notes that her subject, Shawn, produced velars first with low vowels ([ɑk] and [æk]) and with the nonhigh back vowel [oʊ] but with no other vowels. (See also Livia in Appendix C.) Thus, not only a backed-tongue position, but also a more open mouth posture facilitated velar production.

Bernhardt and Stemberger (1998) discuss a child, Terry (age 4-7), who showed CV interactions involving both height and tenseness. Generally, [w] was a default substitution in onset position for /t/, /k/, the fricatives, and the affricates, as below.

tickle	tɪkl̩	wɪʔoʊ
coffee	kʰɑfi:	wɑʔi
five	faɪv	wʌɪ
sis	sɪs	wɪʔ

However, before the high tense vowels [i] and [u], Terry produced a palatal fricative [ç] or a velar fricative [x]. Palatals are considered both dorsal and coronal (as is the vowel /i/).

teeth	tʰi:θ	çi
key	kʰi:	çi
shoe	ʃu:	xu
tooth	tʰu:θ	çu

The [Dorsal] and [+continuant] features of the vowel /u/ spread to the consonant slot, resulting in a velar fricative [x]. The [Coronal] feature of the palatal fricative either arose as a match with the coronal of the target (*teeth, tooth*) or spread from [i]. The substitutions in front of high tense vowels, although unusual, resulted in closer approximations to the adult target than was the case for the [w] substitution. Voiceless obstruents are redundantly [+tense]. Thus, the child was trying to match aspects of the target pronunciation as best he could, and the tense vowels afforded that possibility through spreading of features. He was effecting his own successive approximation strategy. In terms of the stops /t/ and /k/, of course, he lost the [−continuant] aspect of the stop (through spread of [+continuant]). He matched one aspect of the aspirated stop, i.e., the [+spread glottis] feature, since both aspirated stops and voiceless fricatives such as [ç] are redundantly [+spread glottis].

As with Marnie, CV interactions were more a strategy than a goal for Terry's phonological intervention. Initial consonant production was one of the many priority goals. Knowledge of the CV interactions gave the clinicians ideas for useful word sets for stop and fricative production (starting with tense vowels) and suggested a strategy of successive approximations through an oral-motor approach.

Terry was slow to progress on initial consonants, although he did improve notably in production of final and medial consonants during the first 4 months of treatment. Among the initial consonants, labiodental fricatives were learned first. The coronal fricatives were learned gradually (not 100% consistent by age 8 because of some lateralization). The initial stops /k/ and /t/ were not acquired until they were targeted directly in therapy (at age 5-3).

8.4. **Vowels Separated by Consonants**

Vowels may show sequence constraints when separated by consonants. Two different vowels may not be allowed across consonants. This is typically observed in cases of vowel harmony, as in the following example.

baby   beɪbiː   bibi

In this case, the first vowel harmonized with the last and more frequent vowel of the target. Recall that the default value for [high] in English may be [−high] (the value for /ɛ/ or /ə/), and that nondefaults spread in assimilation repairs. Here, the nondefault [+high] of /i/ spreads to the first vowel slot.

We are not sure how common vowel sequence constraints are in development, although they are most likely when the child uses full syllable reduplication, as in *baby* above. Sometimes harmony appears when only part of the syllable is reduplicated, as in Roland's production of *bagel* as [gɛbgɛ] (Section 8.2.4). Sometimes only the vowel harmonizes, e.g., *music* as ['mʊhʊ]. In reduplication, it is often the stressed vowel that is reiterated (as in *bagel*). That is not necessarily the case, however, as the words *baby* and Roland's production of *vitamins* as [mlɛmlɛ] show.

Vowel harmony is not highlighted on the scan, but we mention it here as something that can be noted and analyzed more if relevant.

If a child tends to have vowel harmony, this may be useful information when choosing words for disyllabic word production. If the focus is on production of C2 in a CVCV word, it might be helpful to use syllables with identical or near identical vowels so that the child can concentrate on the consonants. As we noted for CV interactions, vowel sequence constraints may suggest intervention *strategies* rather than being *intervention goals* themselves.

8.5. **Final Comments**

Sequence constraints can result in variable and inconsistent data. They can affect neighboring or distant consonants, neighboring consonants and vowels, and distant vowels. Among the sequence goals, clusters are probably the most common intervention targets. Other sequences may also be targets for intervention (depending on their relative prevalence). In addition, such sequence constraints often need to be considered when choosing therapy words for other goals (avoiding difficult sequences when some other goal is paramount).

Vowels

**Analyses in This Chapter
(page 8 of the scan)**

- overall vowel system
- specific vowel targets
- vowels and syllable timing

9.1. Vowels in Phonological Intervention

Vowels are much less often the target of phonological intervention than consonants. There are several reasons for this:

- In comparison with consonant development, vowel development is generally faster and usually less impaired in cases of phonological disorders.

- Not much research has been done on typical or disordered development of vowels, and hence clinicians have perhaps less information than they need to assess the vowel systems adequately.

- Vowels tend to be more difficult than consonants to transcribe reliably, particularly for children, and hence vowel deviations may be missed. Dialectal differences may also make it difficult to determine whether a particular child's vowels are disordered.

- It is difficult to teach vowels because there are less precise articulatory configurations to demonstrate. A child's vowel space is different acoustically from an adult's, and hence both the clinician and the child have to rely more on acoustic matches than on a combination of acoustic and articulatory matches, as can be done with many consonants.

- Children's vowel accuracy can improve simply as a result of consonant intervention (Bernhardt, Major, & Stemberger, 1996).

That being said, some children do seem to need intervention focused on vowels (Bernhardt, 1990; Pollock, 1994). There are several situations in which this may arise:

- A child may have an extremely low proportion of consonant *and* vowel matches (see Section 9.2).

- After intervention focusing on consonants, some (or many) vowels may remain unchanged, in a way that is impacting significantly on intelligibility (see Sections 9.3 and 9.4).

- Mastery of vowel length may be connected to development of timing within the syllable or stress in some way. For example, a child may be able to produce lax vowels and codas, but no codas after long vowels or diphthongs (Section 9.4); a child may produce no diphthongs, at least in part due to timing restrictions in syllables (Section 9.4); or a child may lengthen vowels in order to be able to produce a weak syllable (see Barry's data in Section 6.2.2).

• Rhotic vowels may cause particular difficulty.

• There may be consonant-vowel interactions such as discussed in Chapter 8.

• Vowel resonance may be unusual, i.e., hypernasal or hyponasal, or excessively pharyngealized ("tunnel voice") or laryngealized ("creaky voice"), etc. In such cases, voice therapy or procedures relating to velopharyngeal control are implicated.

• A person may wish to change his or her vowels to reflect the ambient dialect.

On the scan analysis form, questions and information about vowels are in two places: on the "Bird's-Eye View" and on page 8. In this chapter, we give examples of vowel analyses and intervention programs for the first three situations noted above. Rhotic vowels can be analyzed along with /r/ in the sections on consonants, and consonant-vowel interactions are analyzed on page 6 of the scan (as shown in Chapter 8). Vocal quality and resonance differences are mentioned for completeness but are beyond the scope of this workbook. Similarly, dialectal differences, while important, are not disorders and also lie beyond the scope of this book.

The expected developmental trends for vowels are as follows:

Early mastery: • The basic vowel triangle /i/, /ɑ/, /u/
                 • Mid back tense /oʊ/
                 • Mid central /ʌ/

Mid mastery: • Back and central lax vowels /ʊ/, /ɔ/, /ə/
               • Low front vowel /æ/

Late mastery: • Front nonlow vowels /eɪ/, /ɛ/, /ɪ/
                • Rhotic vowels

See Stoel-Gammon and Herrington (1990) and Otomo and Stoel-Gammon (1992).

9.2. Low Vowel and Consonant Match

Children with very limited lexicons may be candidates for vowel intervention in addition to consonant intervention. Many such children are considered to have a language impairment or dyspraxia in addition to (or instead of) a phonological impairment, but a phonological approach to intervention may be effective (Bopp, 1995). In such cases, vowels may be the first intervention targets, or they may be taught along with consonants. Sometimes these children have difficulty with different place sequences. This may impede production of CV sequences and, hence, words (as discussed in Chapter 8). If this is the case, it may be efficacious to choose therapy words in which (a) consonants and vowels have the same place of articulation, e.g., *boo(m), more, tea, knee, need, go, coke;* or (b) there are placeless glottals in onset, e.g., *hi, head, hit, who, I, eat,* etc. Generally, it is also important to find words that are communicatively useful.

The child whose data we present in brief here had a very limited lexicon but showed the capacity to produce most vowels and consonants *in imitation* in at least one word during assessment.

9.2.1. The Child

Colin: Age 5-0. Severe phonological and language production disorder.

Colin had no obvious cognitive or motor impairments. His language comprehension appeared to be average. He had very few recognizable words (his mother understood about five of his words). In spontaneous speech (accompanied by a rich gestural system) he used the following "default" words primarily: [gak], [gagak], [gaha], [bap], and [bahə], as shown in the data set in Table 9.1.

9.2.2. Analysis and Intervention

Overall Vowel Match

The predominant vowel in Colin's speech was [a]. During the "Bird's-Eye View" analysis, it was clear that vowels were significantly disordered in his speech and would need deeper analysis than is generally necessary. Given the low frequency of accurate vowels, it was considered important to calculate a vowel match proportion, both to compare with consonants and as a baseline measure. Table 9.1 was set up in such a way as to allow for quick calculation of vowel match (a match and a nonmatch column). In the selection of words chosen for this table, the vowel match was 10% (2/20).

Table 9.1. Low Vowel Match: Colin's Data

Word	Adult Pronunciation	Child Pronunciation	S/I	Target Vowel	
				Match	Nonmatch
egg	(ʔ)ɛg	nã	S		ɛ
mask	mæsk	gak	S		æ
		bap	I		æ
me	miː	hãĭ	S		i
mouth	maʊθ	gak	S		aʊ
		bɐɪk	S		aʊ
pie	pʰaɪ	gak	S		aɪ
		baɪ	I	aɪ	
buzzing	bʌzĭŋ	bahəʔ	I		ʌĭ
TV	tʰiːviː	gagak	S		i, i
two	tʰuː	kʰuː	S	u	
throwing	θroʊĭŋ	gahaː	S		oʊ, ĭ
radio	reɪdioʊ	gaha	S		eɪ, i, oʊ
		bəhə	I		eɪ, i, oʊ
TOTALS				2	19
% V Match				2/21 (10%)	

Note. S = spontaneous, I = imitated.

During assessment, a vowel match was calculated over a sample of 170 words, and the PVC (percent vowels correct) was actually 25%. The importance of larger samples is clear from this comparison, although in either case, a vowel match of 25% or lower is most definitely severe.

Elicitation Context

Just as for consonants, it is often relevant to consider elicitation context in vowel production. During the assessment, it was found that Colin's imitated words were more likely to have matching vowels. (Note that Table 9.1 includes a column for context: spontaneous versus imitated productions.) Across the sample, even though PVC and PSCC (percent singleton consonants correct) were 25% and 13%, respectively, Colin did produce in imitation at least one accurate token of all vowels and consonants except /l/ and all diphthongs (there were two instances of [aɪ], once as a match and once as a nonmatch). This was considered a positive prognostic indicator, although it was not clear why he was not using those consonants and vowels if he was immediately stimulable for them.

Rationale for Vowel Intervention

Although three of Colin's four *immediate* goals for the first 6 weeks of intervention were for consonants, the low vowel match indicated a need for one set of vowel targets also. If imitation of adult models was to become an effective learning strategy (which it had not yet become in his natural environment), then vowels (which rely on accurate listening and acoustic matching) would be useful first intervention targets.

But what do you choose when someone needs almost everything? The concept of the basic vowel triangle (the vowels that are usually mastered earliest) came to mind:

$$i \qquad\qquad u$$

$$ɑ$$

In Colin's spontaneous words, there were a few occurrences of [u] and [i] and of course many instances of [a], which, for child speech, is often a (fairly acceptable) variant of /ɑ/ (see Bernhardt & Stemberger, 1998). If he learned the value of imitation through production of these most discrete points of the acoustic vowel space, perhaps the rest would fill in gradually. But rather than just focusing on single vowels (which he already produced spontaneously), we decided to target the diphthongs /aʊ/ and /aɪ/. This strategy (a) included vowels at the corner points of the vowel triangle, (b) addressed the syllable structure need for vowels with two timing units (i.e., diphthongs, VV), and (c) presented an opportunity to make successful imitation rewarding.

The halves of the diphthong were rhythmically supported (as moras; see Chapter 11), with "frog leaps" in the case of /aɪ/ (ah-EE!) and with "howling at the moon" for /aʊ/ (ah-OO!), making the targets salient and the imitation immediately reinforcing. (*Note:* The "ah" of "ah-EE" is produced in a squat position. On the "EE," parent, clinician, and child leap.)

Intervention Outcomes

The approach to vowel intervention was a successful strategy. By the end of the first 6 weeks of intervention (which included three other goals), the overall vowel match had improved to 61%, with diphthongs /aʊ/ and /aɪ/ at 53% match proportion. (For further details on Colin's program, see Bernhardt & Stemberger, 1998, Chapter 8).

This escalation continued throughout the program (diphthongs were targets in the second cycle of treatment also).

By focusing on the structural property of the diphthongs as two timing units (a nonlinear perspective) and utilizing pronounceable segments (even if two were marginal at assessment), notable gains were made in *both* segmental inventory and syllable structure matches.

9.3. After Consonant Intervention

Gordon: Age 6-0 at assessment, age 6-4 at probe 3; moderate phonological disorder, severe language production disorder.

If vowels are not the initial targets of intervention, but vowel accuracy is lower than expected even after consonant intervention, vowels may become targets of intervention. Gordon (Bernhardt, 1990) provided such a case. In addition to his phonological and language production disorders, Gordon had a mild cognitive delay, as well as some production processing and oral motor difficulties.

Gordon had 12 weeks of consonant intervention focusing on /l/, /r/, palatoalveolars, and clusters (late-developing elements). At the initial assessment it was noted that vowels were also impaired. By the end of the second of three 6-week blocks of intervention (three times per week), vowel accuracy had not increased substantially. Gordon produced all vowels, but only some were sufficiently established: low and mid vowels (except for /ɛ/ and /æ/), /i/, and the diphthongs, as follows:

```
i
eɪ        ʌ/ə      oʊ
                   ɔ(ɪ)
a{ʊ/ɪ}             ɑ
```

The lax vowels /ɪ/, /ɛ/, and /ʊ/, rhotic vowels, and the high-tense vowel /u/ presented notable difficulty and became targets for intervention in the last treatment block of the study. Of these, all except /u/ are expected to be later-developing (although not as late as age 6). The absence of /u/ shows he did not have the basic vowel triangle (generally the earliest mastered set of vowels). (See Table 9.2 for match percentages.)

Table 9.2. Gordon's Nonmatching Vowels Over Time

Vowel	% Match		
	Assessment	After Consonant Intervention[a]	After Vowel Intervention[a]
ɪ	53.8% (21/39)	64.5% (20/31)	66.7% (22/33)
ɛ	31.8% (7/22)	15.4% (4/26)	37.5% (9/24)
ʊ	45.8% (11/24)	0% (0/3)	41.2% (7/17)
u	8.0% (2/25)	5.6% (1/18)	39.0%[b] (16/41)

[a]The consonant intervention period was 14 weeks. The vowel intervention period was 7 weeks, with an exclusive focus on vowels during 2 of those weeks.

[b]The only vowel showing significant gain after vowel intervention was /u/.

How can nonlinear phonological theory explain this? Thinking of the status of features as defaults versus nondefaults, and as *individual features* versus *features in simultaneous combination* elucidates Gordon's difficulties.

9.3.1. [+high] a Nondefault?

Three of the four nonmatching vowels were [+high] (/ɪ/, /ʊ/, and /u/). According to Stemberger (1992), the feature [+high] is a nondefault (and [−high] a default) in English. Segments with nondefaults often develop later, especially when they have to combine with other nondefaults in the same segment. For /ɪ/, height and place were maintained in repair patterns, and tenseness was the vulnerable feature (see below); but for the back vowels, place (and often tenseness) was maintained, and [+high] was the vulnerable feature, as shown in the examples below. The combination of two nondefault features, [Labial] and [+high], possibly made the back high vowels particularly challenging.

Word	Adult	Child	Repair		
middle	mɪɾl̩	midoʊ	[−tense]	>	[+tense]; [+high] correct, but not *with* [−tense]
good	gʊd	goᵊd	[+high]	>	[−high]; nondefault > default
boot	buːt	boʊt	[+high]	>	[−high]; nondefault > default

9.3.2. [−tense] and Timing

The other common problematic feature was [−tense], either as an individual feature or in combination with other features. There were three lax vowels in the nonmatching group (/ɪ/, /ɛ/, and /ʊ/). As noted, /ɪ/ tended to surface as its tense counterpart, [iː], and /ʊ/ tended to surface as [+tense] [oʊ] or lax [ɔ]; /ɛ/ surfaced as other lax vowels: (frequently) [a], or [ʌ], as in the examples.

Word	Adult	Child	Repair		
present	pʰrɛzn̩t	pʌ̃n̪ᵗθin	[−back]	>	[+back]; [+back] default?
bed	bɛd	baᵊd	[−low]	>	[+low]; nondefault [−back], default [−high] maintained (at expense of [−low])

According to syllable theories, the feature [−tense] (for the lax vowels) is correlated with the moraic (timing unit) structure in English: lax vowels may appear only in closed syllables and are short. For a child with a motor processing deficit, short vowels with nondefault features may have presented more difficulty because of the limited time available for the production of the syllable. By lengthening the vowels or using a vowel with default features, he may have reduced the processing load during speech production.

9.3.3. Vowel Intervention Outcomes

Two of the last six weeks of Gordon's intervention were devoted exclusively to vowels, although there was a general focus on vowels throughout that treatment block. The most improved vowel after treatment was /u/. Long vowels are perhaps easier to teach, because they can be elicited in open syllables and can be prolonged more easily than inherently short vowels. Gordon had actual difficulty maintaining a tongue position for /ɛ/ (see also Pollock, 1994, who reports similar results for another child with a vowel disorder). Interestingly, his predominant repair pattern changed for /u/ also. Whereas he initially produced [oʊ] 63% of the time for the high back vowels, his primary substitution for /u/ after intervention was the lax counterpart, [ʊ] (68%). Thus, although the high back lax vowel was only partially established itself, it served as a substitution, showing that the feature combination [Labial] and [+high] was becoming more possible, even when short and lax. This pattern was somewhat surprising, since lax vowels were generally difficult for him.

9.4. Timing Units: Vowel Length and Codas

Both Colin and Gordon showed constraints relative to timing units and vowels (that directly affected vowel production). Constraints on the number of timing units in the rime may affect both consonants and vowels, as was the case for Sean below. Although this is more of an interactive effect (the subject of discussion in Chapter 8), we present it here because it is related to Colin's and Gordon's data above. What it implies for intervention is the possible need to consider *both* vowel timing units *and* consonant timing units when addressing either independently.

Sean: Age 3-4–4-0 during the nonlinear intervention study (Bernhardt, 1994a). Severe phonological and language production disorder.

Sean had above average nonverbal intelligence and average language comprehension.

At assessment, 54.5% of Sean's monosyllabic words were open CV(V) syllables. CVC targets had codas 29% of the time (excluding /r/ and /l/ codas). A number of patterns occurred relative to rime timing units:

- Lax vowels were usually produced with offglides or were lengthened (e.g., *big* as [bɛːkʰ], *man* as [mæᵊ]).

- CVC words usually had lax (i.e., short) vowels.

- Open-syllable diphthong targets appeared as matches (12 out of 27) or with lengthened monophthongs (e.g., *pie* as [pɑːᵊ]).

- Closed-syllable diphthong targets had only 2 diphthong matches (out of 17 targets) and otherwise had short vowels and codas (e.g., *house* as [ʔas]), or long vowels or diphthongs with no coda (e.g., *boat* as [boʊ] or [bɔʔ]).

Sean appeared to have a constraint on the rime, limiting the number of timing units to two. Either he could produce a short vowel with a coda, *or* he could produce a long vowel or diphthong in an open syllable. Thus, timing unit constraints were affecting *both vowels and consonants*.

Constraints on the number of timing units within the rime continued for some time throughout Sean's intervention program. After the first 6-week block focusing on CVC as one of four goals, CVC's increased significantly (81% match), but he still rarely produced diphthongs in the CVVC word shape. In fact, diphthong use in general decreased. Perhaps the focus on VC as two rime timing units resulted in an overgeneralization whereby VV was considered a less optimal rime (a regression for vowel timing units).

In the second block of treatment, diphthongs thus became one of four targets. This resulted in establishment of diphthongs in open syllables, where two riming units were present in the rime (CVV) but *still not in closed syllables.* It was only after the third block of intervention that CVVC with diphthongs became established. (Interestingly, CVCC, another word shape with three rime timing units, emerged only with /s/-clusters; the sonorant nasal clusters (e.g., *mp*) did *not* arise spontaneously and had to be targeted 6 months later.)

Sean's data show that it can be important to look at both vowels and consonants in terms of their timing unit status.

9.5. Final Comments

It may be necessary to target vowels in intervention for a number of reasons, whether because of a general low match overall, lack of change following consonant intervention, or timing unit restrictions in the rime of the syllable. In terms of nonlinear phonological theory, the following concepts are useful when trying to understand patterns:

- the status of vowel features as nondefaults or defaults
- the relative difficulty of feature combinations
- the status of vowel timing units in the rime, particularly for diphthongs
- the relationship between vowel and consonant timing units in the rime
- the relationship between consonants and vowels in terms of place of articulation (Chapter 8)

ᴈ φ ω'
α ᶜ ꝑ ₒ ꝼ
λ ꞃ ꝑ

Chapter 10

Interactions Between Phonology and Grammar

Because all meaningful units (words and morphemes) are expressed phonologically, the phonology can have a strong effect on them. In the most extreme instances, grammatical morphemes (such as *the, is, on,* and plural *-s*) may be absent because they require phonological skills that the child does not possess. Sentences may be limited to a single word because of constraints on sequences of segments. It is important to investigate the effects of phonology before assuming that there is a grammatical problem. On the flip side, the grammar may lead to the occurrence of sequences that might be impossible within a single word.

10.1. Phonological Aspects of Grammatical Morphemes

The following characterization holds true for most grammatical morphemes in English (plural, possessive, and present-tense *-s;* past and perfect *-ed;* progressive *-ing;* adverbial *-ly;* comparative *-er;* superlative *-est; is, can, will, should, in, on, with, the, a,* etc.):

- A coda consonant is added (*flies* /flaɪ-z/).
- A complex coda is created (*needs* /niːd-z/, *laughed* /læf-t/).
- A final unstressed syllable is created (*horses* /ˈhɔrs-əz/, *John'll* /ˈʤɑn-l̩/).
- An initial unstressed syllable is created (*a cat* /ə-ˈkæt/, *with me* /wəθ-ˈmiː/).

As noted in Chapters 1–3, all of these are potentially absent from a child's speech. In addition, the particular phonemes involved (such as the /z/ of plural *-s*) may be late developing. Further, particular sequences may be created (such as the /ks/ of *rocks* /rɑks/) that may be impossible within a simple word.

The same types of repair processes occur as are found for uninflected words. Deletion is a common option.

Constraints: No codas, complex codas, or unstressed syllables possible
Repair: Deletion

- of the coda consonant (*flies* /flaɪ-z/ [faɪ])
- of a consonant in the complex coda (*needs* /niːd-z/ [niːd] or [niːz])
- of the final unstressed syllable (*horses* /ˈhɔrs-əz/ [hɔrs])
- of the initial unstressed syllable (*a cat* /ə-ˈkæt/ [ˈkæt])

In most instances, the result is the same as if the grammatical morpheme was absent (e.g., see Gerken, 1991, on articles). What is a phonological problem may at first appear to be a grammatical problem. Note, however, that some deletions may preserve the grammatical morpheme, as when /dz/ is pronounced [z]. Note also that irregular forms may be unaffected by the same constraints. If no codas are possible, the difference between present tense and past tense may still be signaled by a difference in vowels:

sink [sɪ]   sank   [sa]

If the constraints allow codas and unstressed syllables but prohibit these weak positions from having independent phonological segments and features, assimilations may instead occur:

Repair: Assimilation—   a bee   /əˈbiː/   [bəˈbiː]

Alternatively, extra syllables can be created to remove a coda or to break up complex codas (epenthesis). However, this seems to be unusual.

Repair: Epenthesis—   dogs   /dɑgz/   [ˈdada]

Grammatical morphemes do not have to be treated the same as equivalent phonological material that is a part of a simple word:

Same deletion:	box	/bɑks/	[bak]	rocks	/rɑks/	[wak]
	balloon	/bəluːn/	[buːn]	the cat	/ðəkæt/	[kæt]
Different deletion:	box	/bɑks/	[bas]	rocks	/rɑks/	[wak]
Only one deleted:	box	/bɑks/	[bak]	rocks	/rɑks/	[waks]
OR	box	/bɑks/	[baks]	rocks	/rɑks/	[wak]
	balloon	/bəluːn/	[buːn]	the cat	/ðəkæt/	[ðəkæt]
OR	balloon	/bəluːn/	[bəluːn]	the cat	/ðəkæt/	[kæt]

Reductions are often the same for both. For some normally developing children, the grammatical morpheme may be present, even though similar sequences are not possible within a morpheme. The grammatical morpheme is supported by meaning and constraints on syntax, and so may be in advance of the phonology found within a morpheme. Especially for children with specific language impairment, grammatical morphemes may be absent most of the time, even when similar sequences within a morpheme are present most of the time, showing a statistical tendency for simple morphemes to be in advance of combinations of morphemes.

For word-final consonant clusters, a vowel may be inserted to prevent a complex coda:

Both augmented: box /bɑks/ [bakəs]   rocks /rɑks/ [wakəz]

However, adding vowels to codas appears to be very unusual within a morpheme (Bernhardt & Stemberger, 1998, Chapter 6). It is more likely to find the addition of a vowel only before grammatical morphemes, since allomorphs such as /-əz/ are present in adult English in other phonological environments:

Only one augmented: box /bɑks/ [bak]   rocks /rɑks/ [wakəz]

We would like to emphasize, however, that grammatical morphemes and equivalent nongrammatical phonological material are often treated in the same fashion.

Exercise

1. The following data come from a normally developing child. Compare the simple words with the past-tense forms. Point out similarities and differences. Explain where the past tense is [d] or [t], and where it has an extra syllable.

Sequence	Simple			Past tense		
/d/	seed	/siːd/	[siːd]	peed	/piːd/	[pʰiːd]
/rd/	beard	/bird/	[bird]	scared	/skɛrd/	[sɛrd]
/mp/	jump	/dʒʌmp/	[zʌmp]	jumped	/dʒʌmpt/	[zʌmt]
/nd/	round	/raʊnd/	[wawn]	turned	/tɝnd/	[tʰɝndəd]
/kt/	act	/ækt/	[ʔæːk]	walked	/wɑkt/	[wɑːktəd]
/st/	last	/læst/	[læːs]	kissed	/kɪst/	[tʰɪstəd]

10.2. Limitations on Syntactic Development

Word combinations can be affected by phonological factors. In extreme cases, the phonology can make two-word sentences quite rare (Bopp, 1995; Donahue, 1986; Matthei, 1989; Stemberger & Bernhardt, 1997).

Several children have been reported who have severe constraints on sequences of features, and whose only two-word combinations are limited to the same sequences that are allowed within words. Roland was such a child (see Sections 8.2.2–8.2.4). The following sequences occurred, in which the consonants were separated by a vowel:

same-place	bib	[bɪb]	night	[nʌt]	cookie	[kʊki]
initial glottal	ham	[hæm]	head	[hɛd]		
[Labial]-[Coronal]	please	[pis] (*rare*)				
[Dorsal]-[Labial]-[Dorsal]	cup	[gʌpk] (*rare*)				

For the most part, two consonants within a word had to have the same place of articulation. At the same point in time, the only two-word combinations that were produced had consonants with the same place of articulation, or one glottal:

[Glottal]-[Labial]-[Labial]	hop up	/hɑp ʌp/	[ʔɑp ʌp]
[Glottal]-[Coronal]-[Coronal]	hold it	/hoʊld ɪt/	[ʔoʊd ɪt]

At age 2-2, the sequence constraints began to lose their force within words, with the appearance of consonants with different places of articulation within words. Immediately thereafter, the child's two-word combinations exploded, with the two words containing consonants that had different places of articulation:

Casey push me down.	[Dorsal]-[Coronal], [Labial]-[Coronal], [Labial], [Coronal]-[Coronal]
Me see.	[Labial], [Coronal]

It appears that two words could not be combined in a sentence if the result would violate constraints on phonological sequences. Syntactic development was being limited by phonological development.

10.3. Effects on Phonology

Combinations of words may create combinations of segments that are impossible within a word. In most cases, the words are pronounced the same way as they are in isolation. However, in some instances the phonological constraints affect the realization of those combinations. In some cases, this leads to an improvement in the pronunciation of a word. In other cases, it leads to a worsening of the pronunciation of a word.

10.3.1. Improvements in Word Pronunciations in Connected Speech

Improvements arise when a sequence allows for a way to rescue a segment or feature that otherwise would be impossible. For example, if codas are impossible, instead of deleting a word-final consonant, the consonant can be shifted into the onset of the first syllable in the next word, if that word begins with a vowel and so has no onset:

| head | /hɛd/ | [haː] |
| (Put your) head over (here). | /hɛd oʊvɚ/ | [.haː.doʊ.] |

A consonant that was deleted when the word was sentence-final or when the next word began with a consonant was pronounced when the next word began with a vowel, for syllable structure reasons.

In some instances, the segment has an improved realization of a feature. If [Labial] is subject to sequence constraints so that it rarely appears in a coda, it may nonetheless surface when the next word starts with a labial:

| Jump! | /dʒʌmp/ | [dʌt] |
| Jump, Papa! | /dʒʌmp pɑpə/ | [dʌp papa] |

The two tokens of the [Labial] feature are merged, leading to one lengthened labial gesture extending over both the word-final consonant and the word-initial consonant. If [Labial] is well established in word-initial onsets (as here), merger across word boundaries allows realization of [Labial] in the coda of the first word.

10.3.2. Deterioration of Word Pronunciations in Connected Speech

Phonological constraints may also lead to a worsening of the pronunciation. For example, if two consonants are never allowed to appear in a sequence (so that the largest two-syllable word would be CVCVC, with no clusters initially, medially, or finally), a problem arises with some two-word combinations:

| Book me. | /bʊk miː/ | [bʊkə miː] |
| Come, Tony! | /kʌm toːni/ | [hʌmə tʰoːni] |

Here a vowel is epenthesized between the coda of the first word and the onset of the second. Such difficulties and repairs can involve any constraint on feature sequences and may be repaired via

- deletion of features or segments (possibly followed by insertion of default features or segments, or by spreading of nearby features or segments);

- separation of the relevant segments by inserting a vowel between them (epenthesis);

- reversal (metathesis) of the relevant features or segments; or

- separation of the relevant features through migration of one feature to a more distant segment.

Pronunciations may be worse within sentences in general, without any particular characteristic of the environment being relevant. This may result from insufficient cognitive resources (or attentional resources) to plan out both the syntax *and* the pronunciations of all the words involved, leading to a general worsening of the processing of the phonological forms of words.

10.4. Final Comments

- What appears to be a grammatical problem may have a phonological basis. It is important to investigate the effects of phonology before assuming that there is a grammatical problem.

- On the flip side, embedding words in phrases may affect the phonology, leading to improvement or deterioration of pronunciation. New sequences of segments are created across word boundaries that may facilitate or hamper production of segments in the two words.

Chapter 11

Intervention Strategies and Techniques

This chapter provides general intervention strategies and techniques that derive from nonlinear phonological theories. (Some of the strategies and techniques may not derive exclusively from nonlinear phonological theories, but we present them as they relate to those theories.) It is beyond the scope of this workbook to present detailed intervention procedures. For more intervention ideas, see Bernhardt (1994b) and Bernhardt et al. (1997). Note that the strategies and techniques to follow do not have to be tied to any particular intervention *approach,* in terms of scheduling of intervention targets, expectations for the child (from passive listening to direct imitation), type of adult facilitator (parent, speech–language pathologist, teacher), or degree and type of cueing support. A variety of approaches have been used in nonlinear phonological intervention projects, depending on the needs of the child, the perspectives of the family and the clinicians, and the time available for intervention (Bernhardt, 1990, 1992; Major & Bernhardt, 1998; Von Bremen, 1990).

11.1. Choosing Words for Therapy

Whatever type of methods or activities is used, word choice is a key factor. The following factors need to be considered for word choice:

- Use available segments when targeting new syllable structures.

- Use available syllable structures when targeting new segments.

- Avoid sequence constraints when first targeting new features or word shapes.

Exceptions:

• *Phonetic considerations:* Sometimes a child just cannot pronounce a particular sound class in the available word positions. Some children may find it easier to pronounce velars, fricatives, or voiceless stops in coda even if CVC is only partially established.

• *Learning potential and rate:* Some children can learn more than one thing at a time, and so goals can be "doubled up," i.e., new segments in new word shapes.

• *Awareness activities:* When a child does not actually have to pronounce anything, a greater range of contexts for segments, or segments for word shapes, can be used.

Each of the following sections, 11.2–11.5, begins with a list of sample goals, which are followed by a number of suggested strategies for meeting those goals. These lists are meant to provide only an overview.

11.2. Word Structure: Length, Stress, Segment Use

Sample word structure intervention goals:

- Words with more syllables
- Words with a greater range of stress patterns
- Consistent use of inventory segments in longer words

General strategies for word structure intervention are as follows.

1. **Fluency strategies:** Model slow and rhythmic speech, creating longer words (or words with new stress patterns, or words with *all* segments pronounced) out of individual syllables. In particular, increase the loudness, pitch, and duration of the unstressed syllables (maintaining a distinction between the stressed and unstressed syllables). As the child shows the ability to pronounce a series of (apparently unrelated) syllables at a slow rate, gradually increase the rate of articulation, moving in the direction of the adult rate, pitch, and loudness and bringing the syllables together into a new word. Choose words that make some kind of sense as parts and wholes, as in the example below.

> "bam!" "boo!" > "bam, boo" > "bamboo!" *Possible scenario:* Two pandas play hide-and-seek in the bushes. They bump into things (*bam*), scare themselves and each other (*boo*), then become excited as they stumble into a much desired *bamboo* patch.

2. **Musical and rhythmic support:** Use music and rhythm to emphasize the number of syllables or the difference between strong and weak syllables. Note: For some children, doing two activities at once (drumming *and* talking) is too challenging. In such cases, the adult provides either the rhythm or the speech models.

3. **Labels:** Give the child the labels to facilitate awareness. For example, label strong and weak syllables. (The weak syllable may be "tiny," but it is "tough" and does not let the strong syllables bully it out of the game.)

4. **Visual support for stress patterns, or syllable number:** Use podium setups (with chairs, stools, or blocks) with the right number of syllables for the stimulus word. The Strong syllable is on the highest step of the podium, but the weak syllables have their own step:

$$\boxed{w}\overline{\boxed{S}}\boxed{w}$$

As the child says the word, someone (or something) is moved from step to step on the podium.

5. **"Strong-weak" as a unit:** Add on syllables to the basic Sw stress pattern. In the example below, a swS word (*kangaroo*) is created from Sw (*Kanga*) and S (*Roo*) words.

> Scenario: Kanga and Roo can't find each other, so they call each other's name: "Kanga!" calls Roo. "ROO!" calls Kanga. Eventually, they find each

other and hug and jump up and down, saying, "KangaROO" together, with the mother being most excited and emphasizing the "ROO" part (the syllable with primary stress).

11.3. Subsyllabic Structure

Sample Intervention Targets for Onset or Rime Development:

- **Onsets:** (a) glottal onset to vowel-initial words rather than consonant (i.e., [ʔæpl̩], not [pæpl̩]); (b) word-initial clusters of various types

- **Rimes:** VC, diphthongs (VV), rimes with clusters, i.e., VCC(C)

- **Onset OR Coda—word position goals:** movement of segments from onset to coda (word-final position) or vice versa

- **Onset AND Rime:** onset-coda (C1–C2) sequences, e.g., [Coronal]-[Labial], [Dorsal]-[Coronal]

General strategies follow for interventions that either focus on the onset or rime, or use the onset or rime as a unit to achieve some other goal.

1. **Verbal stimuli that focus on onset or rime:**

- onset—alliteration, tongue-twisters
- rime—poetry, songs, nursery rhymes

2. **Analogies and visual support for onset and rime:** Old metaphonological awareness strategies such as a *head* or *engine* for onsets, a *body* or *train coach* for the vowel nucleus of the rime, and *tails* or *cabooses* for codas of the rime are useful ways of organizing stimuli for presentation in therapy, so that metaphonological awareness training is built directly into phonological intervention activities.

3. **Sneaking up on sequence constraints:** To circumvent sequence constraints, it can be useful to target sequences first in larger phonological units that can be separated in time (similarly to what is done when creating longer words, as in 11.2 above). The onsets of each syllable are more likely to survive if they are separated in time one from the other. For example, when trying to eliminate a [Coronal]-[Labial] sequence constraint, start with two syllables pronounced in slow sequence, in which the first onset is a coronal consonant and the second is a labial (as in *Beany* below). Gradually decrease the interval between the two syllables until C1VC2V is produced. (This can also be useful when the goal is production of CVCV *as a word shape,* as it was for Dylan in Chapter 5 and Mandy in Chapter 7.)

"Bee" "Knee" > "Bee, Knee" > "Beany"

C1VC2V can be a starting point for a C1VC2 monosyllable, by eliminating the final rime "y."

"Beany" > "Bean, y" > "Bean" "y" > "Bean"
CVCV   > CVC,V > CVC V" > CVC

Another strategy to eliminate sequence constraints in CVC is to separate the onset and rime at first. This necessitates use of consonants in the onset that can be lengthened, either by increasing the aspiration phase (adding more [h]'s), or because the consonant is [+sonorant] (e.g., a nasal or glide), or [+continuant] (fricative).

[tʰʰ] [ap] > [tʰap]

[sːː] [ɑː] > [sɑː]

4. **Introducing a coda—VC > CVC:** Begin with awareness and imitation of a VC rime, then introduce an onset, either by alternations of VC (see #5), or by onset prolongation (as in #3 above for CVC).

5. **Moving consonants from the rime to the onset:** If a child does not use certain consonants in onset (either singletons or clusters) but uses them in coda, alternations of VC can lead to production of the target consonants in onset, as in "up up up" > "pup," "est est" > "test."

6. **Word-initial clusters with sonorants in C2:** (as in [sm̱], [sw̱], [bṟ], [pḻ], etc.) Treat the segments of the cluster as an indivisible unit, i.e., "friend sounds," which go around and join up with vowels and longer rimes, as in "sn" "ow" > "snow," or "sue" "L" > "swell" ([suːʔɛl̩] > [suːɛl] > [swɛl]). This works best when the second consonant of the cluster is a sonorant (nasal, glide, liquid).

Sample Moras and Edges Intervention Targets:

- Add vowel moras (CV > CVV, as in diphthongs).

- Add consonant moras after short (lax) vowels (CV to CVC, as in *bit* and *bet*).

- Add consonants to the *edges* of syllables "outside" the mora structure (at the beginning or end of syllables), as in the following examples: C+CVV (*s* + *top*), CVC + C (*bit* + *s*), CVV + C (*boo* + *t*).

This section gives general strategies for syllable structure development that utilize the concepts of syllable weight units (moras) and (weightless) syllable edges. Note that onsets are weightless, and thus strategies that separate the onset from the nucleus (as suggested in the previous section) can also apply here. The concept of weight does give additional strategies, however, and we focus on those here.

1. **Rhythmic and visual support for adding moras:** When syllables have only one mora (short vowel), typical additions are long vowels, diphthongs, and lax vowels with coda consonants. Use rhythmic support (one beat per mora) and visual aids to emphasize the two parts.

- long vowel: *bee* = 2 beats (wing flaps?) for the vowel [iː]
- diphthong: *bye* = 2 beats (waves?), 1 for [a] and 1 for [ɪ] of [baɪ]
- CVC, lax V: *mi* + *tt* = 2 beats (mitted hand claps?), 1 for [mɪ] and 1 for [t]

This may seem counterintuitive at first, because in typical rhythmic clapping, monosyllables receive only one clap. Here the goal is to draw attention to the moras. Children have less experience with clapping traditions and adapt to the strategy.

2. **Adding edges:** Add one by one to the edges of existing syllables. For example, for the /s/ of an /s/-cluster, the /s/ is added to the outside of an existing word (no beats here, since the edges have no weight). This is particularly helpful for /s/-stop clusters, but can be used for any clusters.

Scenario: Cinderella in her th-rift s-tore rags, with her b-room. The b-room makes a s-wishing sound [s], [s], [s]. Cinderella goes, "Weep, weep, weep." All of a sudden her (good s-peech) fairy godmother (in one of her many s-parkly th-rift s-tore gowns) hears the s-wish and comes along and asks Cinderella what she wishes for and s-wishes for. Cinderella says, to make the broom "s-weep" all by itself, so she won't have to "weep" or "s-weep" any more. . . . The End, *or,* if necessary, the p-rince can come by too, with his magic s-lipper . . . and they can "s-weep" off s-tage with their th-rift s-tore robes s-wishing behind them. . . . The Alternate End.

Note on CVC and CVCV

It is often facilitative to work on CVC and CVCV together to draw attention to the C2 position (the typical locus of difficulty). To focus attention more precisely on the moraic structure of the words, use words with short *lax vowels* in the stressed syllable. Lax vowels have only one mora, but English syllables require two moras, and thus *a coda consonant is required.*

The CVCV word appears to have two obvious beats (one for each vowel), but, according to moraic theory, CVC also has two beats, one for the V and one for the second consonant. By tapping the two obvious beats of CVCV and then the two less obvious beats of VC in CVC, attention is drawn to the importance of C2 of CVC (e.g., *Mi-ckey* as two claps, but, alternatively, *Mi-ck* as two claps).

Activities that remove the vowel from CVCV, or add it back to CVC, also emphasize the importance of the C2 and the relationship between the two word shapes.

Scenario: Missy, the letter carrier, is walking along carrying a mailbag with her name on it. Whoops, the *y* falls off of her mailbag into a hole, leaving *Miss* with only part of her name. She "*misses* her y," because without it, her name is only half there. She goes back searching for it. "Y,* where are you? I miSS you." Y calls, "Missy, here I am. Miss, see?" When she finds it, there is great rejoicing as the *y* and *Miss* are reunited.

*pronounced /i/

11.4. The Phrase

Phrasal (sentence)-level restrictions are usually described in syntactic or morphological terms. However, grouping of words into intonation contours may result in further restrictions on output (see Chapter 10). Phrasally unstressed words may be particularly susceptible to omission when children have phonological encoding difficulties.

Sample Intervention Targets at the Sentence or Phrase Level:

- production of words in phrases, first in stressed positions and then in unstressed positions, with gradual increase in length and complexity of syntactic structure

- production of a given consonant-consonant or consonant-vowel sequence in single words first, then across words, or vice versa (see Roland's data, Chapter 8)

General strategies for intervention for grammatical morphemes are as follows.

1. **Prominent phrasal positions:** First put the problematic grammatical morpheme in a stressed phrasal position, such as sentence-final position, a tag question, or somewhere with contrastive emphasis.

A pronoun: The girl is nice, isn't *she*?
The verb *be:* I wonder where it *is.*
An article: Not *a* dog, *the* dog.

2. **In Sw sequences:** Next, create Strong-weak sequences in which the problematic grammatical morpheme is in an *expected* and easily pronounced Strong-weak sequence, instead of being the weak syllable in a more difficult weak-Strong sequence (the final type of phrase to accommodate an unstressed grammatical morpheme, as in the example with the article *the* below). Use rhythm and visual cueing to support the alternation of strong and weak syllables.

FIRST USE: [Hit *the*] [big ba][lloon].

                       S w   s w   S

NOT: *The* [yellow ba][nana is] [big].

                w   S w   w   S w w   S

3. **Songs and story choruses:** The rhythm of a song or chorus offers opportunities to emphasize grammatical morphemes by giving active beats to all the syllables.

GOAL: Production of *do* in questions.

SONG: /What/—/do you do/—/with a/—/si//lly/ /sai//lor/?

8-BEAT RHYTHM: 1   2 and 3   4 and   5 6 7 8

11.5. Segmental Goals

All usable techniques apply to facilitating production of new segments. As with other phonological approaches, implications of nonlinear theory suggest targeting groups of segments that have the target feature in common (the category of "fricatives" or "velars" or "voiced" segments). Facilitative contexts for segment production are also suggested because of the interaction between segments that share features. Thus, velars may be targeted with back vowels; or the first clusters might share place, e.g., /st/ or /sn/. Phonetic tendencies are taken into consideration when choosing word positions in which to target new segments (providing that the child is capable of producing some segment in a given word position). Thus, voiceless obstruents *tend* to be easier to articulate word-finally than voiced obstruents, whereas voiced obstruents tend to be easier to articulate prevocalically or intervocalically. Fricatives, nasals, and velars are often easier to produce word-finally.

Successive approximation is a long-used technique for helping someone learn to pronounce a new speech sound. The concept of segments as feature combinations suggests strategies for successive approximation, such as in the examples that follow.

1. **Combining [+continuant] with oral articulation (getting fricatives from [h]):** When a child can produce [h] but no fricatives, fricatives can be taught

with the [+spread glottis] and [+continuant] [h] as a starting point. With the airstream of [h] and different occluding positions of the tongue, lips, and teeth, oral place fricatives can result. Possible analogies: air rushing through a "tunnel" (the mouth), with its narrow points trapping the air and making little storms; water running over rocks, creating turbulent rapids, etc.

2. **Combining [+continuant] with Laryngeal for [h] (getting [h] from fricatives):** If a child already has an oral place fricative, the obstructions of the oral cavity can be lifted to allow for smooth airflow ([h]). The tunnel can be cleared to let the storms pass and calm wind to escape, or the canoe can come into calm waters without rapids.

3. **Combining [+continuant] with [−sonorant] (getting fricatives from vowels):** If a child has only sonorant [+continuant] sounds (vowels, glides), making the high front vowel voiceless (whispering) will lead to production of a palatal fricative [ç], which can be shaped into [ʃ] or [s] or [h].

4. **Combining [+spread glottis] of [h] with initial stops to produce aspirated stops:** By rapidly repeating a word like *hot* or *hop,* an aspirated stop can result:

hop hop hop[ʰ] > [pʰɑp]

5. **Moving from /r/ to /l/ or /l/ to /r/:** By retracting an [l], an [r] can result. Similarly, by moving an [r] forward, an [l] can result. Words that can be useful for this strategy include, e.g., *wheeler dealer, gir-l, poo-r l-amb, ca-r l-ot.*

6. **Moving from labiodental to coronal fricatives or vice versa:** If stops are already produced at the targeted place of articulation, there is already some experience with that place of articulation. What is needed is a combination of place and a new manner.

From [f] to [s]: Raise the tongue for /t/, articulate [f], and let go of the labiodental articulation. When oral air pressure is maintained, air will escape as [s].

7. **Making glides from vowels:** By rapidly articulating a vowel sequence, glides will intervene naturally as onsets, as in creation of [w] from /u/:

/u/ > [w] through alternations: [a u a u au] > Wow!

11.6. Final Comments

Theories will continue to change as they always do, but we believe that many concepts presented in this book will be valid for clinical application for some time to come. One of the exciting parts of the clinical application of theory is the inventive aspect. The forms used for analysis and the therapy strategies presented here are our suggestions. Readers may (and are encouraged to) create better forms and new therapy strategies and techniques. We hope that what we have presented here will be a springboard for such creativity.

IPA Symbols Used in This Book

		bilabial		labio-dental		dental/alveolar		retro-flex		palato-alveolar		alveo-palatal		palatal		velar		uvular		pharyn-geal		glottal		labio-velar	
		vcls	vcd	vcls	vcd	vcls	vcd	vcls	vcd	vcls	vcd	vcls	vcd	vcls	vcd	vcls	vcd	vcls	vcd	vcls	vcd	vcls	vcd	vcls	vcd
stop	oral	p	b			t	d	ʈ	ɖ					c	ɟ	k	g	q				ʔ			
	nasal		m		ɱ		n		ɳ		ɲ				ɲ		ŋ		ɴ							
fricative	grooved					s	z	ʂ	ʐ	ʃ	ʒ														
	ungrooved					θ	ð					ɕ	ʑ	ç	ʝ										
	noncoronal	ɸ	β	f	v											x	ɣ	χ	ʁ	ħ	ʕ	h			
affricate						ts	dz			tʃ	dʒ	tɕ	dʑ												
glide					ʋ				ɹ						j		ɰ								w
lateral	liquid						l		ɭ						ʎ										
	fricative					ɬ	ɮ																		
"r"	trill		ʙ				r												ʀ						
	tap/flap						ɾ																		

Unrounded Vowels

	front	central	back
HIGH	i	ɨ	ɯ
	ɪ		
MID	e	ə	ɤ
	ɛ	ʌ	
LOW	æ		
	a	ɑ	ɒ

Rounded Vowels

	front	central	back
HIGH	y	ʉ	u
	ʏ		ʊ
MID	ø	ɵ	o
	œ		ɔ
LOW	ɶ		ɔ

Diacritics

aspirated:	Cʰ	dental:	C̪
voiceless/unvoiced:	x̥	rounded:	ɹ̹
unreleased:	C˺	palatized:	Cʲ
syllabic:	C̩	labiovelarized:	Cʷ
nasalized:	x̃	long:	x:
retracted:	xˤ	raised:	x̂
advanced:	x›	lowered:	x̌
		lateralized:	Cˡ

Appendix B
Answers to Exercises

Chapter 1

1.

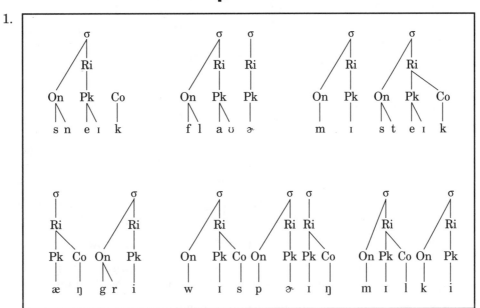

Figure B.1. Answers to Chapter 2, question 1.

2. (ɑ, u) (w, r) l (n, m) v (s, θ) g (p, t) (ties in parentheses)

3. smile: /s/   task: none   plunk: none
   glance: none   stroll: /s/   sphinx: initial /s/ *and* final /s/

4. carry   buckle   coffee   city

5. a. no problem

   b. problem: initial /sk/
      repairs: deletion   ([suːt]/[kuːt])
                  epenthesis   ([səkuːt])

   c. problem: initial syllable
      repair: epenthesis   ([ʔɑɪsi]/[hɑɪsi]/[wɑɪsi], etc.)

   d. problem: final /sk/
      repairs: deletion   ([æ])
                  epenthesis   ([æsəkə])   *unlikely*
                  movement   ([skæ])   *unlikely*

    e. problem: /sw/
        repairs: deletion   ([sɪŋ]/[wɪŋ])

e. problem: /sw/
  repairs: deletion ([sɪŋ]/[wɪŋ])
     coalescence ([fɪŋ])
     epenthesis ([səwɪŋ])
     make syllabic ([.su.ɪŋ.]) *unlikely*
     movement ([.sɪʊŋ.]) *unlikely*

f. problem: second syllable lacks onset
  repairs: syllable deletion ([ʃaʊ])
     epenthesis ([ʃaʊdɚ])
     lengthening ([ʃaʊwɚ])
     make nonsyllabic ([.ʃaʊr.]) *unlikely*

6. Sw wS Sww Sww
  wSw Sw Sw wS
  Sww Sw wSww wSw

7. a. constraint: no wS
   repair: delete initial weak syllable

  b. none

  c. constraint: no Sww
   repair: delete first unstressed syllable

8. s | Sww   S | s   Sw | sw   S | sw
  sw | Sww Sw | sw Sw | sw wS | s
  Sw | s   sw | Sw Sw | sw sw | S

9. .CV.CVC. .CVC.CV. .CCVVC. .CV.CVVC.CV. .CVVC.CV.CVVC.
  .CV.CV. .CCVV.CV.V. .CVC.CVC. .CVC.   .CVV.

10. fin   —no coda, but stranded timing unit lengthens vowel

  feet   —only two moras per syllable, but [fiːt] has three moras
        —delete one of the moras of the vowel, thereby shortening it

  ketchup—stressed syllables should be heavy
        —to make the first syllable heavy, insert a mora
        —insert the second half of a diphthong to fill the new mora

Chapter 2

1. a. +sonorant,−consonantal,+continuant,+voiced,Dorsal,−high

  b. −sonorant,+consonantal,−nasal,+voiced,−s.g.,−c.g.,Coronal

  c. +sonorant,−consonantal,+continuant,+voiced,Labial,+round,Dorsal,+back

  d. +continuant,−nasal

  e. −nasal,+voiced,−s.g.,−c.g.,Dorsal,+high,−low

2. a. [u]—[+high,(+tense)]

  b. [w]—[Labial,+back]   [æ]—[+low,(−tense)]

  c. [u]—[+round]   [k]—[−voiced]   [b]—[−back]   [ɑ]—[+low]

  d. [p]—[Labial]   [t]—[+anterior]   [tʃ]—[−anterior,+grooved]
    [g]—[Dorsal,+voiced]

e. [n]—[+nasal,−continuant]   [l]—[+lateral]   [w]—[Dorsal]
   [ɫ]—[−sonorant]   [r]—[−anterior]

f. [m]—[+nasal,−labiodental]   [d]—[−distributed]
   [v]—[+labiodental]   [ʃ]—[−anterior,+grooved]

g. [s]—[+grooved,+anterior]   [e]—[−high,−back]
   [g]—[+high,+back]   [m]—[+nasal,Labial]
   [h]−(has no place features)

3. a. Labial, /v/
   > ∅Labial Coronal,+anterior,−distributed,+grooved [z]
   (*Note:* ∅ means the feature is irrelevant for that segment and hence is
   neither [+] nor [−].)

   b. Labial, [+high], [−low] /u/ > ∅Labial−high,+low [ɑ] (?tense?)

   c. −nasal > +nasal

   d. +lateral, etc., /l/ > −consonantal,−lateral,−anterior,+distributed,
      Dorsal,−back,+high,− low [j]

   e. −consonantal, etc., /w/ > −sonorant,+consonantal,−continuant,
      −round,0Dorsal [b]

   f. −continuant, etc., /k/ > +sonorant,−consonantal,+continuant,
      0Dorsal [h]

   g. −tense /ʊ/ > +tense [u]

   h. −distributed, +grooved /s/ > +distributed,−grooved [θ]

   i. −nasal, etc., /k/ > +sonorant,+nasal,+voiced [ŋ] (−tense)

4. a. Labial, −labiodental, +sonorant
   b. none
   c. Dorsal, +back
   d. +continuant, −nasal
   e. Coronal, +sonorant
   f. All features are the same.
   g. −sonorant, −nasal
   h. +continuant, −nasal

5. a. [oʊ]   delete consonant
      [doʊ]   delete [+nasal,+sonorant]   (faithful to [−continuant,−lateral])
      [loʊ]   delete [+nasal,−continuant,−lateral]   (faithful to [+sonorant])

   b. [ʊt]   delete consonant
      [sʊt]   delete [Labial]   (faithful in that still has [Place])
      [hʊt]   delete [Place]   (has no nontarget place features)

   c. [aʊs]   delete /m/
      [naʊs]   delete [Labial]   (faithful to [+nasal])
      [baʊs]   delete [+nasal]   (faithful to [Labial])
      [naʊf]   [Labial] migrates to another segment
      [baʊn]   [+nasal] migrates to another segment

   d. [aɪ]   delete consonant
      [haɪ]   delete [Place]
      [jaɪ]   delete [Labial]   (insert [Coronal])
      [vaɪ]   delete [−consonantal]   (insert [+consonantal, −sonorant])

6. a. calf: k → t   substitution   [Dorsal] → [Coronal]
                                     nondefault → default   *expected*

   b. mud: d → t   substitution   [+voiced] → [−voiced]
                                     nondefault → default   *expected*

              m → b   ?substitution [+nasal] → [−nasal]
                                     nondefault → default   *expected*

                      ?assimilation   *not expected*

   c. pen: n → t   ?substitution [+nasal] → [−nasal]
                                     nondefault → default   *expected*

                      ?assimilation   *not expected*

   d. muddy: d → b   assimilation   [Coronal] → [Labial]
                                     default → nondefault   *expected*

   e. down: d → n   assimilation   [−nasal] → [+nasal]
                                     default → nondefault   *expected*

   f. corn: k → t   ?substitution [Dorsal] → [Coronal]
                                     nondefault → default   *expected*

                      ?assimilation   *not expected*

   g. fish: f → b   substitution   [+cont] → [−cont]
                                     nondefault → default   *expected*

                                     [−voiced] → [+voiced]
                                     default → nondefault   *not expected*

                                     [+s.g.] → [−s.g.]
                                     nondefault → default   *expected*

              ʃ → t   substitution   [+cont] → [−cont]
                                     nondefault → default   *expected*

                                     [−anterior] → [+anterior]
                                     nondefault → default   *expected*

                                     [+grooved] → [−grooved]
                                     nondefault → default   *expected*

   h. movie: m → v   assimilation   [+nasal] → [−nasal]
                                     nondefault → default   *not expected*

                                     [−cont] → [+cont]
                                     default → nondefault   *expected*

Chapter 3

1. a. rʌ   rʌp   rʌbə   rʌr   bʌb   brʌ
   b. əræf   ʔəræf   rəræf   ʤəʤæf
   c. ɛs   sɛs   dɛs   nɛs   .iɛ̬s.
   d. ɛd   tʰɛd   sɛd   dɛ
   e. teɪ   teɪt   teɪkə   keɪk

2. a. not adjacent on C-plane, but adjacent because there is no token of [Labial] between them

    b. adjacent on the C-plane, but not adjacent on the timing unit plane

    c. not adjacent by any definition because separated by a very different consonant

3. a. teɪ ~ eɪk   teɪt   keɪk   keɪt
    b. ir   wir ~ lir ~ zir ~ (etc.)   jer
    c. mʌni ~ bʌdi   bʌji ~ bʌhi ~ (etc.)   .bʌ.i.
    d. tɑɪs ~ wɑɪs ~ (etc.)   pɑɪs   tɑɪf ~ tɑʊs ~ tɔɪs   təwɑɪs

Chapter 10

1. —same for singleton /d/, /rd/, nasal-voiceless stop (all possible sequences)

    —different for stop-stop, fricative-stop, nasal-voiced stop (all impossible sequences)

    Simple: C2 deleted. Result: no cluster in coda.

    Past tense: -ed doubled. Result: no cluster in coda, cluster split between syllables (e.g., [.wak.təd.]).

ℛ φ ω ʾ
ɑ̣ᶜ ɓ ̊ ꜰ
λ ᶜ ᶰ ɓ

Appendix C
Data Sets for Extra Practice

Word Length, Word Shape

Jeremy: Age 3-4. Mean length of utterance, Brown's Stage I; average language comprehension. (Bernhardt, 1990; Bernhardt & Gilbert, 1992; Bernhardt & Stemberger, 1998.)

	Adult	**Child (I = Imitated)**
mom	mᴧ̃m	mᴧ̃m
mommy	mᴧ̃mi	mᴧ̃mi
monkey	mᴧ̃ŋki	mᴧ̃ɲɪs (I), mᴧ̃ɪ
no	noʊ	noʔ
present	pʰrɛzn̩t	pʰɛs (I)
banana	bənænə	nᴅ̃ə (I)
bib	bɪb	bɪs (I)
combing	kʰoʊmĩŋ	komĩn (I)
go	goʊ	goʊ
finger	fĩŋgɚ	fɪs (I)
fun	fᴧ̃n	fᴧ̃n
funny	fᴧ̃ni	fᴧɪ/faɪ (6 times); fᴧ̃n (Pause) ni (once)
screwdriver	skru:draɪvɚ	nũwᴧəʃ (I)
sleeping	sli:pĩŋ	mɪs, beɪsˀ (I)
rabbit	ræbət	wɛɪs (I)
radio	reɪdioʊ	wɪsˀ
happy	hæpi:	ʔæpi: (4)

Hints: Pay attention to the default [s] coda and the word reduction.

Stress Patterns

	Adult	**Child**
apple	ˈæpl̩	æˈpʊ:
open	ˈopn̩	oˈpɚn
monkey	ˈmᴧ̃ŋki:	mᴧ̃ŋˈki:
picture	ˈpɪkʃɚ	pɪkˈʃɚ

elephant	'ɛləfn̩t	ɛəˈfɪnt ˈɪt
banana	bəˈnænə	ˌnæˈnɑː
potato	pʰəˈtʰeɾo	ˌtʰetʰeˈtʰoː
dinosaur	ˈdɑɪnəˌsɔr	nɑɪˌnɪsˈhɔr
octopus	ˈɑktəˌpʊs	ɑˌpʌˈpɪs ~ ˌɑpɪtˈpɪs
telephone	ˈtɛləˌfon	tɛˌvʌˈhʌm
alligator	ˈæləˌgeɾɚ	ɛˈdɝ ~ hɑˌdʌ.ʌˈdɝː
helicopter	ˈhɛləˌkɑptɚ	ˌkʰæˈtʰɝ
chimpanzee	ˌtʃɪmpænˈziː	ˌtʰɪmtʰiˈtʰiː
kangaroo	ˌkæŋgəˈruː	kʌˌwɑˈoː ~ ˌkɔɪjəˈoː
avocado	ˌævəˈkʰɑɾo	ˌkʰædæˈdɒː
Cinderella	ˌsɪndəˈɛlə	ˌlɑˈblɑː ~ hɛˌlɑbəˈlɑ

Source: M. Kehoe, 1995, 254–264.

Clusters

Serena: Age 4-6. Average language comprehension and production; severe phonological disorder.

	Adult	Child
plum	pʰlʌ̃m	plʌ̃m
pretend	pʰriːtɛ̃nd	pitɛ̃æ̃
black	blæk	plæ̃
brushing	brʌʃĩŋ	plʌʔhĩ
tractor	tʰræktɚ	bɛʔɔ̃
truck	tʰrʌk	fæː
clown	kʰlãʊn	saʊ̃ː
crayons	kʰreɪ(j)ã:nz	faɪjã:
quiet	kʰwaɪ(j)ət	faɪɛ
glasses	glæsəz	sæ̃ʔɛ̃
growl	graʊl	gaɪɛ̃
flying	flaɪ(j)ĩŋ	faɪɛ
frog	frɑːg	fwɑː
three	θriː	fiː
smooth	smuːð	muː
snow	snoʊ	noʊː
spoon	spũːn	fũː
sticker	stɪkɚ	gɪʔɬ
scarf	skarf	goã:
screwdriver	skruːdraɪvɚ	fufaɛə
sleeping	sliːpĩŋ	ʂĩpɛ̃
sweater	swɛɾɚ	fæʔʔɛə

Hints: Compare deletion, segment substitution, and coalescence patterns.

Consonant-Consonant and Consonant-Vowel Sequence Constraints

Livia: Age 5-11. Severe phonological disorder; reduced phrase length; average to above average comprehension; slight sensorineural high-frequency hearing loss. (Holdgrafer, MacFarlane, & Bernhardt, 1996.)

	Adult	**Child**
machine	məʃiːn	tʰĩːn
me	miː	miː
pig	pʰɪg	pɪd
plum	pʰlʌ̃m	pʌ̃m
boot	buːt	buːt
teeth	tʰiːθ	tiːt
TV	tʰiːviː	tiːdiː
toothbrush	tʰuːθbrʌʃ	tubʌtʰ
doll	dɑːl	gɑː
cake	kʰeɪk	keɪt
coffee	kʰɑfiː	kɑtiː
cook	kʰʊk	kʊk
cup	kʰʌp	kʌt, kʌk
key	kʰiː	t̪iː
feather	fɛðɚ	pɛd̪æ
soap	soʊp	kot
shoe	ʃuː	tuː

Hints: [Coronal]-[Dorsal] place interactions for vowels and consonants. [Labial] constraints for consonants.

Appendix D
Nonlinear Scan Analysis Form

Nonlinear Scan Analysis

$$\boxed{\text{Page 1}}$$

Identifying and Summary Information

Date of scan analysis _____ Date of sample (if different from scan) _____

Child's name _____ Child's birthdate _____

Caregiver names _____

Address _____ Phone number _____

Other biographical information: _____

_____

_____

General communication needs: _____

_____

_____

Goal order from summary sheet: _____

_____

_____

Referrals: _____

_____

_____

Treatment schedule: _____

_____

_____

Bird's-Eye View: 5-Minute Checklist

Segments (Phonemes)

Consonant sound classes in sample: (Circle if present; use parentheses to indicate limited numbers)

Stops, nasals, fricatives, liquids, glides

Labials, coronals [dentals, alveolars, palatoalveolars], velars

Voiced/voiceless

Missing sound classes from above: _____

Major segmental substitution patterns: _____

_____

_____

Vowels

Substitutions:

Defaults:

Diphthongs:

Analysis needed: ☐ Yes   ☐ No
(See final page of scan)

Syllable and Word Structure

Syllables added to words: ☐ Yes   ☐ No   If yes, ☐ Often ☐ Seldom

Syllables missing from words: ☐ Yes   ☐ No   If yes, ☐ Often ☐ Seldom

Patterns specific to a given word position:

General omission: ☐ Initial   ☐ Medial   ☐ Final

Reduced clusters: ☐ Initial   ☐ Medial   ☐ Final

Position-based substitution
    pattern: ☐ Initial   ☐ Medial   ☐ Final

Other General Observations

Unusual prosody: ☐ Yes   ☐ No

Unusual oral–motor characteristics: ☐ Yes   ☐ No

Variability

Same word: ☐ Yes   ☐ No   If yes, ☐ Often ☐ Seldom

Same speech sounds: ☐ Yes   ☐ No   If yes, ☐ Often ☐ Seldom

Assimilation/metathesis (Possible sequence constraints): ☐ Yes   ☐ No

Proceed to scan, doing relevant sections. No or minimal counting.

Syllable and Word Structure Analysis

Unusual prosodic factors? (circle) pitch, voice/resonance, duration, rate, rhythm, intonation, loudness

	Word Length	Stress Patterns	Word Shapes
Basic inventory	1 syllable 2 syllables 3 syllables 4 syllables Other:	Sw Ss Sww Sws Ssw wS wSw swS Other:	V(V) (C)V(V)CV(V) V(V)C CV(V)CV(V)C CV(V) CV(V)CCV(V)C CV(V)C Other: (C)VCC CCV(V)(C)
Matches by category	1 syllable 2 syllables 3 syllables 4 syllables Other:	Sw Ss Sww Sws Ssw wS wSw swS Other:	V(V) (C)V(V)CV(V) V(V)C CV(V)CV(V)C CV(V) CV(V)CCV(V)C CV(V)C Other: (C)VCC CCV(V)(C)
Child's maximum			
Child's most frequent	1 2 Both Other:	Sw Other:	V(V) CVC CV(V) CVCV Other:
Child's developing forms (some matches)	2 syllables 3 syllables 4 syllables	wS Other:	CV(V) CVC CVCV CCV(V) (C)VCC CVCVC Other:

Comparison with adult targets	Syllables missing?
	
	Syllables added?
		Missing:
		    Weak syllables
		    Strong syllables
		Stress shift?
		
		Equal stress?
		
		Segments differ on repetition of multisyllable words?
			Missing C's:
			    WF WI SIWW SFWW
			    Clusters
			[?] or Glide for C:
			Missing V's:
			    Diphthong
			    WF WI Medial
			Added C's:
			Added V's:

Context differences? Spontaneous vs. imitated Single word vs. phrases			
Need to count? What?	Variable?	Variable?	Variable?
Other data needed? What?			
Needs? (Add to Goal Summary page, Goal 1, page 7)			

Consonant Analysis

Overuse? (circle) labial, dental, alveolar, palatal, velar, lateral, nasal, uvular, pharyngeal, glottal, other

Phonetic inventory: First 2 rows. List non-English phones also. **Substitutions:** On row for the specific feature.

Feature	Adult Targets	Word-Initial	Medial, Syllable-Final	Medial, Syllable-Initial	Word-Final
[+consonantal] inventory	All but glides below				
[−consonantal] inventory	ʔ h w j r				
[+lateral]	l				
[+nasal]	m n ŋ				
[−continuant]	p t k b d g ʔ m n ŋ				
[+continuant] (&[−sonorant])	f v s z θ ð ʃ ʒ				
[−continuant]-[+continuant]	ʧ ʤ				

Manner Default Summary: Expected: [−cont], [−nasal]; [−cons] for /l/   Other:

Feature	Adult Targets	Word-Initial	Medial, Syllable-Final	Medial, Syllable-Initial	Word-Final
[+voiced] obstruents	b d g v z ð ʒ ʤ				
[−voiced] obstruents	p t k f s θ ʃ ʧ				
[+spread glottis]	h; Asp. stops; (vl. fricatives)				

Laryngeal Default Summary: Expected: [−voiced]   Other: ʔ or h default:

Feature	Adult Targets	Word-Initial	Medial, Syllable-Final	Medial, Syllable-Initial	Word-Final
Labial	p b m f v w				
Coronal [+anterior]	t d n l s z θ ð				
Coronal [−anterior]	ʃ ʒ ʧ ʤ j r				
Coronal [+grooved]	s z ʃ ʒ ʧ ʤ				
Coronal [−grooved]	θ ð				
Dorsal	k g ŋ (w) (j)				
Coronal & Labial	r				

Place Default Summary: Expected: Coronal [+anterior]; [+grooved]   Other:

Variable? (circle) Spontaneous/imitated?   Connected/single words?   Same word?   Same C?
Count what?   **Data needed?**

168

Consonant Analysis: Summary

Feature	Summary of Substitutions (from page 4)	Goal Type 2: Feature Marginal or Not Used at All	Goal Type 3: Feature Marginal or Not Used in Specific Feature Combinations*
[+consonantal]			
[−consonantal]			
[+lateral]			
[+nasal]			
[−continuant]			
[+continuant] (&[−sonorant])			
[−continuant]-[+continuant]			

Manner Defaults Needing Change:

[+voiced] obstruents			
[−voiced] obstruents			
[+spread glottis]			

Laryngeal Defaults Needing Change:

Labial			
Coronal [+anterior]			
Coronal [−anterior]			
Coronal [+grooved]			
Coronal [−grooved]			
Dorsal			
Coronal & Labial			

Place Defaults Needing Change:

*See box at top of page 6

Go to Goal Summary page and enter feature data.

Goal Type 2: New features—has no or marginal use of a feature. List strong and missing individual features.

Goal Type 3: New simultaneous combinations of features: **Has some segments within a sound class but not all (uses both features in *other* segments).** List strong and needed feature combinations. **Focus on nondefaults.**

Goal Type 1: Pick strong segments to make new word shapes. List those in Segments to Use in New Structures cell in the Goal 1 column.

Goal Type 4: Word Position and Sequence

A. Inventory of segment and feature classes missing *in a given word position (but occurring elsewhere).*

Word-Initial	Medial: Syllable-Initial	Medial: Syllable-Final	Word-Final

B. Sequences of segments and features: Check between-word variability, assimilation, and metathesis for clues to sequence constraints (Circle or give examples)

Consonant Assimilation (top > [pɑp]) **OR Dissimilation** (tot > [tɑp])	**Coalescence (fusion)** (/tr/ > [f])	**Epenthesis** (tray > [təweɪ])
		Metathesis (fish > [ʃɪf]) **OR Migration** (cup > [pʌ])
	CV Assimilation (bee > [di]; do > [bu]) **OR Dissimilation** (boo > [du])	**Other Patterns**

Clusters Produced: (circle matches)

Missing Clusters: (compared with adult targets)*

Cross-V Sequences Produced: (Circle those produced. Put checkmarks over ones that match targets.)

    Lab-Lab, Cor-Cor, Dors-Dors, Lab-Cor, Cor-Lab, Lab-Dors, Dors-Lab, Cor-Dors, Dors-Cor; nonnasal-nasal; other

Missing Cross-V Sequences: (compared with adult targets) (circle)

    Lab-Lab, Cor-Cor, Dors-Dors, Lab-Cor, Cor-Lab, Lab-Dors, Dors-Lab, Cor-Dors, Dors-Cor; nonnasal-nasal; other

Context Differences for (A) or (B): Spontaneous/imitated? Connected/single word? For same word? For same C?
Need to count?   **What?**
Other data needed:

*Cluster substitutions can be noted here (e.g., /pl/ > [pw])

Go to Goal Summary page: List both *position* and *sequence* strengths and needs.

Goal Summary

Level	Syllable and Word Structure		Features and Segments	
Goal Type	**Goal Type 1** Structure	**Goal Type 4** Word Position and Sequences	**Goal Type 2** Individual Features	**Goal Type 3** Feature Combinations
Strengths	Word length Stress patterns Word shapes	Segment and feature classes by word position Sequences		Manner-Laryngeal Manner-Place Place-Laryngeal
Needs	Word length Stress patterns Word shapes	Word position Sequences		Manner-Laryngeal Manner-Place Place-Laryngeal Place-Place
Strengths To Use To Support Needs	Segments to use for structure goals	Segments to use for structure goals	Word shapes to use for feature goals	Word shapes to use for feature goals
Interactions (prosody, perception, morphology, motor)				
Social Factors				
Immediate Goals				
Treatment Strategies				
Goal # in Program (order)				

Vowel Needs (from page 8):

Notes on Goal Selection

1. Give high weight to social factors: child/caregiver concerns, motivation, attention, scheduling, and so on.

2. Consider interactions with other parts of the linguistic, perceptual, and motor systems.

3. Consider all aspects of the phonological system. Although a child may not have needs in all areas, knowing strengths helps in strategy development. For the first period of intervention (4–8 weeks), choose about three to four major goals, with a balance between word structure and feature goals, and between "old stuff" to be used in new ways and completely "new stuff." Developmental "norms" and immediate stimulability are not necessarily critical factors for goal selection.

4. A general rule of thumb is to target new segments in old word positions and new word positions or shapes with old segments. However, sometimes a child tolerates or needs the introduction of a new feature into a totally new word position or shape. For some children velars and fricatives (new features) are easiest in word-final position and may be useful segments to help consolidate (C)VC (word shape goal) if targeted word-finally first.

Vowels

(Circle occurring ones. Put checkmarks over matches.)

i ɪ e ɪ ɛ æ a ʌ ə ɚ ɝ u ʊ o oʊ ɔ ɑ ɔɪ aʊ aɪ   Other:

Vowel Features

[+tense]: i, u, e, o

[−tense]: ɪ, ɛ, ʌ, ə, ʊ

[+low]: a, æ, ɑ, (ɔ)

[−back] (Coronal-Dorsal): i, ɪ, e, ɛ, æ, a

[+back] (Dorsal only): u, ʊ, ɔ, o, ʌ, ə

[+high]: i, ɪ, u, ʊ

[+round] (Labial-Dorsal): u, ʊ, ɔ, o

[−high], [−low]: ɛ, ʌ, ə, o, ɔ, e

Note: For diphthongs, see features for each part of the diphthong. Tenseness is unclear for low vowels in English.

Vowel feature inventory:

Vowel feature matches:

Individual vowel feature needs:

Vowel feature combination needs:

Any CV interactions noted on page 6?

172

References

Bernhardt, B. (1990). *Application of nonlinear phonological theory to intervention with six phonologically disordered children.* Unpublished doctoral dissertation, University of British Columbia, Vancouver, Canada.

Bernhardt, B. (1992). The application of nonlinear phonological theory to intervention with one phonologically disordered child. *Clinical Linguistics and Phonetics, 6,* 283–316.

Bernhardt, B. (1994a). Phonological intervention techniques for syllable and word structure development. *Clinics in Communication Disorders, 4,* 54–65.

Bernhardt, B. (1994b). The prosodic tier and phonological disorders. In M. Yavaş (Ed.), *First and second language phonology* (pp. 149–172). San Diego, CA: Singular Publishing Group.

Bernhardt, B., & Gilbert, J. (1992). Applying linguistic theory to speech–language pathology: The case for non-linear phonology. *Clinical Linguistics and Phonetics, 6,* 123–145.

Bernhardt, B., Major, E., & Stemberger, J. P. (1996, November). Effects of consonant intervention on vowel systems in disordered phonology. Poster presented at the American Speech-Language Hearing Association convention, Seattle, WA.

Bernhardt, B., Ruelle, H., Edwards, S., Haynes, T., & Major, E. (1997). *Nonlinear phonological therapy manual.* Unpublished manuscript.

Bernhardt, B. H., & Stemberger, J. P. (1998). *Handbook of phonological development: From the perspective of constraint–based nonlinear phonology.* San Diego, CA: Academic Press.

Bernthal, J., & Bankson, N. (1998). *Articulation and phonological disorders* (4th ed.). Englewood Cliffs, NJ: Prentice-Hall.

Bopp, K. D. (1995). *The effects of phonological intervention on morphosyntactic development in preschool children with phonological and morphosyntactic disorders.* Unpublished master's thesis, University of British Columbia, Vancouver, Canada.

Davis, B., & MacNeilage, P. (1990). Acquisition of correct vowel production: A quantitative case study. *Journal of Speech and Hearing Research, 33,* 16–27.

Dinnsen, D. A. (1996). Context effects in the acquisition of fricatives. In B. Bernhardt, J. Gilbert, & D. Ingram (Eds.), *Proceedings of the UBC international conference on phonological acquisition* (pp. 136–148). Somerville, MA: Cascadilla Press.

Donahue, M. (1986). Phonological constraints on the emergence of two-word utterances. *Journal of Child Language, 13,* 209–218.

Edwards, M. L. (1996). Word position effects in the production of fricatives. In B. Bernhardt, J. Gilbert, & D. Ingram (Eds.), *Proceedings of the UBC international conference on phonological acquisition* (pp. 149–158). Somerville, MA: Cascadilla Press.

Edwards, S. M. (1995). *Optimal outcomes of nonlinear phonological intervention.* Unpublished master's thesis, University of British Columbia, Vancouver, Canada.

Gerken, L. (1991). The metrical basis for children's subjectless sentences. *Journal of Memory and Language, 30,* 431–451.

Gierut, J. (1996). An experimental test of phonemic cyclicity. *Journal of Child Language, 23,* 81–102.

Gierut, J. A., Cho, M.-H., & Dinnsen, D. (1993). Geometric accounts of consonant–vowel interactions in developing systems. *Clinical Linguistics and Phonetics, 7,* 219–236.

Grunwell, P. (1985). *Phonological assessment of child speech.* San Diego, CA: College-Hill Press.

Hayes, B. (1989). Compensatory lengthening in moraic phonology. *Linguistic Inquiry, 20,* 253–306.

Hockett, C. (1955). A manual of phonology. *International Journal of American Linguistics, 41*(4), part 1. Memoir 11.

Holdgrafer, G., MacFarlane, L., & Bernhardt, B. (1996). University of Alberta Phonology Project database. Unpublished manuscript, University of Alberta, Edmonton, Alberta, Canada.

Ingram, D. (1974). Fronting in child phonology. *Journal of Child Language, 1,* 49–64.

Ingram, D., Christensen, L., Veach, S., & Webster, B. (1980). The acquisition of word-initial fricatives and affricates in English by children between 2 and 6 years. In G. Yeni-Komshian, J. F. Kavanagh, & C. A. Ferguson (Eds.), *Child phonology: Vol. 1. Production* (pp. 169–191). New York: Academic Press.

International Phonetics Association. (1989). Report on the Kiel Convention. *Journal of the International Phonetics Association, 19,* 67–80.

Kehoe, M. (1995). *An investigation of rhythmic processes in English-speaking children's word production.* Unpublished doctoral dissertation, University of Washington, Seattle.

Lowe, R. (1996). *Workbook for the identification of phonological processes* (2nd ed.). Austin, TX: Pro-Ed.

Major, E., & Bernhardt, B. H. (1998). Metaphonological skills of children with phonological disorders before and after phonological and metaphonological intervention. *International Journal of Language and Communication Disorders, 33,* 413–444.

Matthei, E. (1989). Crossing boundaries: More evidence for phonological constraints on early multi-word utterances. *Journal of Child Language, 16,* 41–54.

Menn, L. (1975). Counter example to "fronting" as a universal in child phonology. *Journal of Child Language, 2,* 293–296.

Otomo, K., & Stoel-Gammon, C. (1992). The acquisition of unrounded vowels in English. *Journal of Speech and Hearing Research, 35,* 604–616.

Pollock, K. (1994). Assessment and remediation of vowel misarticulations. *Clinics in Communication Disorders, 4,* 23–37.

Smit, A., Hand, L., Freilinger, J. J., Bernthal, J. E., & Bird, A. (1990). The Iowa articulation norms project and its Nebraska replication. *Journal of Speech and Hearing Disorders, 55,* 779–798.

Stemberger, J. P. (1992). Vocalic underspecification in English language production. *Language, 68,* 492–524.

Stemberger, J. P., & Bernhardt, B. H. (1997). Optimality Theory. In M. Ball & R. Kent (Eds.), *The new phonologies* (pp. 211–245). San Diego, CA: Singular Publishing Group.

Stoel-Gammon, C., & Dunn, C. (1985). *Normal and disordered phonology in children.* Austin, TX: Pro-Ed.

Stoel-Gammon, C., & Herrington, P. B. (1990). Vowel systems of normally developing and phonologically disordered children. *Clinical Linguistics and Phonetics, 4,* 145–160.

Stoel-Gammon, C., & Stemberger, J. P. (1994). Consonant harmony and phonological underspecification in child speech. In M. Yavaş (Ed.), *First and second language phonology* (pp. 63–80). San Diego: Singular Publishing Group.

Von Bremen, V. (1990). *A nonlinear phonological approach to intervention with severely phonologically disordered twins.* Unpublished master's thesis, University of British Columbia, Vancouver, Canada.

Williams, A. L., & Dinnsen, D. A. (1987). A problem of allophonic variation in a speech disordered child. *Innovations in Linguistics Education, 5,* 85–90.

About the Authors

Barbara Handford Bernhardt, PhD, is an associate professor at the University of British Columbia, Vancouver, BC, Canada, in the School of Audiology and Speech Sciences. She has also been a clinical speech–language pathologist since 1972. Her areas of specialization are phonological and phonetic development and disorders, although she also teaches about and works with children with a variety of developmental communicative challenges. The methodologies demonstrated in this workbook have been developed in clinical research projects, clinical practice, and academic courses and are being utilized by speech–language pathologists in several Canadian provinces. The alternate domains of parenting, music, dance, theater, sports, cycling, and mountains have contributed in their own unique ways to the development of these clincial procedures.

Joseph Paul Stemberger, PhD, is a professor at the University of Minnesota, Minneapolis, Minnesota, in the Department of Communication Disorders and in the Graduate Program in Linguistics. He received his PhD from the University of California, San Diego, in 1982, in Linguistics. His areas of specialization are phonology and morphology, especially within adult psycholinguistic processing and within child language development, but also within linguistic theory. He teaches courses in phonetics, phonological theory, normal and disordered phonological development, and the psychology of language. He is also active in parenting, music, and cycling and is a member of three amateur dance groups that perform traditional English dancing.